THE NEW AMERICAN SMALL TOWN

THE NEW AMERICAN SMALL TOWN

Lessons for Sustainable Urban Futures

JENNIFER MAPES

WEST VIRGINIA UNIVERSITY PRESS
MORGANTOWN

Copyright © 2025 West Virginia University Press
All rights reserved
First edition published 2025 by West Virginia University Press
Printed in the United States of America

ISBN 978-1-959000-47-1 (paperback) / ISBN 978-1-959000-48-8 (ebook)

Library of Congress Control Number: 2024038415

Cover and book design by Than Saffel.
Cover image by Jennifer Mapes

NO AI TRAINING: Without in any way limiting the author's exclusive rights under copyright, any use of this publication to train generative artificial intelligence (AI) technologies to generate text is expressly prohibited. The author reserves all rights to license uses of this work for generative AI training and development of machine learning language models.

For EU safety/GPSR concerns, please direct inquiries to WVUPress@mail.wvu.edu or our physical mailing address at West Virginia University Press / PO Box 6295 / West Virginia University / Morgantown, WV, 26508, USA.

CONTENTS

List of Figures vii

    Introduction: The Myth of the American Small Town 1
1 Defining and Describing Small Towns in the US 8
2 The Small Town in the American Imagination 33
3 New Urbanism and the New Small Town 51
4 Small Towns and the Rise of Donald Trump 69
5 Dreaming Big in Small Towns 87
6 Sustainable Futures for Ordinary Cities 107
    Conclusion: Transforming the American Small Town 127

Acknowledgments 135
Notes 137
Bibliography 147
Index 165

FIGURES

I.1	Schuylerville, New York, in 1998	2
I.2	Location of case study towns and other towns mentioned in the book	6
1.1	Defining cities, towns, and rural areas in Northeast Ohio	15
1.2	Stow/Kent/Akron urban area	20
1.3	Bellefonte/State College urban area	21
1.4	Small town cluster analysis maps	25
1.5	Case study histories	32
2.1	Small towns in TV and film map	46
3.1	Prairie Crossing, Illinois	53
3.2	Aerial image of Crocker Park, Westlake, Ohio	62
3.3	Crocker Park, Westlake, Ohio	63
3.4	Hudson, Ohio, downtown	65
3.5	Kent, Ohio, downtown	66
4.1	Slag in Anaconda, Montana	72
4.2	Old Works Golf Course, Anaconda, Montana	73
4.3	Fourth of July parade, Wellington, Colorado	77
4.4	Ohio voting patterns	83
5.1	Man-made stream and beach in Steamboat Springs, Colorado	91
5.2	Saratoga Springs, New York	97
5.3	Brown Ranch proposal, Steamboat Springs, Colorado, map	100
5.4	Quincy, Washington, houses	101
6.1	Wellington Brewery, Wellington, Colorado	115
6.2	Amatek flags, Kent, Ohio	116
C.1	Hayden, Colorado, Granary interior	132
C.2	Hayden, Colorado, Granary at dusk	132

THE NEW AMERICAN SMALL TOWN

INTRODUCTION
The Myth of the American Small Town

In 1990, James Howard Kunstler published a scathing portrait of my hometown in the *New York Times Magazine*. The article, "Schuylerville Stands Still," ran with the tagline "The 80's boom came and went, but this upstate New York town missed it entirely." And so began a Manhattanite's nostalgic sojourn into small-town America,[1] *my* small-town America (Figure I.1). Kunstler's critique of America's built landscape—expanded on three years later as *The Geography of Nowhere*—is at the intersection of the two most common small-town stereotypes: the notion that small towns should be (or *are*, or *were once*) models of community, safety, and sustainability, but at the same time, that they are in decline: abandoned outposts of America's past. In the article, he wrote: "Here in Schuylerville, and in many other old industrial towns up the Hudson River . . . it wasn't morning in America at all. It was more like 4 P.M. on the first day of winter."[2] But later he wrote, "I believe that we are entering an era when small towns will be valued again, and that out of necessity we will reinvent truly local economies using local assets and resources."[3] Kunstler continues today to be a popular (if divisive) urban critic: The planning blog Planetizen recently named *Geography of Nowhere* one of its top 20 Urban Planning Books of All Time.[4]

In 1993, the same year Kunstler's book was published, the Congress for the New Urbanism proposed design principles set to resolve the sub/urban ills he described. At the heart of New Urbanism is support for "traditional neighborhood design": replication of what the architects viewed as the best qualities of the American small town.[5] Proponents argued that new urban development should include a mix of uses in each building and neighborhood, with apartments above and retail below and offices and retail near homes; diversity in income and housing style; front porches and community open spaces;

Figure I.1. The Schuylerville of Kunstler's *Geography of Nowhere*: Broad Street in 1998. Photo by author.

higher density; increased walkability; and greater connectivity. Today, the New Urbanist platform—once primarily used by developers building new communities on city outskirts—is integrated into the community master plans and zoning codes of cities large and small. Its principles reach far beyond the US into city planning in countries around the world.

Why replicate small towns? Andrés Duany and Elizabeth Plater-Zyberk argued that small town characteristics promote a wide range of sustainable features: they enhance economic development, preserve natural environments by building densely and conserving open space, reduce greenhouse gas emissions and sprawl, and provide for more equitable and diverse neighborhoods.[6] Dense urban development, New Urbanists and others recognize, is key to a sustainable future, a future that balances economic viability, environmental health, and social equity. Given the inevitability of urbanization, we should develop the "right" way by following a dense traditional urban pattern rather than the auto-centric path of the twentieth century. New Urbanism remains popular and certainly has had many positive impacts on city planning. But at the same time, some developers took a cafeteria-style approach to the menu items offered by New Urbanists and chose those that best suited their economic interests, leaving behind any interest in balancing these with social equity or environmentalism. This replication of small towns is done uncritically, without looking more closely at what can be learned by looking at how these towns function in real life.

That New Urbanism has sold so well, even in its watered-down form, is only further evidence of many Americans' need to believe in the myth of the American small town as the American ideal. This can also be seen in calls to "Make America Great Again," a slogan and philosophy that celebrates the Mayberry era when small towns were thriving—for some. The small town of many white Americans' imagination is white like them, a myth that propagates much of American anti-urban sentiment as well as a sense that white rural America is being "left behind."[7]

While the small-town ideal informs our understanding of community and neighborhood, the small-town reality is of much less interest to traditional urban geographers. For the most part, we acknowledge instead the rise of the world city and with it the belief that small towns don't matter much in our globalized society: London, Tokyo, and New York are where everything happens. And yet, despite a general dismissal of small towns by the intellectual elite, occasionally the small town returns as a place of interest. Most recently, the 2016 and 2020 presidential elections highlighted the small town as a place that "matters again" due to presumed support of Donald Trump.[8] It mattered little to pundits that precinct-level data showed many small towns voted blue (or at least bluer than their rural counterparts).[9] The idea of the American small town rallying to protect its economic dignity by voting for Trump makes for a great narrative.

The demise of the American small town is an important part of this story. It fits well with what we say about America more broadly: From pundits both left and right we've heard about the demise of our American values and policies. Thus, the small town that we rally around we also mourn. Shuttered main streets, the success of suburbia and the fall of the shopping mall, closed factories and declining middle class—all these play into an idea that we've lost our "middle America." In this book, I challenge the idea that small towns are uniformly a dying breed. Forces of globalization and new technologies have certainly brought change to these towns, just as they have in larger cities, but for as many employers as these forces have shut down, they've also opened other opportunities.

I didn't read Jim Kunstler's article and book until college. In the twenty-five years since, I've committed to learning enough about small towns to dispute, agree, and add nuance to this story of Schuylerville and, with it, the story of the American small town. My research as a graduate student and now professor involves studying how we talk about small towns and learning about the demographic, environmental, economic, and cultural shifts of the twentieth and twenty-first centuries. I argue that geographers, planners, and indeed citizens need to take these places seriously, and that our perceptions of small towns matter in the national discourse. My goal is to broaden our understanding of small towns, encouraging researchers to include these places when discussing "the city" and recognizing that they need to be separated from rural areas to truly understand places where people live.

The Dream of the American Small Town

I believe in the promise of a small town: That's why I live in one. Kent, Ohio, is a college town, which gives it economic stability thanks in large part to a university that employs hundreds and keeps a constant stream of students and their parents' wallets nearby. Retail and restaurants thrive downtown, and the political atmosphere is (for me) comfortably blue in a purple state of rural reds. The art and particularly music scenes are vibrant, and festivals abound; I've counted about fifteen annually. Despite all this, the city remains distinctively Rust Belt in that it is not popular enough for houses to be expensive. My beautiful hundred-year-old house, with a two-car garage and a large, treed backyard, cost $130,000 in 2012. I walk my kid to school, then walk the six blocks to work; if I've got a few extra minutes I stop at Starbucks on the way. I walk to yoga in an old mill along the river. I can do most errands on foot or bicycle. It's my own mini-Manhattan.

Not long into writing this book, I read a magazine article that argued that a lack of community is "destroying families"; the author lives in suburban San Francisco. I lived in Los Angeles for five years, so I understand when she talks of the difficulty of meeting people for simple outings—everyone lives on the edges, and in opposite directions. But in my town, it's easy. Most of our friends live within a mile of one another in different neighborhoods, but no one's more than a mile and a half away. We walk to meet up with our kids at the library or downtown for coffee.

But I'm also a realist. Not everyone can live in small towns: jobs, cost of living, and family pull us elsewhere. And small towns are no utopia. Many have lost their original functions, leaving behind places that geographer Ben Marsh described as having "meaning but not means."[10] Even many well-off towns are more set dressing than the functional live/work/play spaces that urbanists dream of. Small towns are often not diverse and can be difficult places to live if your race, ethnicity, gender, or sexual identity feels (or is seen by others as) out of place. While on average, they're not nearly as homogenous as you'd expect, this average is deceptive given the number of towns that are a vast majority

Black or Hispanic. Like so many other places in America, they're mostly segregated by race and class.

Economic diversity can be hit-or-miss as well. Some cities like mine have a mix of incomes, but others (exurbs, for example) can be unaffordable to most, and some are primarily low-income given their reliance on service or agricultural work. Nor are small towns everyone's cup of tea. They're missing airports, sporting venues, spas, high-end restaurants, choices of retail, and organic grocery stores. They're "great to raise kids in" if your kid doesn't stick out, or until you realize your kid is a musical savant or decide that a 6/10 school rating is not enough, and specialized school choices are lacking. I've heard all these complaints from more cosmopolitan colleagues who feel trapped living in our small town. There are days when I miss the fast pace of Los Angeles or long for the easy access to woods and trails that I enjoyed growing up surrounded by forest and farmland.

In the end, though, I wouldn't be writing this book if I didn't see promise in the American small town. I believe in the promise of dense, walkable neighborhoods to create a stronger community and decrease dependence on the automobile. I also believe that if small towns are to be our starting point for discussing a more livable city, we need to look at the lived experience of the American small town, not only our imagined ideas of what this might be. More importantly, we need to recognize just how much there is to be learned from the small town: not only its economic and social reality, but from how we talk about, dream about, and mythologize the small town.

Exploring Myths, Dreams, and Realities of Small Towns

In this book, I examine the stories told about small towns. We tell these stories in popular media—television shows and movies—but we also tell them through nonfiction, in the news media. At the same time, New Urbanist planning policies reflect a small-town ideal and drive development. Examining what others have written about small towns brings me to the core of my research question: What is the reality of the American small town today? And what does this—together with our small-town narratives—say more broadly about America and Americans? This broad question necessitates a starting point in which I define "small town," a topic that remains contentious. The ability to separate out small towns from suburbs and hamlets is essential for describing demographics and tracking change over time. Oddly, Americans both are certain that they would know a small town when we see it but also easily throw around the term to include suburbs and rural areas as it benefits the narrative they're trying to sell. This book will look closely at how to effectively delineate

Figure I.2. Case study towns (diamonds) and additional places (circles) mentioned throughout this book. Map by author.

small towns and use these data to compare small towns to rural areas, suburbs, and large cities. The second important part of examining the "new American small town" is finding a way both to recognize nuance and differences in these places and to identify similarities and themes.

I pursue this through a multitude of quantitative (primarily census data) and qualitative sources. In 2008 I selected seven different small towns in the West to visit for three weeks to three months (Figure I.2). I lived cheaply (in an RV park cabin, a flophouse, and camping on the Yampa River) and spent this time walking through the town, observing the landscape, searching through newspaper archives, and stopping by visitors' centers. Most importantly, I interviewed about ten key stakeholders in each city. In these interviews, I quickly found that a key question was "What factors are creating change in your community, and to what extent do you feel you have control over these changes?" Through this question, I learned about the hopes and fears of residents, was able to think through the influence of national and global change on these small places, and saw the impact of what Doreen Massey called "a global sense of place": that it was possible to be both independent of the world and dependent on it at the same time.[11]

Over the next decade, I remained in contact with some of my interview subjects, and in 2016, I returned to these towns to see what had changed and what hadn't. I found specific stories and issues in these towns to be telling and was fascinated to see what eight years meant. For example, in Ellensburg, Washington, a push to connect to the economy by permitting big-box retail at its interchange dried up with the recession. But if anything, this left the downtown more vibrant: Five downtown grocery stores within walking distance is a problem many cities would love to have. Just outside of Steamboat Springs, Colorado, its smaller cousin Hayden is both like every other town with a railroad and a grain elevator that belong to a bygone era and not at all like any other town because of its wealthier neighbor and because of a couple who refused to let it die, buying the grain elevator for a dollar and turning it into a successful coffeeshop and gathering space. In Anaconda, Montana, where a mound of slag from copper smelting looms over the town, residents hope again that maybe this time, a new project and new promises will bring jobs to replace its closed smelter. While I spend the most time looking at them through an academic eye, it's impossible to keep this book focused on my "study sites," as I also think about small towns, the global economy, and sustainability in places I've lived, visited, and read about, so stories from these places also play a role in my analysis of American small towns.

Altogether this book is a triangulation of data from multiple sources: interviews, landscape analysis, demographic data, promotional material, academic literature, newspaper articles, and local news websites. The lived experience is a mishmash of the hard numbers of employment and population change and income levels, together with the perception and experiences of how this plays out in our everyday lives. How residents think their lives have changed and will change is just as important as measuring the change itself: We act on our perceptions, not just on our realities. The same is true for the small town as subject: How we think about small towns, what we think is going on there, and if we think that they're dying or thriving affects everything from the national election narrative to how we plan larger cities and suburbs.

At its heart, this is a book about sustainable urbanism. It recognizes that living in urban places, at high densities, can help us move to a sustainable future, and that smaller cities can help us use the existing urban fabric to find a middle ground between moving to the core of large cities versus living in attractive but destructive suburbia. It's also about how small towns, for all the nostalgic yearning for their heart and soul and what that says about America, can let us down again and again. These can both be true—that small towns can be an ideal but also heartbreakingly flawed—and we can learn from these contradictions as we move toward a sustainable urban future.

CHAPTER 1

DEFINING AND DESCRIBING SMALL TOWNS IN THE US

The American small-town ideal is built on the stories told about America's founding, and a belief that a sense of community gained through these small, dense places is being lost as the United States urbanizes. Small towns are often seen as places that are small enough to know your neighbor yet large enough to live, work, and play within the same town. A definition rooted in cultural ideals and nostalgia (which will be discussed in detail in chapter 2) helps us to understand the perception of small towns, but it is of less help in studying *real* small towns using social science. Studying these small towns means being able to identify specific cities and their inhabitants, to quantify economic and social trends, and then to differentiate between different types of small towns. From a qualitative perspective, this specificity is important because it allows those who study small towns to develop a rigorous methodological approach to learning about experiences specific to these types of places.

There are many different opinions about what should count as a small town. I'll start by looking for common ground. To begin, it's important to ask: What is *small*? And what is a *town*? These are complicated questions that attract a fair amount of disagreement among everyone from residents to politicians to planners to academics. It would be easy to set a maximum population for a large city and call every other city a "small town." But this would be a mistake. Our city boundaries are far more cultural and political than they appear. Cities like Columbus, Ohio, and Los Angeles, for example, are large in area due to a series of water supply–related annexations, so some parts of these cities are more suburban in character despite being part of the city proper. In the Southeast, what Charles Aiken called "underbounded municipalities" retain white political power by refusing to annex dense Black neighborhoods at their fringe.[1] And suburbs, while often small enough in population to appear on paper as small cities, and with separate municipal governments, are at the same time socially and economically integrated within the urban fabric of a larger city. It is also possible for the municipal boundaries of a small city to not account for surrounding suburban populations that increase its overall load of population and services to an entity that is much larger than its official population. Despite recognizing that these settlement types are a continuum rather than black and white, the need to identify and label persists.

Differentiating types of settlements is an increasingly complex task in the twenty-first century as automobiles reduce space and time between the city and the country. Much of the attention placed on classifications is focused on separating rural areas from urban areas. These definitions are used to measure population loss and gain from specific types of settlement: According to the US Census, the US was 80 percent urban in 2020. These definitions are used for more than just record keeping and reporting. Government funding can be dependent on whether a place is urban or rural. A designation of urban is typically required for a location to receive a Community Development Block Grant from the Department of Housing and Urban Development.[2] The Health Resources and Services Administration website provides a "Is your area rural?" search tool to establish grant eligibility. The United States Department of Agriculture (USDA) Economic Research Service focuses its attention on rural areas and excludes urban places from its research.[3] Medicare reimbursements are tiered based on metro (urban) or non-metro (rural).[4] Definitions of urban and rural vary from agency to agency and have changed over time. Work by those at the USDA and the US Census have helped to tease out some workable definitions, but many flaws and exceptions remain.

I see four core elements for identifying small towns in the United States:

1. *Small towns are dense.* Small towns are not equivalent to rural areas; their population is concentrated at their core and there is a distinct edge where density drops off, just like larger cities. In most cases, this includes a historic downtown (central business district).
2. *Small towns are small.* There should be an upper limit of population. Once the town goes above this number, it's a mid-sized city.
3. *Small towns are not that small.* They are not hamlets or housing developments. This is one of the most challenging identifiers to establish,

because few can agree on how small "small" is, but capping the lower end of population is necessary.
4. *Small towns are not suburbs.* They are not solely residential: they have at least some basic services. They may have exurban characteristics, with commuters traveling to a distant large city, but they are not physically and economically connected to larger urban places the way suburbs are.

This framework integrates concepts from previous research to create a starting point for distinguishing between small towns, large cities, suburbs, and rural areas. Identifying small towns then allows me to take a closer look at demographics and change over time in these places, and to propose a typology that distinguishes between small towns with very different social and economic characteristics.

Federal Definitions of Small Towns

There is general agreement that small towns are somewhere between urban and rural. A simplistic definition of small towns would be to cap their population. Some would say at 5,000, or 10,000, or perhaps at 50,000. This maximum is quite arbitrary. It also raises the question of boundaries, and if these definitions should only include incorporated places (municipalities, with governing bodies), or should they also include all densely populated areas surrounding this official boundary? No matter which of these are selected, the simple population maximum runs into a problem when we start to consider the number of suburban "cities" that are just primarily residential subdivisions at the edge of a larger city. These are clearly not small towns but are included by virtue of their "small" population and municipal independence. The use of population alone is a frequent mistake, resulting in research on small cities that groups together cities that are functionally quite different: examples range from academic to popular media.[5] Mayer and Knox make the bold statement that "In the US, more than 97% of cities have less than 50,000 residents."[6] I suspect that the 97 percent figure means that they put no cap on the minimum size of the settlements, nor do they require that they be independent "cities." They can be subdivisions, suburbs, hamlets, or even smaller: In 2020, some census-designated places had a population of zero, and 5,541 of these places were under 100.

One way to alleviate these definitional dilemmas is to use Census-defined metropolitan and micropolitan areas. These start with high-density cores that are above 10,000 people but extend the boundaries of these places to counties when most of the people in the county live in or commute to the central high-density urban area. The cut-off between micropolitan and metropolitan areas is 50,000 people, but both must have the same minimum density. Micropolitan, a term added by the US Census in 2003 to differentiate between types of rural areas, is often used synonymously with small town.[7]

Differentiating metropolitan and micropolitan areas is useful because county boundaries are static, and therefore it is easy to measure change over time. However, the variation in the size of counties by region is quite problematic. In the Riverside–San Bernardino–Ontario MSA in California, for example, high-density neighborhoods are at the far west of the massive Riverside and San Bernardino counties (7,303 and 20,105 square miles). These counties include extremely high-density cities and moderate-density suburbs, but also large swaths of land to the east with zero people per square mile, including Joshua Tree National Park and the Mojave Desert. So, while the total population (and its demographic characteristics) is likely reflective of this metro area, the land area is not. Additionally, the low-density population and any small towns in these counties are subsumed and labeled as part of a metro area. Any demographics attributed to this metro area are averaged across this large land area. Even in smaller counties, this can be a problem. My own county, Portage, is part of the Akron, Ohio, metro area even though most of the county is rural. Kent is at the county's far western edge, with economic and social connections to Akron and its suburbs, but the rest of the county is far more rural than urban. These problems with a county-based urban identification are well known and acknowledged by the Census, yet they remain a reminder of the challenges of identifying and distinguishing between urban and rural.

Commuting patterns can help separate suburban places from small towns. Rural-urban commuting area (RUCA) codes, established by the USDA, are applied at the census tract level. They fall into ten categories, distinguishing between metro, micro, small town, and rural, as well as the extent to which commuting flows are internal or external.[8] Because this approach was developed before micropolitan areas were defined, it calls these non-metro areas with a population of 10,000–49,999 large towns, and other core areas with a population of 2,500–9,999 small towns.[9] One problem with RUCA codes is that they require complex calculations and some manual decision-making. As such, they are not frequently released. As of 2024, they are based on 2006–2010 American Community Survey data, so are more than ten years out of date.[10]

Another approach being considered by the Census for identifying urban areas is that taken by the global human settlement layer (GHSL), developed by the European Commission's Joint Research Centre. This method eliminates all political boundaries as a tool for identification and uses only remote sensing data to delineate areas of dense settlement. This approach separates land areas into eight categories:

1. Urban center (high density, 50,000+ population)
2. Dense urban cluster (high density, 5,000–49,999 inhabitants)
3. Semi-dense urban cluster (moderate density and population)
4. Suburban or peri-urban grid cells (urban, but low density)
5. Rural cluster (low density, low population)
6. Low density rural grid cells (lowest density, lowest population)
7. Very low-density rural grid cells (uninhabited or nearly uninhabited)
8. Water[11]

The category *dense urban cluster* identifies small towns with surprising accuracy, although some areas appear to be more suburban in nature as they are adjacent to suburban grid cells and are slightly higher density but lack the independence from larger cities that small towns would have. This approach also misses some smaller villages with basic retail and services due to the 5,000-person cutoff in its population definition. Many of these places would culturally be identified as small towns but are too small under this definition. The GHSL approach to defining small towns—and its successes and failures—helps to illustrate the challenges of balancing numeric (population, density) definitions with functional (location of work, retail, historic downtown) definitions.

In my dissertation, I argued that the closest match for a small town is the *urban cluster*, a short-lived term in use by the US Census from 2000 to 2022.[12] When first used in 2000, the term expanded upon the existing definition of urban to differentiate between smaller cities (urban clusters) and larger cities (urbanized areas), all of which are considered "urban areas." Before 2000, only places in this category with a population of 50,000 or more were included. In 2000 and 2010, the urban cluster identified cities with populations between 2,500 and 49,999. What is most important about this definition is that it is based on density rather than municipal boundaries. The Census uses its smallest unit, the census block, and identifies blocks that create a central core of high density (1,000 people per square mile or more) and then identifies adjacent blocks that are above 500 people per square mile. The boundaries of each urban cluster and urban area are redrawn with every decennial census as people move and areas become more dense or less dense.[13]

Urban clusters also require a distinct separation from larger high-density areas, which distinguishes them from suburbs of urbanized areas. Once population density drops below 500 people per square mile, this is identified as a rural area. Unlike with the GHSL, urban clusters are connected to existing city names, which allows for a much better understanding of the small town's on-the-ground presence. Just as in urban areas, this results in the inclusion of all high-density areas: both the "official" city and adjacent inner-ring suburbs. But unlike metro areas, the land parcels included are identified at the fine-scale census block level rather than the county scale.

While there were many benefits to using the urban cluster to identify small urban places, there were also drawbacks. Cluster boundaries and names changed at each decennial census. While in some cases, this was due to population growth or decline, in others, it was due purely to adjustments made by those working at the Census Bureau. For example, in 2000, prisons or towns that were dominated by these or other "institutional" uses were often counted as urban clusters. In the 2010 definition, at least 1,500 people needed to live outside the prison to qualify as an urban area. Other definitional shifts were aimed at refining what was counted as urban: gaps between high-density census blocks were reduced from 2.5 miles to 1.5 miles, but land cover of undevelopable area that might create this gap was now allowed as a mitigating factor. Airports and areas of impermeable surfaces (such as commercial strips) were added to account for areas that were "urban" yet uninhabited.[14]

This increasingly nuanced approach to delineating urban areas was useful for learning about the geography of urban versus rural places in the US within each census year, but it was problematic for showing change over time. An analysis of the changes in urban clusters from 2000 to 2010 illustrated how difficult it is to connect and compare these places from decade to decade. It is problematic, then, to report that there was a decline in urban cluster population from 2000 to 2010 (or an increase in urbanized area population), because these shifts are so strongly affected by definitional changes rather than migration patterns or other causal factors. A density-based definition for the boundary of urban areas would seem to be an excellent way to track urban sprawl, but the shifting rules and definitions made any analysis of these changes basically meaningless. Unfortunately, the benefits of defining urban areas by density were also its larger drawbacks.

In 2022, the Census announced yet another change in its approach to identifying urban areas. When 2020 urban areas were released in December 2022, they no longer were divided into urbanized areas and urban clusters. The minimum population was 5,000 (rather than 2,500) or, alternatively, a minimum number of housing units: 2,000. Urban area cores are now identified by aggregating census blocks that have a housing unit density of at least 425 per census block.[15] This resulted in 955 of 3,093 urban clusters from 2010 no longer being designated urban, and the remaining urban clusters being grouped together with all (large) cities. From the perspective of a small-town researcher, these changes are disappointing as, despite some drawbacks, urban clusters were a useful tool in identifying small towns.

Applying Statistical Definitions to Real Places

How do these multiple definitions play out in the real world? Quite differently, it turns out, but many of the differences have to do with the granularity of the data: whether spaces are defined at the county, census tract, or census block level. Figure 1.1 illustrates four different definitions using the example of Northeast Ohio: urban areas, metropolitan and micropolitan areas, RUCA codes, and the GHSL.[16]

There is agreement on the three major cities: Cleveland, Akron, and Youngstown. In the metro area and RUCA definitions, Canton is combined with Akron, but in all others, the two cities are separated. In reality, the two cities are twenty-four miles apart, with farmland, subdivisions, strip malls, and an airport between them. The metro definition that identifies places as urban is not surprisingly clunky, as it includes large swaths of rural areas when only small portions are part of the urban/suburban areas connected to Cleveland, Akron-Canton, and Youngstown. RUCA codes are an improvement, but they tend to conflate suburban areas with urban places, as well as primarily rural areas that are included only due to the large size of census tracts in these low-population areas. East of Cleveland and Akron, only three census tracts are identified as rural, something that does not jibe with the lived experience.

What I'd like to focus on here though are three small towns that will help to better understand the challenges (and successes) in identifying small towns using these four definitions. The first town is my current home, Kent. There is not complete agreement, even here, that Kent is a small town. According to the Census, Kent is a suburb of Akron, and yet more than 30 percent of our 30,000 residents work in Kent. I consider this fact, our strong job base overall, and our historic downtown retail center to solidify this place as a small town. More specifically, we make Blake Gumbrecht's list as a "college town," as more than 20 percent of our residents are college students at Kent State University.[17]

The second town I consider is Alliance, Ohio, south of Kent, east of the nebulous boundary between Akron and Canton, and equally distant west from Youngstown. Alliance is our closest passenger train stop. It's a classic Rust Belt town, with a population (21,672) that boomed with the railroad and manufacturing in the early twentieth century but has been declining in population since 1960. Regionally, it is known for being home to the Troll Hole Museum

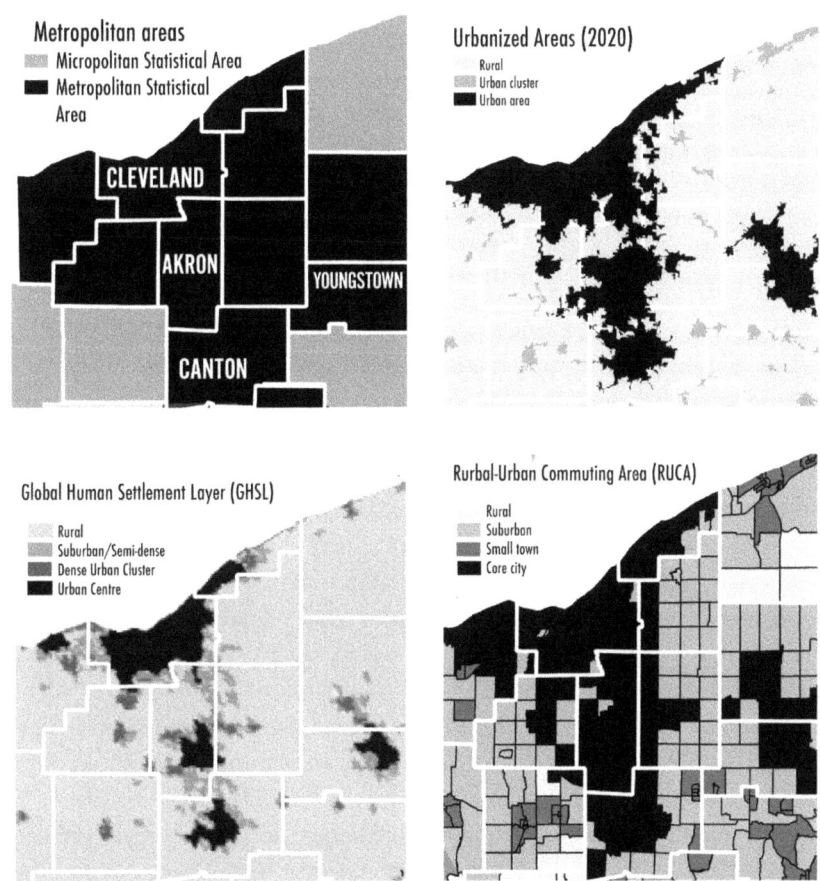

Figure 1.1. Comparing four definitions of urban/rural in Northeast Ohio: urban areas and clusters (outlined), metro areas, RUCA codes, and the global human settlement layer. Map by author.

and the Cat Fanciers' Association, both of which are housed in historic buildings downtown.

The third small town is Chardon (population 5,242), Geauga County's seat. In keeping with its Connecticut Western Reserve heritage, the town's retail is built around a town common with a central white gazebo. The town long served as an agricultural center for the nearby maple syrup industry. In 2012, it was named one of America's top ten small towns by Livability.com. An interurban electric railway once ran from Chardon to downtown Cleveland, which today is a forty-minute drive.

Under the four different definitions, there is little agreement about whether these are small towns. Kent is either suburban, metropolitan, a core city, or a small town; Alliance is either a small town or metropolitan; Chardon could be a small town, metropolitan, rural, or suburban. To better understand why these definitional differences exist, it helps to look at the towns through the lens of my argument that small towns are dense, small, and "not suburbs."

Small Towns Are Dense

At the heart of the designation of "urban" is density. The small town in the American imagination is built on proximity to neighbors, activities, jobs, and schools. These are not places of scattered farmhouses, but entire communities created by interdependence and shared resources (churches, schools, stores). Small towns are small cities.

Small towns are quite dense, but they're no Manhattan. The census tract where my mom was born, in New York City's Greenwich Village—full of prewar walkups—today has a population density of 134,463 people per square mile. Follow her family as they moved out to the inner-ring suburbs (Carle Place, Long Island), and the density goes down to 7,323 people per square mile. Head out to today's exurbs, to the village where my dad is from, Chester, New York, and it is down to 1,072. But small towns can still be quite dense: my current census tract in Kent (which includes apartments and student house rentals) is 5,351 people per square mile. Campus—an exception, for sure—is 10,590 people per square mile. Ravenna, a few miles down the road and minus the college students, is still in the 3,000–6,000 range. All of these towns fall above the 1,000 people per square mile minimum set by the US Census's definition of urban.

A density-based definition has its drawbacks. The artificial boundaries that we use to determine density can strongly affect how dense these places appear to be on paper. An examination of municipalities (mostly equivalent to census-designated places) illustrates how a tightly drawn boundary can produce an exceptionally high population density, but a widely drawn boundary that includes homes on multiple acres or farms or that adds in office buildings, an airport, or a shopping mall can quickly draw down the average population density.[18]

The urban cluster attempts to deal with boundary issues by drilling down to the smallest unit, the census block, requiring a central core of at least 1,000 people per square mile. While this core is typically related to a city center, it can also be mimicked by other types of population clusters. A classic foil to demographic understandings of place is the prison. With high densities and the potential for large populations to match or surpass their surrounding town, many prisons ended up in the initial 2000 Census list of urban clusters. Modifications made in 2010 attempted to deal with this by requiring that at least 1,500 people be not institutionalized within a town for it to count as an urban cluster. However, this does not account for the initial artificial density created by the prison. In Dannemora, New York, for example, the Clinton Correctional Facility takes up nearly half the land in town, and 3,000 out of its 4,000 residents are incarcerated. Compact suburbs with many residents are also difficult to distinguish using density alone, although they don't have a true central core or provide retail or other services.

So how well does population density speak to the three small towns in Northeast Ohio? Using the GHSL works well for Kent because the town center is well above the density and population minimums, and it recognizes the lower-density suburbs that split Kent and the larger city of Akron. However, Chardon does not make the cut due to its low population, despite a high population density at its core. At the census tract level, Chardon is barely above the 1,000 person per square mile cutoff because the census tract itself is quite large and encompasses the entire city and includes unpopulated areas well beyond the city center, creating a lower overall population density. Alliance fits the density definition with no problem at all, with 2,000–3,500 people per square mile in each of its seven census tracts.

Small Towns Are Small

Identifying density is a start, but this also identifies large cities as well as housing developments or prisons. So, a maximum and minimum size can help to distinguish between large cities, small towns, and small clusters of houses (hamlets) or institutions (prisons, college campuses).

The urban cluster definition sets these limits at 2,500 to 50,000. The GHSL model increases the minimum population to 5,000, a level that would decrease the number of urban clusters in the US from 3,090 to 1,775. The lower end of the scale is where our culturally driven idea of a small town enters in. Michael Woods discusses the qualities of a rural places as guided by social representations of rurality and population (or lack thereof). In his examination of what makes a place "rural," Woods addresses many of the definitional questions that I will discuss here as they relate to small towns. He notes that population definitions vary greatly from country to country. For example, in Canada, the maximum population for a rural place is 1,000, whereas in the US, it is 5,000 (as of 2022; previously, it was 2,500), and in England the upper level is 10,000.

The United Nations limit is even higher at 20,000 before the place is deemed "not rural." The term Woods uses here, *rural settlement*, is in and of itself an oxymoron and raises questions of how you can tally a settlement that does not have a center or density or boundary.[19]

Even at the relatively low bar of 2,500, the urban cluster skips over some small towns. My hometown of Schuylerville, New York, is not considered a small town under this definition due to its low population. Schuylerville is a former mill town on the Hudson River about four hours north of New York City. Schuylerville and its adjacent village, Victory Mills, are two block groups that together total 1,781 residents. The Schuylerville block group is high density: 2,135 people per square mile, and Victory is 1,071. The census tract including these two villages is 1,717 people per square mile, so well above the minimum density. Dense small towns fit the small town of the American imagination. That is, they provide for a walkable small town where everyone lives close to one another. In a square mile of Schuylerville, you can find two gas stations, a grocery store, a hardware store, a bank, many restaurants, and the entire K-12 school system.

But in terms of population, even adding to these villages a few adjacent census blocks of high density (a few new developments, totaling about 300 residents), Schuylerville is just over 2,000 people. There are no hamlets close enough to tie in to increase the population to the 2,500 threshold, and it certainly does not meet the new Census requirement of 5,000 people. This is partly due to topography: Schuylerville lies along the Hudson River, with a steep climb only about half a mile in from the water's edge. It is also an agricultural town, with land at its edges more valuable as farmland than as subdivisions (for now).

Just to the east across the Hudson River, Schuylerville's high school rival, Greenwich (pronounced *Green-which*; their team nickname is the Greenwich Witches) made the cut as an urban cluster with the help of a few lines drawn to include nearby hamlets, bringing it to a population of 2,551 (in 2010 when urban clusters were most last identified). In 2000 and 2010, this 500-person difference was enough to make Schuylerville rural and Greenwich urban. The Census's 2022 higher population requirement means that Greenwich is now also considered rural.

The urban cluster definition limited population of the combined census blocks to 49,999. Above this, and these places are considered urbanized areas: large cities. In 2010 there were 486 of these places in the US, ranging from Pascagoula, Mississippi, to New York City. Of course, with a hard and fast line between large and small cities, this results in some cities moving between being considered small towns and large cities through only a small population loss or gain.

Small Towns Are Not Suburbs

The functionality of small towns as urban places is one of the most important criteria, yet it is the most difficult to discern using demographic data. A true small town would retain at least some basic retail and services for consumers. Central place theory suggests a hierarchy in which hamlets typically offer only a few services, and small towns (sometimes referred to as villages) offer more, setting them apart. Hamlets may have a post office, gas station, and church, while small towns are more likely to have restaurants, high schools, and doctors' offices.[20] While acknowledging that all the tenets of central place theory do not apply in today's world (the theory was introduced in 1933), I offer this as an understanding of what makes a town less rural than the surrounding countryside. So, while most small towns would not offer higher-order central place functions like airports, hospitals, or sports stadiums, they would be expected to have more than just a lower-order central place service like a gas station. Part of the understood definition of a small town is that it will have some combination of a school, bank, doctor, restaurants, library, hair salon, and other places that could both provide services to residents and offer employment opportunities.

The urban cluster definition attempts to address this with its core density rule, but as mentioned previously, this is easily thwarted by large housing developments that are purely residential. Most urban geographers would agree that these are not cities. But New Urbanist, mixed-use developments raise another question (addressed further in chapter 3): Are these created-from-scratch towns truly small towns? If we're using population size, density, and central place functions, many would qualify. But do they have their own government? Do they have political independence? Does this matter? If we use municipal identity as a litmus test for small-town-hood, this could separate out housing developments.

A municipal boundary, however, does not mean a city is not dependent on a larger city for jobs and services. Most urban geographers would also agree that suburbs are not small towns. Far too many articles—both academic and popular press—define small cities by population alone. The result is lists of "the best small towns" that are made up primarily of suburbs. The data used to assess these towns are not incorrect (although they don't necessarily make sense to a social scientist), but the data is reflective of places that are far more suburban in character than urban or small town.

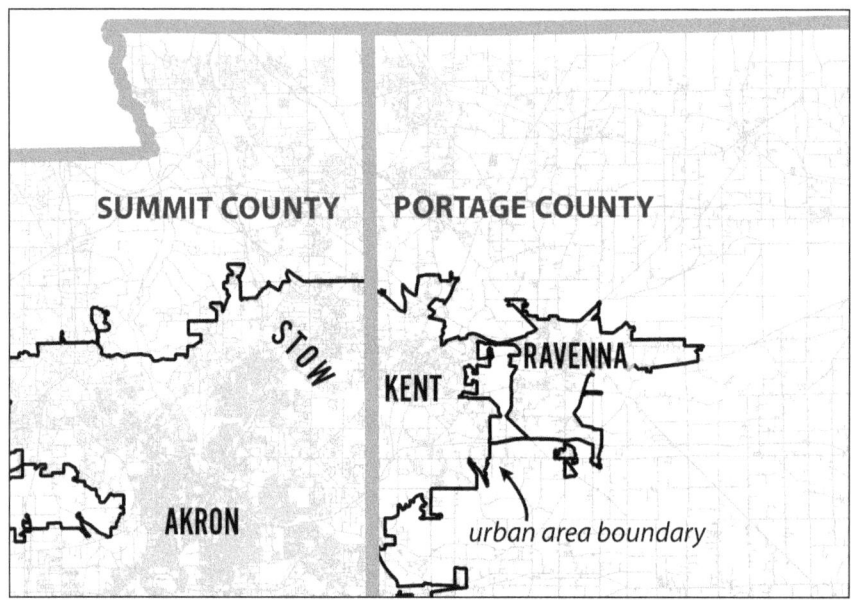

Figure 1.2. The suburban connection between Akron and Kent, Ohio, is the city of Stow. Map by author.

The urban cluster definition requires that a rural disconnect of low-density census blocks exist for an urban cluster to be distinguished as independent from a nearby larger city. Unfortunately, this definition does not allow for any overlap between urban areas and urban clusters. Take a closer look at Kent, Ohio. Originally a mill town, then a manufacturing town, then a college town, Kent is not often referred to as a suburb of Akron or Cleveland. By far the largest group of those employed work and live in Kent. Everyone else's place of employment is broadly distributed between Akron, Cleveland, and suburbs of these cities, as well as other small towns and rural areas surrounding Kent.

The geographic issue that prevents Kent from being designated as its own urban cluster is a suburb, Stow (Figure 1.2). One of the original townships of the township and range system (Town 3, Range 10), Stow lacks the dense downtown center of nearby Akron and Kent. Instead, it is primarily low-density single-family homes, with several commercial strips and big-box developments. Its residential areas have a high enough density, though, to extend from suburban Akron through to Kent. Kent's historic downtown and high-density core are not accounted for because it shares a suburb with Akron. Unlike Cleveland and Akron, the census definitions do not allow for separating out distinct urban clusters from each other or from urban areas.

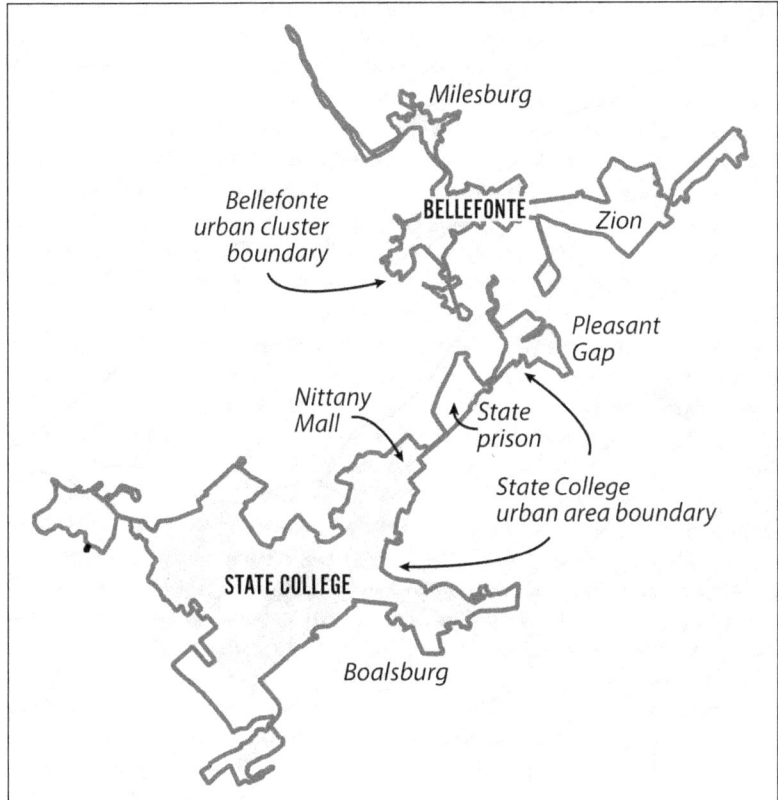

Figure 1.3. Despite their proximity, there is a small rural gap between the urban areas of Bellefonte and State College, PA. Map by author.

Meanwhile, Bellefonte, Pennsylvania, Peirce Lewis's famous "model small town," avoids being subsumed as a suburb of State College, illustrating how similar city-to-town relationships can produce different results due to the automated nature of the urban area identification process.[21] The State College urban area includes most, but not all, of the Pennsylvania State University campus. It also includes several new suburban developments and the small census-designated place (CDP) of Boalsburg (population 4,577 in 2020). To the east of State College, the urban area also includes a commercial area with Nittany Mall, a state correctional institution, and another CDP, Pleasant Gap (population 3,208). But to the northeast, there is a very small gap, and the small town of Bellefonte (population 6,079) is separate and therefore is considered an urban cluster under the 2000/2010 urban area definitions (Figure 1.3). Like Greenwich, it also falls into a rural category under the new 2020 definitions.

These examples illustrate that while definitional tools like RUCA codes, the GHSL, and urbanized areas provide some quantitative help in identifying small towns as we may qualitatively understand them, a closer look shows their imperfections. Beyond this challenge, even when small towns seem to be accurately identified, their boundaries can be questionable, as some include rural areas or suburban areas that do not identify themselves as part of that small town. While this may make little difference for larger cities, exclusions or inclusions of inappropriate areas can impact the overall demographics of the region.

Essential Elements of Small Towns
Throughout this book, I recognize that three elements—density, municipal core, and population—respond to the uniquely American concept of small towns and their qualities that affect more broadly how we think about cities and sustainability. There is no such thing as a perfect definition, but the work done to try to define small town is an important starting point in learning more about what these places are experiencing in the twenty-first century.

Beyond identifying small towns, grouping them by similar demographics can help illustrate trends and patterns specific to towns with certain profiles. Some towns are stable or declining, others are growing steadily, and still others are booming. In addition to population growth (or decline), a closer look at age, race, ethnicity, poverty levels, and median home values of small towns can also provide a sense of the different types of small towns in the US. But they provide only a *sense* of this. It's the specific experiences of events and changes and how they affect the town as a whole and their residents as individuals that I think really tell the story of the new American small town.

A Typology of Small Towns
While boundary issues and other definitional challenges to some extent hamper our ability to use urban clusters to identify small towns, for now, these clusters still provide a valuable starting point. Clusters identified in 2010 can be matched with census-designated place (CDP) names and, from there, can be matched to the 2017–2021 American Community Survey to provide updated data on people within a relatively static boundary (the boundary of the city). So, in this book, while I identify what is considered a small town using density and population through urban clusters, any demographic descriptions are of the city's CDP and are updated with data released by the Census in March 2022.

Combining CDPs and urban areas using GIS allows a comparison of demographics in large cities, suburbs, small towns, and rural areas.[22] Small towns are primarily white, but not as white as rural areas. A greater percentage of their residents are Black and Hispanic than in rural areas, but these percentages are still well below those of large cities, slightly lower than those of suburbs, and lower than the US average. In terms of Asian residents, small towns fall far below suburbs and large cities, but still have a higher percentage than rural areas. Small towns are older than cities, with a median age of 38.9, but not as old as suburbs and rural areas. Only cities are younger, with a median age of 35.6. Small towns are far more diverse on average than rural places, but less diverse than cities. Overall, small towns are whiter than America as a whole, but not as dramatically so as common narratives may suggest, and they are very close to the national median age.

One place where small towns stand out compared to rural areas is in journey-to-work data. On one hand, small towns have the highest percentage of residents who drive a car or truck to work, but they also have the second-highest percentage of people who walk to work (albeit only 3.2 percent). However, where small towns do stand out in these data is in their commute time: They have the highest percentage of people who travel less than fifteen minutes to work—nearly half of people who work outside the home—and the smallest percentage of commuters who spend more than forty minutes driving to work.

Economically, small towns have far lower median income levels than cities and suburbs, but their homes are also less expensive. The average income in small towns is like that of rural areas, but home values are higher although still far below the median value of homes in suburbs and large cities. The poverty rate in small towns matches that of cities and is much higher than that of rural areas and suburbs. Small towns also have a lower percentage of residents with a college degree than any of the other settlement types. Broadband internet subscriptions, which may be seen as a measure of access (and the twenty-first-century equivalent of radio or telephone) is somewhat equal, but small towns fall behind all other settlement types, with the greatest gap between small towns (83 percent) and suburbs (90 percent).

These data show that at least when averaging the thousands of places in each settlement type, small towns generally fall statistically between large cities and rural areas. But of course, averaging all 3,030 small towns can only tell us so much about these places. Among settlement types, small towns themselves contain multitudes. While qualitative examples (the bulk of the focus of this book) can tell us more about the unique experiences of these towns, we can also take a closer statistical look at these places through cluster analysis, which groups towns with similar demographics together.

The cluster analysis[23] offers a sense of the different types of small towns in the US by grouping those with similar socioeconomic characteristics. In this case, I chose to use population growth (2010–2020), median age, percentage below the poverty level, and percentage with a college education in my analysis. In the past, I've included race data in my work with cluster analyses, but I discovered that racial differences between towns were so strong that they statistically determined the clusters. I decided to instead look at data on race and ethnicity *after* the grouping based on other socioeconomic factors was complete, and these data certainly remain quite different between the clusters. Cluster analysis involves testing a different number of clusters with the goal of not ending up with any individual cluster that is too large so as not to offer much detail, or too small so that the data is not generalizable. In this case, clustering the 3,030 small towns into six groups provided clusters of larger than 100 but less than 1,500. The clusters reveal a typology of small towns in the United States (Figure 1.4 and Table 1.1).

Cluster 1 (33 percent of towns) is younger and growing, with average to above average economic indicators. These towns are growing steadily. Of all clusters, they experienced the greatest decline in poverty rate between 2010 and 2020, although the 2020 rate is still above the national average. The average median age in these towns is below the national average, and the average percentage of residents who are children is higher than the national average, comparable to the youth also seen in Cluster 6. While these towns are still more white than the national average, they are among the most diverse of the small towns studied with a higher average percentage of Hispanic residents compared with most other small-town types. The percentage of Black residents living in these towns, however, is smaller than most other types of towns. These towns have the highest percentage of residents who were born outside the United States. Unemployment is much lower than Cluster 3 or 5, as is poverty, and median income and home values are higher. While only 1.8 percent of residents work in agriculture, this is the second highest amount after Cluster 3.

Towns that fit into this cluster are generally economically successful, following a more traditional model of small towns but with enough economic diversity to buffer them against economic downturns. Others rely on a specific source of income for this success. In the case of Manchester, Tennessee, it's Bonnaroo Music Festival. The festival brings tax revenue to the town as well as a "symbiotic" relationship of festival owners who frequently donate to help support the town, through donations to schools and nonprofits.[24]

Cluster 2 (28.2 percent of towns) is made up of older, declining manufacturing towns—when pundits write about "the left behind" and dying small towns,

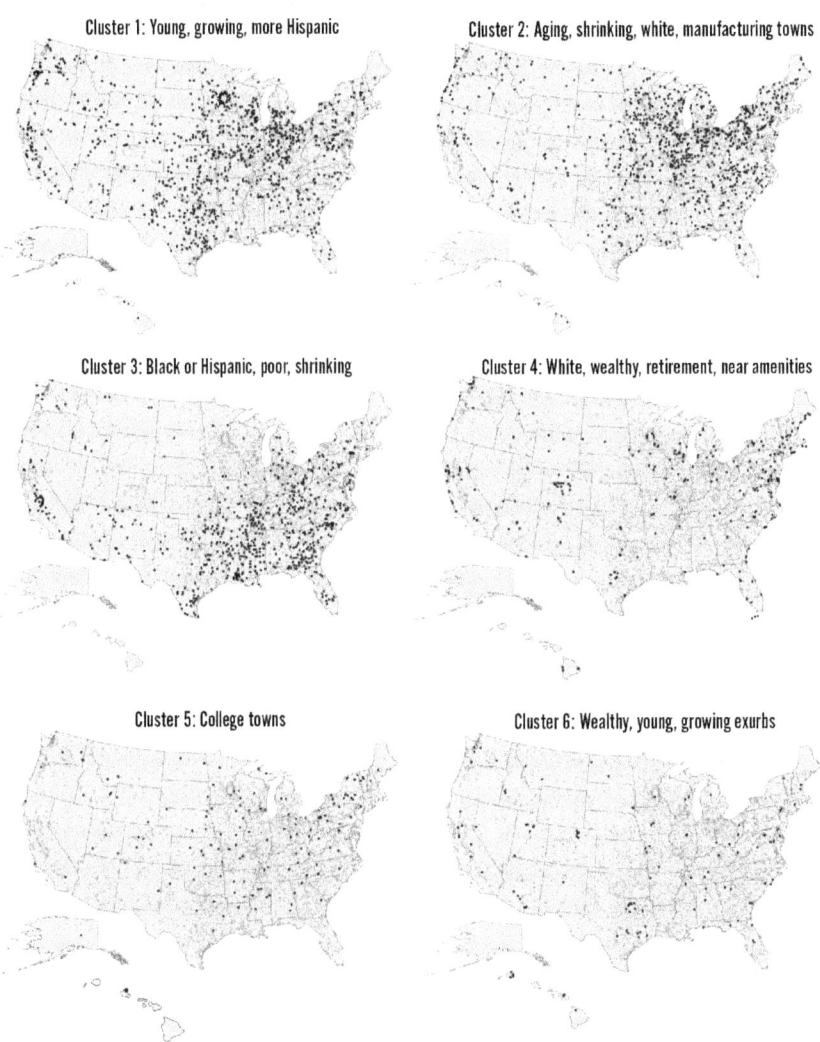

Figure 1.4. Locations of the small towns in each cluster by type. Map by author.

these are the places they're writing about. Population decline in these towns is significant, at –3.8 percent from 2010 to 2020. They also tend to be smaller in size, with an average population of just over 6,000. The median age is forty-four, well above the national average, and it's increasing: median age was forty-one in 2010. These towns also had the second highest average of residents over age sixty-five of town types. It is the least Hispanic of all town types, and mostly white. Nearly 10 percent of working residents are employed in manufacturing,

TABLE 1.1. Cluster analysis results

	Cluster 1	Cluster 2	Cluster 3	Cluster 4	Cluster 5	Cluster 6
	Improving economy, young, children, Hispanic	Aging, manufacturing, shrinking, white	Low income, declining economy, nonwhite	Growing, older, white, wealthy	College town	Growing population, wealthy, children
Population change	6.3	-3.8	-2.9	8.3	3.6	60.3
Median age	35.5	44.0	36.0	47.8	25.8	37.0
Median age change	1.4	9.1	3.2	9.4	2.4	3.9
Under 18	25.4	20.3	25.4	18.7	17.2	27.0
Under 18 change	-1.1	-2.8	-1.1	-2.2	-0.3	-1.0
65+	15.2	22.0	16.5	25.3	11.2	14.3
65+ change	1.5	3.6	1.7	6.1	1.3	3.3
Black	5.7	6.8	24.0	2.9	9.0	6.5
American Indian	1.4	0.9	3.6	0.7	1.0	0.6
Asian	1.2	0.9	0.8	2.1	2.7	2.6
2+ races	4.7	3.2	4.5	3.9	4.1	5.2
Hispanic	17.5	6.9	18.9	8.2	7.3	13.8
Hispanic change	2.6	1.0	2.2	0.8	1.9	2.6
NH white	71.7	82.0	50.5	83.4	77.0	73.2
NH white change	-3.8	-2.0	-4.0	-1.8	-3.9	-4.1
Unemployed	5.0	5.5	8.9	4.1	6.1	4.1

Unemployment change	0.1	0.7	2.5	0.5	1.5	-0.1
Farm/forest/fishing	1.8	0.9	2.8	0.5	0.7	1.3
Farm/forest/fishing change	-2.6	-1.8	-2.7	-0.9	-1.3	-1.4
Manufacturing	9.7	9.8	9.8	4.1	4.6	5.2
Manufacturing change	-4.8	-5.2	-3.9	-4.2	-2.5	-4.8
Below poverty level	13.4	15.9	30.4	8.1	22.0	8.9
Poverty change	-2.5	-1.5	1.9	-0.9	-2.0	-2.0
Med household income	$54,399	$46,434	$35,091	$74,966	$48,273	$78,458
Med household income change	27.2	23.8	17.4	28.5	27.4	33.4
Mean travel time to work	22.3	21.4	21.9	24.6	16.1	29.1
Foreign born	6.8	3.2	6.4	5.9	5.4	6.6
Median home value	$154,646	$125,904	$100,107	$337,885	$188,171	$255,991
Median home value change	22.6	14.2	15.1	15.6	18.9	30.4
Bachelor's degree or higher	19.6	18.9	13.5	42.0	41.5	30.3
Bachelor's degree or higher change	2.6	2.6	0.8	7.3	4.6	5.4

but this is no longer the highest in the town types. These places had the lowest increase in median home value, which is next to the lowest among the types.

Many of these towns are hit by overlapping problems: the decline of manufacturing over decades, the opioid crisis that slid into the space left behind, and natural disasters often exacerbated by climate change. One example is Rutland, Vermont, just over the New York border in the center of the state. Rutland's population peaked in 1970 but is now down to its 1920 population (about 15,000) and dropping. The city was once a railroad boom town and thrived on its marble quarries and manufacturing, but like hundreds of other small towns, it saw declines in these jobs in the 1980s and '90s due to automation and the North American Free Trade Agreement. The resulting poverty made the town a prime spot for high rates of drug use and overdose deaths; the city had twenty-eight deaths in 2021 (a rate of 48.1 per 100,000, compared to 32.4 nationally), a significant increase from previous years.[25] In 2011, Tropical Storm Irene destroyed bridges and roads across southern and central Vermont and killed five Rutland residents, including the city's water manager.[26] Like other small towns with lagging economies and declining populations, disasters—both human-induced and natural—can further restrict recovery.

Cluster 3 (21.5 percent of towns) is young, and most are declining in population and have poor economic indicators. Population in these towns is declining by an average of 2.9 percent, and these towns have the highest poverty rate, highest unemployment, lowest income, and lowest home value of all the types of small towns. They're also the least white, with the highest average percentage of Black, Native American, and Hispanic residents. About half of the towns in this cluster are majority minority: majority Black towns in the Southeast or majority Hispanic towns in the Southwest. These towns have a median age of thirty-five, and the highest average percentage of residents under age eighteen. This cluster has the highest percentage of those employed in farming and manufacturing, many of those with high agricultural employment in California's Central Valley and another subcluster that are manufacturing towns in the South. These towns also have the lowest percentage of residents with a college degree.

Despite *Southern Living*'s claim that the HGTV show *Home Town* saved Laurel, Mississippi, the town still falls into Cluster 3, with more than one-third of its population below the poverty line.[27] The show did bring attention to the town, which was originally a mill town that processed cotton and lumber, thanks to its location on the railroad. After the Civil War, historians note that much of the timber wealth of the city left the area with Northern investors. Laurel struggled economically in the 1970s and '80s as the oil industry—its replacement for timber and cotton—faltered, and eventually people found new jobs in electronics and poultry processing.[28] In 2021, the median household income was $33,149, and the median home value was only $88,900. While *Home Town*'s mostly white featured families would suggest otherwise, the town is 61 percent Black. Like many towns in the South, in Laurel, racial segregation and a lack of investment in the community persist.[29] Only 3 percent of Laurel High School students are white, and 100 percent of students enrolled there are considered "economically disadvantaged."[30] This is a characteristic of many Cluster 3 towns, as is (white) population loss beginning around 1970, when mandatory school integration began, adding to (Black) population loss before this during the two Great Migrations. White students whose families did not move often transferred to private schools, a tradition of segregation that continues today.[31]

Cluster 4 (8.7 percent), like Cluster 1, consists of towns that are growing rapidly, at 8.3 percent. However, they have a much higher median age (forty-eight) and a high percentage of seniors, with fewer children. The median age there has increased by nearly 10 percent in the past ten years, suggesting not just an aging population but also that these towns may be destinations for retirees. The cluster's towns are by far the least diverse, with 83 percent non-Hispanic white residents on average and only 3 percent Black residents. There are slightly more Hispanic residents here compared to Cluster 1, a population that basically stayed the same over the past ten years. Unemployment is very low in these towns, and the percentage of residents below the poverty level is also low. Meanwhile, the median household income in these towns is high, and median home value is the highest of the clusters. The percentage of residents with college degrees is similar to that of college towns.

A look at the list of these towns shows a variety of cities near amenities: Steamboat Springs and Leadville in Colorado; Cody, Wyoming, outside of Yellowstone National Park; Brattleboro and Bennington in the Green Mountains of Vermont; and Montauk on New York's Long Island. Yellow Springs, Ohio, is a politically liberal small town, home to Antioch College, which was founded there in 1850 and first led by Horace Mann. More recently, the town was famous as home to comedian Dave Chappelle, and for being the only town in Ohio that allows non-US citizens to vote in local elections. Chappelle made national news after he threatened to pull local investments if a development was rezoned to allow for affordable housing.[32] Yellow Springs' housing values are nearly double those of surrounding towns, but residents were concerned about the density of the proposal that was meant as a response to a housing needs assessment.

Cluster 5 (4.8 percent of towns) consists of mostly college towns. The impact of students can be seen through the towns' low median age and low percentage of residents over age sixty-five. It's important to note that college students are counted in these towns by the Census Bureau because they live there on April 1 of the year the census is conducted: this can have a dramatic impact on the town's demographics, including age and income (since many are not working or working part time at minimum wage). College towns are relatively diverse, with the highest percentage of Asian residents of all the town types. They have the largest percentage of people employed in education and health, and the highest rate of college degrees at more than 40 percent. They also have the lowest median travel time to work at sixteen minutes.

These towns are broadly distributed geographically, but nearly all have public or private colleges: Ellensburg's Central Washington University, State University of New York in Plattsburgh, Oberlin College in Ohio, Tuskegee University in Alabama, Morehead State University in Kentucky. These towns have college faculty and staff as consistent well-paid employees, as well as students and their parents as visitors and shoppers. These are places that are unique economically and culturally. As Blake Gumprecht writes: "They differ in fundamental ways from other cities and the regions in which they are located. They are alike in their youthful and comparatively diverse populations, their highly educated work forces, their relative absence of heavy industry, and the presence in them of cultural amenities more characteristic of big cities."[33]

Cluster 6 (3.7 percent of towns) is a small group of towns that is growing dramatically, by more than 60 percent between 2010 and 2020. The growth in these places is driven by families, as a high percentage of residents are children, and a smaller than average number are over sixty-five. These towns are close to the national average in terms of percentage white and sit somewhere in the middle among the clusters in terms of Black and Hispanic residents, with among the highest percentage of Asian residents and foreign-born residents. Unemployment in these places is low, as is the percentage below the poverty line, and the percentage employed in manufacturing is half that of Clusters 1, 2, and 3. These towns have the highest median income and the greatest increase in income since 2010. They also have the highest mean travel time to work at nearly thirty minutes, suggesting these may be exurbs of larger cities. Housing values are high and growing, and college education rates are high but not the highest among clusters.

Examples of these exurban small towns include Wellington, twelve miles north of Fort Collins, Colorado (and an hour north of Denver); Snoqualmie, Washington, twenty-nine miles east of Seattle; and Aubrey, Texas, forty-nine miles north of Dallas. These are all towns that were very small a few decades ago but have grown rapidly as housing prices in the cities and close suburbs

TABLE 1.2. Case study town demographics

	Cluster	Population 2020	Pop. change since 2010	% NH white	% NH white change	% Black	% Hispanic
Ellensburg, WA	5. College town	19,331	6.3	77.1	-9.3	1.5	12
Quincy, WA	1. Young, improving econ	7,543	11.7	21.5	2.9	0	75.4
Anaconda, MT	2. Shrinking, aging, manuf.	9,424	1.3	89.6	-2.8	0.5	3.7
Steamboat Springs, CO	4. Growing, wealthy, old	13,215	9.3	80.5	-11.4	0.2	8.9
Wellington, CO	6. Booming, young, wealthy	11,053	75.8	80.2	-5.9	0.9	17.1
Silver City, NM	3. Nonwhite, declining	9,706	-5.3	44	-5.8	1.2	51.3
Safford, AZ	1. Young, improving econ	10,126	5.8	43.8	-20.5	2.4	42.9

	Household income	% Change income	Med. home value	% Change home value	% Below poverty	% Internet at home
Ellensburg, WA	$53,730	99.3	$346,700	59.9	20.9	91.2
Quincy, WA	$69,628	101.7	$236,800	92.7	16.6	85.8
Anaconda, MT	$46,436	31.5	$175,700	71.2	22.9	77.5
Steamboat Springs, CO	$93,280	51	$776,300	46.5	8.1	91.8
Wellington, CO	$101,259	52.2	$413,800	98.5	11.3	96.4
Silver City, NM	$36,853	11.3	$150,100	26.6	21.9	86.1
Safford, AZ	$64,860	73.4	$178,400	33	14.6	82

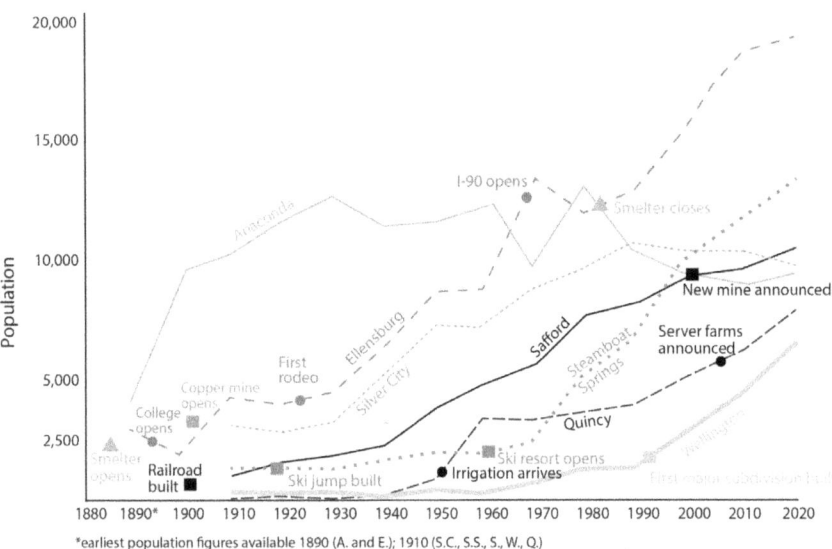

Figure 1.5. Population changes and key events in case study towns. Illustration by author.

increased and technology allowed for more work flexibility. From 2000 to 2010, Snoqualmie grew by nearly 400 percent. The growth here was in large part due to the state's Growth Management Act, which designates certain land as places where housing development should be focused, both in large cities and small towns. Snoqualmie both allowed growth and was "close enough" to Seattle, and this promoted a boom in new wealthy homeowners.[34]

Beyond a Typology of Small Towns

When I began research on small towns, this typology provided a method for selecting seven demographically distinct small towns to study (Table 1.2). At the time, I focused on the Western United States, so I could visit these towns in one spring and summer season. But as my research continued, I've seen many similarities between the stories I heard there and those I've heard in many other small towns across the country (Figure 1.5). The final three chapters in this book discusses the clusters identified here along with stories from towns across the US to describe and critically assess common themes in perceptions, lived experiences, and outlooks for the future of today's small towns.

CHAPTER 2

THE SMALL TOWN IN THE AMERICAN IMAGINATION

For many, small towns are a "way of life," Small Town Institute director Ken Munsell once told me. He saw small towns as places defying simple definitions, relying instead on the sentimentality of those imagining what they might be like, or are, or used to be. While it is important for comparative reasons to set a demographic limit of what qualifies as "small" (as discussed in the previous chapter), it is also valuable to consider how Americans *think* about small towns, how we represent these ideas, and how these representations and perceptions affect our everyday lives in the United States. To understand the geography of small towns—in both present and future forms—we must understand their role in the American imagination.

Small towns have a unique place in American culture. Their history as the primary form of settlement in the formative years of the United States established small towns as important parts of the country's cultural heritage. Over the past century, America's sense of place, as well as nostalgia for days gone by, has molded the small town into a myth: an idealized landscape of community togetherness, safety, and serenity. Though small towns went through a period of critique by those who found them isolated and backward, much of American culture never lost its affection for the small town of days gone by. The idealized small town has recently resurged in media portrayals as a dream of escape for disillusioned urbanites, and today the small-town lifestyle and small towns' ability to balance a sustainable quality of life remains an object of cautious desire for many in the US.

Places, Spaces, and the Stories We Tell about Them

How people perceive and experience places affects the reality of American small towns. Geographers distinguish between space, which is absolute, and place, which is relative to the everyday lives of those who experience it.[1] We recognize that space acquires meaning through interaction and is filtered through culture and human thoughts and various proclivities, all unique to the individual.[2] Discussions of how space transforms into place emphasize experiences: how the everyday lives of humans affect their understanding of the spaces they encounter in their daily lives.

There are three ways that space becomes place, thus affecting the spaces of small towns, which in turn affect our perceptions of small towns. First, place is the result of *everyday experience*, of humans interacting with their environment and, often, developing an attachment to it. Second, place is the result of *past experiences*, the merging of history and space to create a memory that is often not congruent with reality—nostalgia. The third category I describe is both the result of the culture that comes from "real" experience and the (re)creation of this culture. Unlike the other forms of place, it is an understanding of place that arises without any direct contact with the original space. It is *place imagined*. It is this constructed reality that David Hummon argues is most important in our overall views of places.[3] The result of these three metamorphoses is places that are both the subject of social stories and cultural representations, a landscape of mythology.

Distance, proximity, landmarks, and positive and negative associations are relative to individuals and groups who experience space. Made visible through such projects as mental (sketch) maps, we can see that how people understand the space they traverse on a daily (or monthly or annual) basis varies depending on individual circumstance.[4] In addition to the manipulation of how we understand physical space, an understanding of these experiences also helps us understand judgments about space. Although there are often patriotic and other positive associations made with what we perceive as home, Yi-Fu Tuan argues that "topophilia" is not the only result of place experienced: "familiarity breeds affection when it does not breed contempt."[5]

It is also important to consider the impact of history on spatial experiences. Once an interaction with space is in the past, it becomes a place we have experienced. Time flavors how we understand places. Perhaps the best example of this is the effect of nostalgia. There is value to hindsight as much as there is the potential of it distorting our views—of place, as well as events.[6] Just as longtime residents may remain attached to a place based on their history with it, visitors, too, may see places through a lens of history.⁷ In these cases, nostalgia is individual, but past experiences can also be collective. Communities often select what they choose to commemorate, manipulating "what really happened" in the process.⁸

While the concept of place often revolves around direct experiences, place can also be perceived through the lens of culture, through how a place is imagined. This understanding of place involves both interpretations and judgments about specific locations. The types of imaginings about places can run from orientalist (a colonialist fetishizing "the other," per Edward Said) to stereotypical but relatively benign. North and South Dakota, for example, do not have such a personalized judgment attached to them, yet remain equally unpopular as places to live.⁹ Negative and positive stereotypes of places near and far abound, both in American minds and in cultural representations.

Experiences (past and present) along with opinions about people, places, and things that we have no direct experience with result in a shared cultural mythology. This mythology consists of (and is reproduced via) social stories and cultural representations. Social stories are stereotypes—both positive and negative—reproduced through interpersonal communication, discussions between friends and relatives and even strangers. These stories can be based on experiences, but not the firsthand experience of those telling them. Cultural representations involve how these stories are shared as in popular culture. Literature, film, television, and music both reflect and impact how we interpret space. The mythology that emerges from geographic experiences and stories is what most strongly affects small towns. The small town in the American imagination is the product of multiple layers of understandings of place, and while there is no one unified story about these towns, there are many commonalities in American cultural myths. Together, these common stories help explain the role of the small town in the United States today.

A Short History of the American Small Town

The role of the past in shaping understandings of small towns in the present is not to be underestimated. Small towns were long the home of most Americans, particularly in the years when resource extraction created a need for shipping points and central places in the country's hinterlands. While in later years the economies of small towns declined, their infrastructure for the most part remained intact, leaving some towns to be revived through theming and historic preservation, while others sat as virtual ghost towns as populations dwindled and businesses closed.¹⁰

In the early years of European settlement of what became the United States, nearly all towns were small towns. While Native American villages were seen as temporary, Europeans made clear that they intended their settlements to be permanent (with varying degrees of success). Most were styled both consciously and subconsciously after the home countries of the settlers, mostly English. Towns were functional, providing services to rural hinterlands, which in turn provided them with agricultural resources. Most were planned with a gridded street system that focused upon a central public space.[11]

Even between towns of common colonial (and later national) government, there was great regional variation. New England towns were established primarily by religious groups, as "city upon a hill" communal utopias.[12] The towns were centered around churches, which doubled as town meeting halls, and the land surrounding the villages were sold to farmers.[13] In New York and New Jersey, early towns were less homogenous, with settlers of multiple national and religious backgrounds filling a variety of economic classes as farmers, merchants, and estate owners.[14]

Towns in the US South had far less structure. The plantation system resulted in a rural settlement pattern, with homes spread out along river outposts, which allowed them to ship goods and travel on waterways rather than roads. While early plantations were isolated, the plantations themselves often served townlike purposes, with a socioeconomic hierarchy.[15] Towns emerged slowly, with crossroads churches and trading posts becoming the center of commercial and social activities.[16] The pace of urban agglomeration picked up following the Civil War as the economies of the South shifted.

In the early West—what is now considered the Midwest—the communal aspect of the village and farming declined, and homesteads become more independent. Towns were built along rivers and, later, railroads as speculative investments rather than religious outposts.[17] "The frontier" is a common theme in histories of the small town from the 1763 Line of Proclamation westward. The small town is seen as being at the edge of civility and wilderness, the last step in the urbanizing of a wild America.[18] Just as William Cronon found that city and countryside are "tightly bound together," the same should be said of urban America and its small towns.[19]

Most towns in the United States were formed before the nineteenth century. The next century saw expansion in towns, particularly as the nation's railroad network grew and needed fuel, water, and freight shipping stops. The railroad opened the possibility for specialized towns: mining towns that shipped out natural resources, company towns for both manufacturing and resource extraction, college towns as the land grant college system took hold, and resort towns that catered to wealthy residents of larger cities.[20] For towns established on the railroad line, the form of the town centered on the railroad rather than the public square of earlier years.[21] Similarly, commerce became the center of towns in the eighteenth century, and Main Street became a source of pride for towns, a symbol of progress and success.[22] While the size of small towns grew, their role in the national economy remained like earlier years, providing a central point of services for rural hinterlands and connections to larger cities.

The nineteenth century was the small-town heyday, but in some ways set the stage for the next century's economic decline. Not all towns declined in the early to mid-twentieth century, but many saw a loss of population, functions, and employment opportunities. Residents moved to larger cities, industries shut down, and farms were sold or plowed under. Historic buildings fell into disrepair or were torn down.[23]

The consolidation of family farms into agri-industry is an oft-cited reason for population loss and economic decline in small towns. As residents transitioned from business owners to employees, the independent spirit of small towns was lost.[24] Profits, rather than being reinvested in town, were sent to corporate headquarters elsewhere. In some regions of the country, decline came not from farms changing hands or consolidating, but from complete shutdown. Faced with competition from milder climates, farms, particularly those situated on land that required heavy manipulation to produce, have failed, and other farms have been replaced by suburban and exurban development.[25]

The decline of the small town was the result of both physical and psychological change brought by the automobile. As small towns became increasingly connected to large cities, residents began to compare the two. Some moved out of small towns, while those remaining sought to modernize their towns and to (unsuccessfully) make them comparable to large cities. The automobile also made residents of small towns less dependent on small cities.[26] Another challenge faced by small towns is that local industries—despite national and regional success in the previous decade—were unable to meet the economies of scale demanded by the twentieth century. Factories closed, and by the early 1970s, Peirce Lewis writes, "a generation and a half of economic woe had overlain the town with an almost palpable blanket of gloom."[27]

Lewis's assessment of small towns found that while their physical state was assured for the near future, both the economy and the spirit of the small towns had suffered. Yet as he wrote these words, the tide was turning for small towns. The 1970s saw the first population increase in rural areas (albeit slight) in the post-European settlement history of the United States.[28] Place preferences turned toward the rural and small town as big-city residents sought "smallness, simple technology, alternative lifestyles and environmental conservation."[29] By the 1980s, John Fraser Hart was optimistically arguing that the future of small towns lay in manufacturing. Hart saw factories moving to exurban small towns to take advantage of the easier commute and an available labor force made up of out-of-work farmers.[30] Unfortunately, as Hart was writing this article, manufacturing was following agriculture in an automation- and globalization-led decline.

Factories did not save small towns, but in the 1980s and '90s, even as non-metro growth faltered, some small towns were able to achieve a renaissance, marketing their restored downtown façades or "themeing" their towns to attract tourists.[31] In recent decades, the once-impractical desire to return to small towns became a possibility with shifts in technology and economy, changes Lewis and Hart may have hoped for but not foreseen in the 1970s and '80s.

The "American small town" has become immortalized in our stories and culture, a reminder of towns past and of America past. So even when small towns were declining in size and economic importance, they remained dominant in the American imagination. As Russo argues: "Perhaps the greatest legacy of the town . . . was that urbanized Americans continued to define community in terms of 'smallness.' . . . So when towns ceased to be their primary community, Americans longed for small places."[32] While the history of small towns in America varies over space and time, in literature and other cultural mythologies, these distinctions blur and the story of many individual small towns became the story of one.

Competing Small-Town Myths of the Twentieth Century

In twentieth-century American film and literature, two of the strongest discourses about small towns are also two of the most divergent. The small town as ideal is perhaps the most enduring image of the small town in American culture. Two of Donald Meinig's three symbolic American landscapes are set in small towns—the New England village and Main Street of Middle America. Meinig finds these symbols not just in literature and film, but in advertising, on Christmas cards, and in national discourses of what America "should be," or how we imagine it to be.[33] Common between the village and Main Street are a connection between past and present, serenity, prosperity, and, most importantly, a focus on *community*. Conversely, a competing story about small towns emerged in the second half of the twentieth century: a critique of these places as isolated and backward. In essence, critics argued that the towns were too focused on community, and they were self-centered to the point of ignoring the outside world. In this way, the depiction of small towns did not change so much as the interpretation of its qualities by authors shifted. In the end, however, it is the positive image of small towns that remains the strongest in American culture.

Often, the dichotomous relationship between the small town and the city is the focus of this narrative. Small towns are quiet, slow-paced, and friendly—they are places where neighbors keep an eye out for each other and where families can be raised safely. This opposes the qualities of the big city: noisy, hectic, uncaring, impersonal and dangerous.[34] Frank Capra's films, most notably *It's a Wonderful Life* (1946) and *Mr. Smith Goes to Washington* (1939), illustrate this story, the triumph of the small-town man versus the corruption of large cities.[35] While large cities are depicted as places of selfish or lonely individualism, small-town movies focus on the value of community, in opposition to both the individual and the demands of broader society.[36]

Small towns are also seen as "havens from change" and romanticized into stuck-in-time creations like Old Sturbridge Village in Massachusetts and Ohio Village outside of Columbus.[37] Here is where nostalgia and affection for place overlap, as landscapes are (re)created with affection and sometimes forgetfulness. Norman Rockwell, who painted primarily small-town scenes, said, "I paint the world as I would like it to be."[38] Rockwell first painted these images, immortalized on 322 covers of the *Saturday Evening Post*, from New York City, but then moved to the small towns of Arlington, Vermont, and Stockbridge, Massachusetts. The Rockwellian portrait of America supports the view of small towns as places of stability, of a more innocent patriotism that may be lost in the modern era. As Lingeman notes, interest in (and appreciation for) small towns reached its height during times of "social upheaval."[39]

While some look at small towns with nostalgic longing, others see them as at best boring and at worst backward, ignorant to their own (declining) place in the world. Barker argues that Americans "possess a subtle schizophrenia" for small towns, celebrating their beauty and sense of community, but critiquing them for their "narrowness of thought and . . . slowness to respond to change."[40] Just as there is a contingent of American authors eager to celebrate the small town, there are also those who are eager to denigrate it. These authors focus on its isolation—its lack of culture and diversity, as well as its inward rather than outward focus.

One of the earliest—and most enduring—critiques of the small town is Sinclair Lewis's 1920 novel *Main Street*.[41] Lewis's primary complaint about the small town is that it is dull. He finds small towns (based on his own hometown of Sauk Centre, Minnesota) backward and, worse still, unaware of their backwardness: "A savorless people, gulping tasteless food, and sitting afterward, coatless, and thoughtless, in rocking-chairs prickly with inane decorations, listening to mechanical music, saying mechanical things about the excellence of Ford automobiles, and viewing themselves as the greatest race in the world."[42]

In her review of small-town literature through 1939, Ima Herron argues that Americans' emotional appreciation of small towns in their heyday did not change. Rather, the critiques of Lewis and others were the result of physical changes in small towns—a reaction to the industrialization of the American pastoral dream. Thus, while literatures remained celebratory of the small-town "tradition," they were critical of changes in these places they had come to idealize.

This critique found a name in the 1931 overview by Carl Van Doren of "new" American literature: He called it "the revolt from the village."[43] This revolt called into question everything Americans held dear in earlier descriptions of small towns.[44] The community spirit of small towns was examined closely and found to be filled with the gossip of the 1957 film (and later television series) *Peyton Place* and the hypocrisy and vicious betrayals of Shirley Jackson's "The Lottery."[45] The small towns of *In the Heat of the Night* and *Deliverance* were seen as anachronistic places of reactionism, at the margins of American society (as well as academic research).[46]

The idea that darkness lurks behind the idyllic scenes of small towns is examined by David Lynch in his television series *Twin Peaks* (1990–1991) and film *Blue Velvet* (1986). Both focus on murderous conspiracies and the hidden darkness behind the white picket fences of small towns. The opening scene in *Blue Velvet* is particularly telling as it shows a tragedy happening as idyllic small-town life continues uninterrupted. Lynch's stories are at the intersection of three common small-town tropes: murder, secrets, and what Motamayor refers to as "smalltown weirdness."[47] In his work, small towns are not immune from crime, but it is often kept hidden and is sometimes brought about by outsiders or the supernatural. But while Lynch's identity seems to revolve around being "Born Missoula, MT. Eagle Scout," as his X (formerly Twitter) biography reads, a closer look at his life shows that he spent only two months in Missoula, Montana, and two years in Sandpoint, Idaho, with most of his childhood in larger cities and suburbs. Nonetheless in interviews he is happy to accept this biography and speaks nostalgically about postwar American small towns: "A lot of small towns were super peaceful at one time and just idyllic, living close to nature, real serene and beautiful. When drugs came, a lot of crime and violence and fear comes creeping in, and sad stories. So I think a lot of these small towns have been perverted."[48]

Author Richard Russo brought the small town to the *New York Times* bestsellers list and HBO, with his stories of dying small towns in upstate New York and New England.[49] Russo, who won the Pulitzer Prize in 2002 for *Empire Falls*, is seen not so much as a critic of the small town as a realist. Even-handed might be a better description, as his work contains both positive and negative stereotypes of small towns. His treatment of small towns illustrates the good and bad of community; it includes both hurtful gossip and the support of a tight-knit place. Some of his characters are "stuck" in small towns, and others "escape," but both recognize that the small town is neither a cause of, nor a panacea for, their own mistakes. As Russo told the *New York Times*, "Small-mindedness is a human quality, not a geographical one."[50]

While literature critical of small towns continued to be produced throughout the twentieth century, it never completely took hold of the American imagination. Even as realists like Russo began to focus on the experiences of towns in decline, the small-town ideal and its decline remains robust in American culture. Small towns in decline are often depicted as "lost" rather than just undergoing change. A sense of loss intimates (as Herron suggested nearly eighty years ago) that there was something special there in the first place, something that could perhaps be rediscovered.

The Small-Town Ideal in the Twenty-First Century

While the tone of the depiction of small towns varied in the twentieth century, the viewpoint of these descriptions remained static. Small towns were seen from afar, from the view of the outsider—the informed urbanite, be they celebrant or critic. In the twenty-first century, small towns have become increasingly personalized places—places not to observe from afar but to participate in, to integrate with. No longer seen as static and distant, small towns are depicted as places that can change us, just as we can change them.

Small-town literature of the late 1990s and early 2000s was increasingly personal. Two very different forms of media carried the same message: that the small town is no longer theirs, but ours. Guidebooks, once focused on small towns as charming places to visit, now present the small town as a charming and peaceful alternative to larger cities as a place of residence. At the same time, television shows have come to embrace small towns and depict them not as entertaining oddities but as places where the average city dweller can escape to and find redemption in. As these stories are told, Americans are increasingly mobile and connected, allowing what were once distant, idealized places to be possibilities.

The first wave of small-town guidebooks came in the 1990s, including several printings of Norman Crampton's *The 100 Best Small Towns in America* and a practical guide for migrants, *Moving to a Small Town: A Guidebook for Moving from Urban to Rural America*.[51] More books followed in the 2000s, including works focused on Southern towns, art towns, and state-specific towns, as well as more general works naming the best small towns in America or advising potential migrants on how to succeed in their move to a small town.[52] There are also numerous lists published in the media that rank small towns.[53] These guides offer insight into how newcomers see small towns and how they may choose which towns they move to.

In most of these guides, the small town is heralded as the hip destination of the new century, the reality of small-town living blending with the idealized vision of life in a perfect locale. Crampton extols the virtues of small-town young people, "reared in an environment where traditional values of family, community, faith, hard work, and patriotism remain strong." He adds: "Small wonder we put our small towns up on a pedestal—they're helping to preserve the American dream."[54] For Juran, a move to a small town is about people wanting to "liberate themselves from their limitations"; they are searching for a simpler life in places that are cleaner, safer, calmer, and friendlier.[55]

Former *Small Town* editor Kenneth Munsell was critical of books like John Clayton's *Small Town Bound*, arguing that they see small towns as foreign places with foreign cultures that will challenge urban newcomers.[56] Clayton offers numerous stereotypes of small towns (including safe, friendly, relaxed, gossipy, conformist, boring, remote, religious, and backward) but offers to break them down between truth and myth. Similarly, Urbanska and Levering recognize the stereotypes of small towns but offer that these need not apply to all small towns. Nevertheless, there does remain within the guides a suggestion that small towns are both alternative (residents are "indoctrinated into this unique culture at an early age," writes Clayton) and romantic.[57]

Americans' ideal small town is frozen in time but historic, prosperous but affordable, scenic and rural but not isolated. Small-town guides, particularly those that rank towns, suggest that some towns are better than others for urban residents in terms of quality of life, but also places where they will fit in with the current residents. These towns, found through guides and using criteria offered by guides, may become magnets for those leaving the city.

Guidebooks offer portraits of small towns that can be populated by city dwellers. In another realm of early twenty-first century media, television shows were also suggesting the merits of this move. The idealized small town has become a popular place to set television shows.[58] Small towns are not new to television—numerous shows have been set in small towns. But most told the stories of small-town residents as "others," as people we might observe and be entertained by but not identify with. In recent years, however, small-town shows have emerged as a home for big-city characters, people the audience are meant to identify with. The opening credits of one television show (*Ghost Whisperer*, 2005–2010) give a short biography of the main character: "I moved to a small town. I opened an antique shop. I might be just like you," she tells the audience. This character, like many others in recent television history, moved to a small town not just to escape the big city but in search of personal redemption.

Redemption through a move (or return to) small towns is a common theme. One reviewer describes the plot involving a small-town returnee (*Ed*, 2000–2004) as "less a tale of a fish out of water than a story about a fish learning how to swim again."[59] In *Ed*, the title character returns to his hometown, Stuckeyville, Ohio, from New York City, bringing his law practice to a local bowling alley. The show includes frequent establishing shots of a charming main street, complete with a diner offering "all the pie you can eat, $6.00." Another popular television show set in a quirky small town, *Gilmore Girls* (2000–2007, 2016), focuses on a woman who moved to the small town of Stars Hollow, Connecticut, from the city to raise her daughter and escape from her wealthy, urbanite parents. *October Road* (2007–2008) offers another New York City escapee, who returns to his small hometown to face family and friends he lambasted in a best-selling book. In *Men in Trees* (2006–2008), a New York City writer is stranded in, then decides to stay in, an Alaskan small town. Though similar in setting to *Northern Exposure* (1990–1995), in which a doctor is sent to a small town in Alaska to practice medicine, one difference is important to note: the main character in the new show *chose* to leave New York City and live in a small town.

Perhaps the best example of this trope in storytelling is the critically acclaimed television show *Everwood* (2002–2006).[60] Even more strongly than the other series mentioned above, *Everwood* is about the dream of the small town and the personalization of this dream in one man's search for redemption. The pilot of *Everwood* focuses on a stereotypical workaholic New York City doctor, who spends little time with his wife and children. After his wife dies in a car accident, the doctor moves his children to the small town of Everwood, Colorado (population 9,000). Through flashbacks we learn that the doctor's wife suggested that if something were to happen to her, he should go to Everwood:

"When I was a kid, I took this train trip with my parents across the country. There was a snowstorm in the mountains, and we had to stop for a day in a town called Everwood. It was the most beautiful place I'd ever seen . . . It was on this hill surrounded by the Rockies. And I remember thinking, even then, this is what heaven must look like." Once in Everwood, the doctor exchanges his suit for a flannel shirt, grows a beard, and opens a practice in the town's long-vacant train station. He befriends residents and seeks to reconnect with his children.

Depictions of Everwood are in some ways like the idealized images described by authors throughout the twentieth century: the small-town diner, folksy townspeople, tree-lined streets, and Main Street markets. But here the idealized image of the small town branches in a new direction. The television series places great emphasis on the transformative powers of relocation and reacculturation for both the doctor and his teenage son. The slow pace of being a doctor in a small town allows time for the repair of their damaged relationship. Their proximity to rural areas allows for bonding through hiking and fishing. The doctor's relationship to his profession is changed as he is transformed from a specialist to a generalist, treating his neighbors and friends, making do without the technology of a big-city hospital, learning to recognize the personal causes and effects of medical conditions. The small town of Everwood is also a place to grieve for his wife with the support of a community that soon realizes he needs the town as much as they need a doctor.

Sentimental and sappy? Certainly. But it is also telling of the new role of small towns in America. Like the guidebooks described earlier, *Everwood* illustrates that small-town life isn't just for small-town people. We see the imprint of the big city / small town dichotomies on the life of "average" (urban) people. Life in small towns (these stories tell us) is slower, cleaner, safer, and friendlier than big cities, and this difference can transform the lives of those who live there for the better.

A More Critical Approach to the New Small Town

Depictions of idealized small towns continued in the 2000s, but with increased skepticism. There was a mix of television shows during the past two decades, falling into two categories. On one hand, some shows were more nuanced portrayals that recognized that small towns are just like big cities (and everywhere else) and were a combination of good and bad. Other shows took this a step further and set up small towns as places that seemed pleasant but had a dark underside—they were perhaps worse than other places because they lure you in with their deceptively utopian appearance. The themes of films and

TV shows focused on small towns reflect this, with some cozy and lighthearted and others emphasizing dark secrets lurking behind a façade of normalcy (Figure 2.1).

Like *Everwood*, Netflix's *Virgin River* (2019–) features an escape from big-city life. The plot: a nurse-midwife leaves Los Angeles after the death of her husband from a car accident (he died from random street violence in the book) and moves to Virgin River. She finds solace (and love, of course) in the isolated but self-reliant town in the redwoods of Northern California. Unlike some other TV shows, *Virgin River* acknowledges the existence of poverty and crime in small towns. The portrayal of the town leans heavily on the idea that small towns can represent the best of America as their smallness forces a commune-like approach to living and their isolation prevents an overreliance on technology. As Neuhaus and Neuhaus argue: "Virgin River evokes not merely an imagined small-town past but rather envisions a possible alternative present day that 'cultivates the dream of a better condition' for humanity."[61] Robyn Carr, the author of the Virgin River novels, said she wants to show the town not as an unreachable ideal but instead as something we should strive for: "we can have that sense of community in our own neighborhood or school or church group or community center or library association. All we have to do is try to create it."[62]

Meanwhile, the NBC comedy *Parks and Recreation* (2009–2015) is far less romantic about its small-town locale. Here the town of Pawnee is portrayed as both unexciting and unexceptional, but still loved and cared for by city employees like Leslie Knope. Hampton Stevens writes that "*Parks and Rec* is extraordinarily rare for it respectful treatment of small-town life—neither mocking nor glorifying it . . . it's a show where being from a small town, the South, or a Red State doesn't necessarily make you dumb . . . On *Parks and Rec*, living in a place like Pawnee doesn't make you anything necessarily, except an American."[63]

Arguably the most famous small town in recent years is *Schitt's Creek* (2015–2020). When they lose their fortune, the Rose family moves to Schitt's Creek, a small town bought as a joke by one family member for another. This vaguely (North) American town (the series was filmed in Ontario) is far from utopian. Unlike the picturesque towns of Stars Hollow and Virgin River, Schitt's Creek is bland at best and a "vomit-soaked dump" at worst (per David's description of the town in the first episode).[64] Several critics have pointed out that Schitt's Creek is far from the stereotypical homophobic small town and instead is a place where differences are embraced (or just overlooked).

The harmless nature of the small towns portrayed in *Parks and Rec* and *Schitt's Creek* is countered by more cautious views of small towns from the

46 / Chapter 2

Figure 2.1. One hundred examples of small towns/themes in TV and film. Map by author.

2010s. The Stephen King dramas *Haven* (2010–2015) and *Castle Rock* (2018–2019) portray small towns as charming in appearance but with evil and bad intentions not far below the surface. These shows take a sharper view of nostalgia, suggesting that this can soften residents' views of those inside their community and make them more concerned about outsiders when the true horror is within.[65] Similarly, the television show *Stranger Things* (2016–) takes a "normal" and "safe" small town and flips it on its head with the alternate dimension called the Upside Down. As Ann Fisher says: "The greater the normalcy, the more contrast you can show with the horror."[66] The fictional town of Ardham, Massachusetts, in *Lovecraft Country* (2020–2021) portrayed the

IN MOVIES & TV

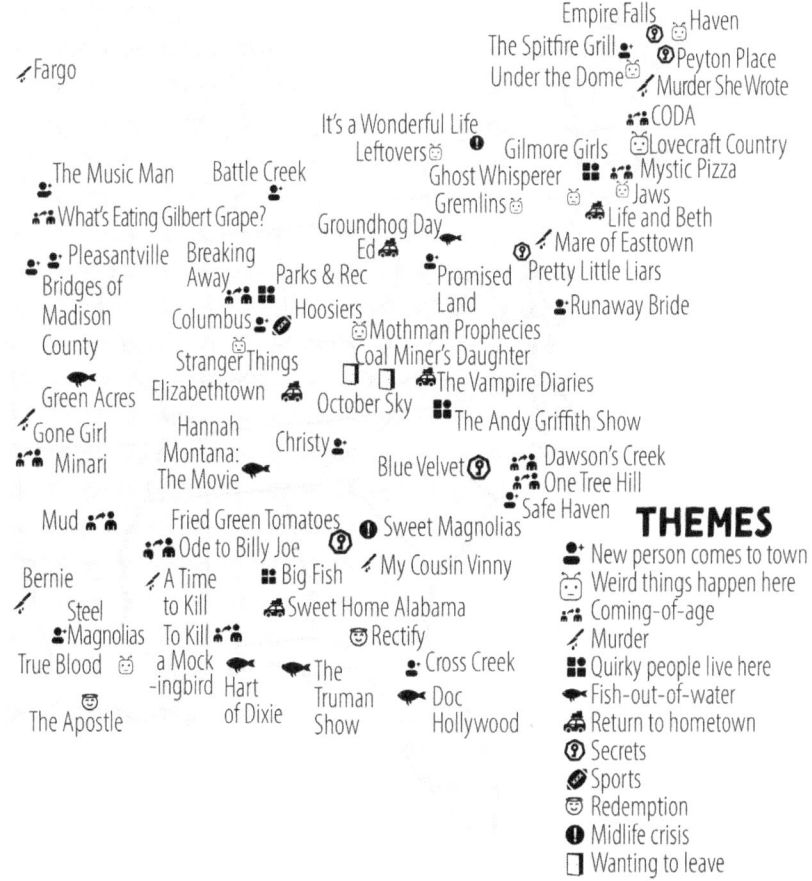

real-life horror of sundown towns in the 1950s, places where Black visitors were warned of deadly consequences for staying in town after dark.[67]

There is perhaps no 2010s television show more indicative of our two-sided relationship with small towns than the return of *Gilmore Girls* in 2016. The first TV series ran from 2000 to 2007 and celebrated small-town life: The centerpiece of the show was Stars Hollow, a small town in Connecticut with town square, gazebo, and dozens of quirky but warmhearted townspeople and shops, all within walking distance. In the four-part return of *Gilmore Girls*, Stars Hollow plays a much more uncertain role. The charm of isolation has seemingly worn off, and instead the lack of cell service and diner owner Luke's attempt to avoid providing Wi-Fi are shown as out of touch with the modern world.

"In this vision of Rory's future," Aja Romano writes, "Stars Hollow becomes a weirdly Lynchian fairy revel from which there is no escape."[68] In the original show, big-city, capitalist, cold Hartford, Connecticut, was set up as antithetical to the warmth, charm, and communalism of Lorelai and Rory's small hometown. But now, it seems trapped in time, and unlike George Bailey, who in *It's a Wonderful Life* returned to Bedford Falls to make good, whenever Rory returns, she seems weighed down by her failure to meet expectations, trapped in a *Groundhog Day* of her teenage years. But as much as some critics saw Stars Hollow through a new, more suspicious lens, others acknowledged that its stuck-in-timeness was part of its charm: "Stars Hollow might be a bubble, but it's a kind, loving bubble," writes Emily St. James. "You might yearn to escape it. You might even *need* to escape it for your own personal growth, but it will always take you back."[69]

"Small-Town Values" and Putting a Value on Small Towns

The twenty-first-century small town saw a brief uncritical revival in which guidebooks and television shows put these places on a pedestal, following a long-established narrative of the friendly small town versus the cold big city. In the last decade, a more critical, nuanced approach can be seen in television portrayals, but overall a warm-and-fuzzy view of small towns remains. This tracks with the Pew Research Center's geographical preference survey: in 2009 and 2014, the top category of place people would like to live was a small town (30 percent of respondents).[70] While it offered expanded categories, a 2018 Gallup poll similarly found 30 percent of Americans preferred a small city or town but had less interest in large cities (12 percent) and a greater preference for rural areas (27 percent).[71] A Pew survey in 2023 found that a slight majority of Americans are looking for suburban or rural communities where people live farther apart (only urban, rural, or suburban were given as options). Meanwhile, 42 percent of respondents preferred walkable communities. These data reflect a return to an interest in walkable communities after a brief increase in suburban popularity during the COVID-19 pandemic.[72]

It would be disingenuous to write about perceptions, preferences, and portrayals of small towns without discussing race. As noted in chapter 1, small towns are more demographically diverse than might be assumed—and those assumptions are most certainly based on TV and film in which most characters living in small towns are white. David Lynch is not the only (white) person dreaming of small towns of the 1950s, towns that were active in segregation and racism in housing, retail, schools, recreation, and nearly every facet of community life. Despite this history and continued perceptions (real and imagined) of small towns as mostly white, there is a strong interest in living in small towns among all demographic groups.

The 2014 Pew survey offers a breakdown of place preference by race. Black respondents to this survey were less likely than white respondents to want to live in a small town (24 percent versus 31 percent), while Hispanic residents were more likely than whites to prefer a small town by a small margin. Both Black and Hispanic respondents preferred cities over suburbs and small towns as a place to live.[73] While the 2023 survey did not break down preferred community type by race, it asked instead about walkability. White Americans (60 percent) are the most likely to prefer spread-out houses. Nonwhite groups are more likely to prefer smaller, more compact neighborhoods, with Asians preferring these at 62 percent, followed by Hispanics (49 percent), and African Americans (46 percent).[74] The 2018 Gallup poll found that nonwhites are less interested in living in a rural area (16 percent), with their place preferences a small city/town or suburb (34 percent for each), 9 percentage points more than white respondents.[75]

While preferences for small towns and walkable communities are not held by a full majority of Americans, they remain popular, thanks in part to generally positive depictions of small towns in American culture. To many, the American small town represents the safety and security of 1950s suburbia and the vibrancy of the "urban village" described by Jane Jacobs. The ideal of the American small town—of community, beauty, and democracy—now surpasses any concern about isolation and otherness. The small town of today is about "us" and not about "them."

In the 1970s a wave of literature also celebrated the small town as a sustainable alternative to the suburb, and authors sought to explain the (short-lived) reverse in rural-to-urban migration patterns. Despite a gloomy description of the 1970s-era small town, Peirce Lewis made the prophetic statement that in the future, "a town may find more economic value in green trees, pure air, and a good architect than in capturing the new facilities of a gray-iron foundry or hosiery factory."[76] Others in the 1970s, extolling the virtues of small towns and noting the population trend toward non-metropolitan areas, suggest something similar: that if only the dilemma of employment were solved, small towns could prove to be a more desired, more sustainable way of living than traditional large urban settlements. If the American myth of the small town involves both ideal and isolation, and a means of dampening or celebrating their isolation was found, what would the result be? If barriers of space are breached and place preferences overcame traditional geographies of employment, would

Americans race (back) to small towns? The answer is complicated, and it shifts place by place, year by year, decade by decade.

Today, the small town is idealized not just by media but also by planners and other urban critics as an exemplar of how cities should work. The "traditional" small town is cited as a role model for the preservation of community and environmental consciousness through sustainable urban design, in particular through New Urbanism. Today many architects and planners extol the virtues of the small town: pedestrian-friendly neighborhoods; commercial buildings that can be reused; an intermingling of retail, office, and residential uses; and streets that slow traffic rather than speed it up. In the last fifteen years, these ideas have been solidified as actual development, planned towns that are "neo-traditional" in nature. Developers seek to capture the home-buying power of the disillusioned American who sees in these places "the magic of urbanism that is denied them in the conventional suburb."[77]

CHAPTER 3

NEW URBANISM AND THE NEW SMALL TOWN

"The future . . . does not have to be imagined so much as remembered," write Andrés Duany and Elizabeth Plater-Zyberk in an article where they herald New Urbanism as "the second coming of the American small town."[1] In decades of writing and speeches and conferences, they and others have called for a sea change in American planning and design. Rejecting the modernism of the previous fifty years, Duany, Plater-Zyberk, and other founders of the Congress for the New Urbanism (CNU) argued that developers need only look to small towns to see the best way to design a settlement. These new neighborhoods would be diverse (socially, economically, and architecturally), walkable, and built to complement local history and ecology. The antithesis of stark suburbs, they would use design to promote a renewed sense of community and place*full*ness.[2] The built outcomes of the New Urbanism movement provide a unique lens for looking at how imagined ideas about the small towns have been transmitted into suburbs and larger cities.

The starting point of New Urbanism at the idealized American small town is clear when paging through the initial guidelines of the movement. These focus on promoting a mix of uses (retail, office, housing) and incomes, pedestrian-friendly streets with sidewalks, and enough density to make both of these work, reducing dependence on cars. As specific design characteristics and real-life examples emerged, the similarity to idealized small towns became clear: front porches, back alleys, town commons, and market squares were all part of these planned communities. The first built New Urbanist community, Seaside, Florida, was modeled architecturally after Southern small towns. Robert Davis, who collaborated with Duany and Plater-Zyberk (as architectural firm DPZ) and provided the land where Seaside was built, spoke nostalgically of the "sense of community" of the 1950s and "the simple genius of a small town."[3] While its earliest routes were in essentially building small-town neighborhoods in suburban greenfields, the movement evolved and changed over the past few decades, both within the movement and beyond as the New Urbanist term became a selling point for new development projects across the country and around the world. Google's Ngram Viewer (which counts the use of words and phrases in books over time) shows a peak of "New Urbanism" in 2004, and a decline over the last twenty years. But its impacts on urban design remain strongly felt in cities, suburbs, and small towns as the ideas of New Urbanism were codified in zoning codes and master plans. In many places, they are now simply considered best practices.

While there are still plenty of cookie-cutter suburbs being built, there is now also an entire subsection of the real estate industry that builds and markets New Urbanist homes. In the suburbs of Pittsburgh last year, I drove past a barn advertising *The Great American Neighborhood*, and of course I needed to dig deeper. It turns out that this development, Meeder (named after the farming family that owned the land for generations), is one of eight built by Charter Homes in Pennsylvania suburbs. Each development has a mix of home types, a central green space, a natural playground (trademarked as TerraPark), walking trails, and a small commercial area with some combination of local pub, yoga studio, and coffee shop. Its website cheers: "More than a neighborhood" and "Walk home full and happy any day of the week." Touring them on Google StreetView, the neighborhoods all look different in architectural style, yet much the same in form and amenities.

The first New Urbanist neighborhood I visited was Prairie Crossing in Grayslake, Illinois, in 2006 (Figure 3.1). It and others I've been to since are indeed charming as places to spend nights and weekends. But what they all have in common is that on weekdays when residents are commuting to work miles away, they're just another suburb. They don't have the population of a small town and so remain dependent on surrounding suburbs and distant cities for jobs, supermarkets, barbers, and dentists. New Urbanist neighborhoods can replicate the small-town aesthetics, but without a much larger population, they can't provide the same functionality for day-to-day activities. More recent applications of New Urbanism, as infill in more urban settings, suggest great promise in meeting the goals described in early New Urbanist promotion,

Figure 3.1. Home and windmill in Prairie Crossing, IL. Photo by author.

and so perhaps we are at a turning point where function will surpass form in the real-life application of the movement.

At its inception, New Urbanism was the ideal small town imprinted on our (sub)urban reality. While in the 1980s and '90s it consisted of only a few projects, mostly on paper, today the characteristics of New Urbanism are written into city master plans, zoning codes, and public and private place marketing. "We don't have to think all that much anymore about how to get urbanism to our town—it just shows up," writes Delgadillo.[4] She argues that while this "ubiquitous urbanism" has not outpaced suburban sprawl, the two are now at least on an equal footing, providing more options for planners and residents. To better understand the role of New Urbanism today as a response to our urban problems, it helps to trace the history of past responses to urbanization and its discontents.

The "Urban Problem"

There was really no time during the age of urbanization that people were not worrying about cities. In Victorian London, cholera tested the limits of the infrastructure needed to remove our own waste.[5] In Chicago, the Great Fire illustrated the power of man-made disaster to nearly erase a city. And in New York City, the photography of Jacob Riis illustrated the dangerous conditions of overcrowded tenements. In addition to health, crime, and other safety issues brought about by rapid urbanization of the late nineteenth century, there was also a broader aesthetic concern that US cities were not measuring up to their European counterparts. One architectural and planning response was the City Beautiful movement, an approach rooted in reforms of the Progressive Era. While its name focuses on beautifying, at the heart of the movement was a focus on improving the quality of life of urban residents. Architecturally, the focus was on grand civic buildings built in the Beaux-Arts style and wide boulevards that mimicked European promenades. While Washington, DC, is probably the most often-cited city that implements the City Beautiful approach, its architectural influence can be seen in cities across the United States.

A second key aspect of this response to concerns about rapid urbanization was a focus on large-scale planning. This approach is most prominently seen in Daniel Burnham and Edward Bennett's 1909 Plan of Chicago. The plan integrated an understanding of urban systems to predict transportation, housing, and employment needs in the future. "The time has come to bring order out of the chaos incident to rapid growth," Burnham wrote in on the first page of the plan. It called for improving the lakefront; creating integrative street, highway, bridge, railway, and park systems; and building civic centers to unify the city. The resulting design was only partially constructed, but the plan itself influenced other cities for decades to come as the first city master plan.[6]

As Burnham's approach gained popularity, it was implemented by less-famous planners like John Nolen, who traveled around the country authoring plans for small towns that followed the same principles as Chicago, New York, and Washington, DC. Nolen, based in Cambridge, Massachusetts, created city plans for Asheville, North Carolina; Bristol, Connecticut; Kingsport, Tennessee; Akron, Ohio; and Schenectady, New York, among many others. His plans called for the establishment of connected park systems and grand boulevards that are still assets to these cities today, but also pushed for decentralization, including moving train stations from downtowns to their suburban edge. Influenced by Ebenezer Howard's Garden City movement, Nolen and others also designed new cities and suburbs from scratch with curvilinear streets alongside wide boulevards and park networks.[7]

During the same period, and in some cases working in tandem with these plans, cities passed zoning laws restricting land use and building construction. Though couched in the language of "safety," many of these laws were really tools of segregation by income and race. They called for separation of uses (industrial, commercial, and residential) as well as separation of housing type and reduction of urban density. While zoning ordinances in New York City and

San Francisco are cited as the first in the United States, it was suburban Euclid, Ohio, that tested the constitutionality of these restrictions at the US Supreme Court. The court found that zoning is within the powers of a municipality.[8]

The New Deal brought an even broader embrace of government intervention into urban planning. A focus on public housing led to the demolition of neighborhoods and the construction of stark cookie-cutter apartment buildings. Planners of the time, plentiful thanks to the need for solid government employment, dabbled in socialism and technocracy as they drew up and implemented large-scale changes in cities. Government-provided housing was seen as a cure-all for the poverty brought by the Great Depression but fell into disfavor during the Cold War. Zoning, meanwhile, became increasingly popular and created the framework for the social and physical divisions of US suburbia.

Post–World War II America saw a dramatic increase in suburban home ownership as cars became affordable, the GI Bill supported mortgages, and urban decline and racism led to white flight from the city to suburbs. Federal support of interstate highways as a national defense mechanism further enabled and encouraged suburban development increasingly distant from city centers. Retailers responded to new residential patterns and increased dependence on the automobile by closing downtown stores and replacing them with strip malls, shopping centers, and parking lots. Population decline and commercial disinvestment led to a cycle of segregation, discrimination, and concentrated poverty in urban centers.

By the 1960s the idea of an "urban problem" permeated both professional and popular literature. Doubling down on New Deal–era policies, federal funding supported the demolition of entire neighborhoods through urban renewal, a policy that, like redlining before it, targeted nonwhite communities. While the tragedy of urban renewal is commonly connected with cities like Chicago, Detroit, Baltimore, and New York, many small cities were also affected, with nearly 75 percent of cities that participated by 1974 below 50,000 people.[9] In Newburgh, New York, for example, 1,300 buildings across 128 acres in two neighborhoods were demolished, including much of the city's downtown. Nearly all the families displaced were Black. The new affordable housing promised to residents never materialized, and for decades the land sat empty.[10] Urban renewal's large-scale "slum clearance" and modernist approach to architecture also led to the demolition of historic structures across the country. These buildings were in large and small cities; they ran the gamut from the monumental (train stations and city halls) to the mundane (main street retail and brownstone apartments). The destruction was not just of physical structures but also of the community fabric and infrastructure that was woven through it.

While urban renewal authorities persist today as a means of large-scale redevelopment, by the 1980s, their destructive capacities lessened as redevelopment took a more piecemeal approach. Historians today credit the heavy hand of modernist urban renewal policies that targeted historic buildings with inspiring the country's first historic preservation movements.[11] In the following decades, cities and towns reassessed the value of their historic buildings and downtowns and sought preservation rather than across-the-board destruction. In 1980, the National Trust for Historic Preservation introduced the Main Street America program, an approach to preservation specifically targeted at small-town downtowns. Today, more than 2,000 communities in the US follow the Main Street America program's guidelines for economic development and historic preservation.[12]

Restoring and Revering Main Street

The restoration of main streets is emblematic of a renewed interest in preservation (and replication) of small towns. All the main streets of small towns I researched have deteriorated to some extent from their early-twentieth-century prime. A few have recovered and are thriving, while others are still struggling. In all cases, there has been a concerted effort to celebrate the historic center of downtown. Five of the towns are part of the Main Street America program. To *celebrate* main street, however, there must *be* a main street, in terms of form, function, and aesthetics. This often involves the re-creation of a main street that has been lost or plans for the restoration of a main street that has been abandoned. Emotional connections to the past—both real and imagined—play a strong role in the creation of the physical landscape of today's small town.

Somewhere in the middle between abandonment and revival is the main street of Silver City, New Mexico: Bullard Street. Like leaders of many other small towns, at the end of the twentieth century, Silver City decision-makers began to see their downtown as an asset rather than a liability. In a 1999 book about the city's historic buildings, Berry and Russell write: "A major paradigm shift has been seen in local thinking, where buildings once considered merely 'old' (used up, worthless, ripe for replacement) are now 'historic' (venerable, intrinsically valuable, filled with potential)."[13]

Thus downtown Silver City, along with two other historic districts in town, became the focus of revitalization and preservation efforts. A Main Street group was formed in 1985. The group hosts downtown events and encourages economic development, infrastructure improvements, and historic preservation. Berry and Russell argue that there is an important connection between long-term economic success and historic preservation: "A future economy, based at least partly on tourism and retirement, will draw upon Silver City's historic architecture as a resource. If there is one thing our past should have taught us, it is to keep the good things that earlier people have left for us. We have nothing to gain by destroying pieces of our own heritage."[14]

In Anaconda, Montana, historic preservation is a reactionary force that has come too late for many buildings. Anaconda's downtown is a juxtaposition of destruction and preservation through neglect. On a block downtown that was bulldozed in the 1970s for a pedestrian mall that never came to fruition, there is a replica of the town's train station. It's now a visitor center. Other lots claimed for urban renewal are now parking lots, and in another unfortunate event of the 1970s, the top two stories of the Montana Hotel were removed. While these stories of destruction are perhaps the strongest story about the town's form, the town continues to use what remains to market itself as conforming to the small-town ideal. Images of the Montana Hotel depict not the current two-story structure with a Subway restaurant and a national investment company as its only tenants, but the four-story building of its past.

For Anaconda's planners—as well as those involved in economic development projects—the historic buildings that remain are central to the town's revival. The county's Growth Policy Statement of Vision (2005) argues for the "enhancement of our turn-of-the-century image," and the "preservation and development of our resources." The Growth Policy goes on to say that "Anaconda's appearance evokes the image of an ideal small town . . . revitalization should take place, ensuring that the 'small-town charm' be retained."[15] An outside planning firm, hired to help the town (which is for municipal purposes consolidated with Deer Lodge County) see its strengths and weaknesses, showed an image of a New Urbanist grid plan at a May 2008 county commissioners meeting and a county planning meeting, noting that Anaconda already has what many developers are trying to create: a strong urban form and a sense of community.

While the destruction and urban renewal has restricted Anaconda's restoration of its main street, abandonment is more common. And in an era of renewed interest in place and history, abandonment may, in the long run, have been an asset for the town. Anaconda has many buildings that it celebrates in tourist literature: the town library, built with a donation from Phoebe Hearst; the downtown theater, which was named among the top five best in the country by *Smithsonian Magazine*; and the county courthouse, a testament to the town's booming copper years. These architectural treasures are increasingly celebrated in representation of the town as reminders of Anaconda's heyday.

In Safford, Arizona, councilman Danny Smith lamented the broken windows and handwritten signs on Main Street. "Everything you see is post-1999 Walmart," he said, looking out the window of a small café on Main Street to an empty storefront across the street. Many of the storefronts, while open, were insurance companies and thrift stores; others had bars on their windows. "You can have all the events down here, and if it's scary to come here and there's no place to shop, no one's going to come. You have to have it all," Smith said.

In response to these concerns, Safford, booming with the success of a new local mine, created a Main Street Vision Plan that suggests improvements to the infrastructure of Main Street and other downtown locales.[16] The plan suggests the addition of street trees, sculptures, and a "park with water feature." It turns an abandoned train depot into a museum, and surrounding warehouses into a mixed-use development. Before and after pictures of Main Street show a vibrant business district with people walking downtown, and new buildings filling empty lots. This plan, and others like it, relied heavily on the ability of a recreated/restored urban form to change the function of the downtown and the broader city. From what I saw when I returned in 2016, this hadn't happened. The change in physical form was remarkable: sidewalk bump-outs at every intersection to prioritize pedestrian safety, new trees planted, benches and flowers that added attractive elements to the once-worn sidewalks. But there were few new stores, and the streets were as empty as a decade earlier.

Like towns, main streets have their booms and busts. Each of the small towns I visited showed an interest in returning their main street to the condition of its heyday, with the belief that a physical transformation would support—or create—economic success. The Ellensburg (Washington) Comprehensive Plan states that "Ellensburg's downtown remains the main retail/commercial/nostalgic center of the city and the lower Kittitas Valley."[17] Zoning rules that followed this plan supported this with restrictions on big-box development beyond the traditional downtown. But many small towns and Main Street programs recognize that it is ultimately consumers who decide if a revitalized downtown will be successful. It was, after all, these consumers who chose to drive out of town to shop at suburban stores, leading to downtown decline in the first place. One of Main Street America's transformation strategies is promotion: attracting customers not just through traditional advertisements and social media, but through coordinated events, improving the appearance of downtown, and promoting local shopping. Community plans and organizations that prioritize downtowns over commercial strips illustrate a recognition by municipalities of the value of promoting their traditional town center as a business center. The re-creation of Main Street illustrates the desire to preserve what residents see as a sense of place, with both geographic particulars and a national understanding of what should constitute a small town.

The Urban Solution: A Short History of New Urbanism

In parallel to the drive to preserve and restore main streets, New Urbanism grew out of a reaction to previous decades of urban renewal and sprawl. In its planning and dedication to order, it reflected the grand civic ideals of the City Beautiful movement. But unlike movements of the past, New Urbanism was driven by architects and developers and was very much a free-market movement. The hope was that, freed of single-use zoning and other restrictions and more responsive to consumer demand, new development could build on nostalgia for cities and small towns of the past and create denser, more urban places: a win-win for developers and environmentalists alike.

In the early years of New Urbanism the movement was as much about public relations as it was about planning and design. For Andrés Duany, the original mission of New Urbanism could be summed up in designing communities that did not require cars to live there: "For the 50 percent of Americans who do not drive, they have a kind of freedom of movement."[18] Despite lofty environmentalist goals, early example communities were small and exclusive, with only 2,000 people living in them in 1995.[19] Seaside, Florida, for example, is a resort town that today is mostly rental properties and second homes, including one owned by former Congressman Matt Gaetz. *The Truman Show*, which depicted a man who discovers he grew up on a reality TV show set, was filmed in Gaetz's childhood home in Seaside.[20] But in the past twenty years, New Urbanist ideas caught on and are increasingly seen in mainstream development across the country. Using *New Urban News* directories and the Congress for the New Urbanism database, Gao et al. found 1,089 New Urbanist developments in 476 cities as of 2021.[21] In 2023, 2,600 people paid the $200 annual membership fee for the CNU, according to the group's website.

Integration into HUD's Hope IV program brought federally financed New Urbanist development to even more cities across the country: 240 sites and 111,000 housing units. In Akron, Ohio, across from the zoo, the $20 million Hope IV housing project looks like any other New Urbanist development, with CNU guidelines determining locations of sidewalks, styles of park benches, and home paint colors.[22] The difference is that this housing is mixed-income and supportive, containing social services within the neighborhood. These duplexes replaced boxlike public housing built in the early 1940s following some of the city's earliest urban renewal demolitions of Black neighborhoods.[23]

The features of New Urbanist development vary greatly depending on where they are built, how constrained they are by local conditions, and how they are funded. In the past few decades, the blank canvas and hefty bank account required to adhere to all tenets of New Urbanism have yielded to a more pragmatic and piecemeal approach in terms of architecture, neighborhood layout, and land use. In some cases, New Urbanist developments follow the CNU guidelines closely, but in others, particularly infill development, the density of the development requires some modifications. Still other New Urbanist developments choose to apply CNU principles more strategically to what is otherwise more traditional low-density subdivisions.[24]

Critics of New Urbanism saw this approach to urban design as greenwashing of sprawl since, in its early years, most New Urbanism development was in greenfields well outside cities. As Roberts writes in *High Country News*: "New Urbanism rests on an unholy alliance between the greedheads and the greens. Developers get to wrap themselves in the mantle of crusaders bravely battling the alienation of the suburbs while protecting the land from the ravages of sprawl. Environmentalists get to envision a society made over according to their agenda, with high-density, automobile-free cities surrounded by open space and wildlife habitat."[25] For others, New Urbanism's flexibility and reliance on market mechanisms encourage developers to skirt directives that would promote economic and racial diversity or environmental protection.[26]

Critics also return to the romantic origin story of Seaside and note that by modeling their town on turn-of-the-century Southern towns, they were building models of towns that were off-limits and sometimes deadly to non-whites. After all, Robert Davis, who spoke so highly of 1950s neighborhood culture, grew up (white) in Birmingham, Alabama. A closer look at Seaside reveals that to copy the midcentury small town is to leave out Black and brown folks, poor folks, working moms, and others who live outside of nontraditional boxes. Karen Falconer Al-Hindi and Caedmon Staddon call Seaside a simulacrum, a panopticon, colonialist, and environmental determinist, among other academic affronts, concluding: "we find such neotraditional developments a dangerous diversion from the search for genuine solutions to real urban problems."[27]

From the start New Urbanists have pushed to separate the movement from perhaps its greatest criticism: that it is just another form of suburban sprawl, not just in its development of greenfields but also in its appeal and availability to wealthy white homeowners. In recent decades, New Urbanism evolved from being focused on planned suburban development (primarily in greenfields) to including development at all scales, with a "special focus" on brownfields. These infill developments offer an opportunity to rebuild neighborhoods lost to urban renewal and to better meet the promise of community building and neighborhood diversity.

Faux Main Streets and Town Centers

Initially focused primarily on residential development, New Urbanism increasingly shows up in new retail projects. Previous iterations of retail agglomeration included the commercial strip, the shopping mall, and the big-box zone. Applying New Urbanism to the basic principles of grouped retail buildings led to a new style of retail: the lifestyle center, also known as a townscape mall. Most of these projects are dominated by retail, with most including offices or residential as homages to the idea of mixed-use. Their main relationship to New Urbanism is aesthetics: they're open-air, with a main street, park benches, and a few green spaces with Adirondack chairs scattered throughout.

This trend gained increasing attention from the shopping mall community and, ultimately, academics and architects. "Malls are now being designed to resemble the downtown commercial districts they replaced. What sweet vindication for urban sophisticates!" observed Blum.[28] By 2018 there were more than five hundred lifestyle centers, according to the International Council of Shopping Centers, most located in wealthy suburbs of major metro areas. Research on lifestyle center hotspots found clusters in the Philadelphia-DC area, Florida, and Denver.[29]

My first experiences with lifestyle centers were in the Los Angeles area: The Grove and Americana at Brand were two of the earliest and more elaborate examples of this type of development. The Grove is nearly a theme park. Americana at Brand in Glendale is more of an outdoor shopping mall, anchored by the Cheesecake Factory, AMC Theaters, and Barnes & Noble. Moving to Ohio in 2012, I was surprised to find some impressive examples of New Urbanist retail developments right in my own backyard. One of the more popular examples is Crocker Park in Westlake, a suburb on Cleveland's West Side (Figure 3.2). The developer of Crocker Park proposed a mixed-use community and jumped through a lot of hoops to get there. A citywide referendum removed strict zoning from the parcel to allow for mixed-use, and the developer also negotiated with the city of Westlake to prioritize residential (must be more than 50 percent) and restrict retail to 35 percent. The city also pushed for most of the parking to be within structures versus open lots.[30]

The end result, which opened in 2004 and continues to grow, now covers 120 acres—twenty city blocks—and gets 20 million visitors a year. It includes

Figure 3.2. Google Earth image of Crocker Park, Westlake, OH.

725,000 square feet of office space, 536 apartments, 100-plus stores, two grocery stores, a hotel, a movie theater, a gym, eight parking garages, a farmers market, a splash pad, and an outdoor stage. But what's even more impressive are the aesthetics: It feels like a small town or even a neighborhood in a larger city, with an eclectic mix of European-style architecture (Figure 3.3). Perhaps overstating a bit, Cope et al. call it "a well-organized, and one might even say artistic masterpiece."[31] A more critical view recognizes that this admiration of its vibe comes from a place of privilege: "There's none of the grit or anxiety associated with the real world. There's an impression that everything is predictable, safe and clean inside the Crocker Park bubble. It's an instant, self-contained village, optimized for the upper-middle-class pursuit of happiness"[32]

Twenty years after it first opened, Crocker Park not only has held up as a destination (keeping many of its original star tenants), but has expanded, adding a hotel on the retail side and American Greetings offices on the other. I've been going there for more than ten years with my in-laws, and the experience of this space with people in their eighties made me rethink my "this is a fake postmodernist hellscape!" first impressions. My in-laws, who lived in Cleveland all their lives (first in the city, then in suburban Bay Village), could go to Crocker Park, have lunch, go book browsing at Barnes & Noble, and pick up some groceries at Trader Joe's. All while safely walking (and later wheeling) around an (admittedly fake) main street. They loved it there, and who could

Figure 3.3. Mixed-use buildings in Crocker Park, Westlake, OH. Photo by author.

blame them? We could go there with them, all have a picnic in the park, then let my kid play in the spray ground while Grandma watched and Grandpa shopped for books. Meanwhile, I could run down to Nordstrom Rack and look for bargains and my husband could run over to the Apple Store Genius Bar to fix his iPad. From an anticapitalism perspective, maybe this does sound like a postmodern hellscape, but from a real-life, this-is-the-world-we-live in perspective? It worked. And it made for many lovely family days together.

As these private commercial developments thrived, suburban municipal governments began to take note. If suburban sprawl was out and dense urban places were in, how could they build themselves a city center? One exceptional example to this is Carmel, Indiana. While Carmel is (in)famous for its 145 roundabouts, the city is perhaps the most successful suburb–to–small town transformation in the United States. In fact, its population grew so fast that it went from a 25,380 population suburb in 1990 to a medium-sized city of more than 100,000 in 2022, briefly passing through the small town stage on its way. To be an independent city rather than a suburb, Carmel attracted large employers, added its own civic center, and completely revamped its transportation system. A strong mayor and a willingness to take on a lot of debt were at the center of these changes. Jim Brainard, a Republican, became mayor in 1996, and the city passed a city center redevelopment plan in 1998. It detailed an ambitious development that brought high-density housing and office complexes into the city center, along with first-floor retail and pedestrian-friendly streets.[33]

Closer to home here in Ohio, three surrounding suburbs have talked about creating a dense(r) town center to host retail and civic functions. Stow, to the west of Kent, Brimfield to the south, and Streetsboro to the north would all love to have a town center. In 2018, Stow (a high-density suburb of Akron) put out a request for proposals to develop a downtown on the sixty-four acres around city hall to include housing, retail, and green space. The city cites the nearby cities of Hudson and Kent as examples of successful, walkable downtowns that they are looking to replicate.[34] However, a more up-to-date description from the city suggests this was scaled back to just a new playground. In Brimfield (a rural farming community) a few years later, township trustees suggested that they could expand their civic center area (town hall and fire department) to include an "entertainment district" that could eventually include "a playground area, boutiques, sit-down restaurants and a brewery," according to one trustee. They said sidewalks from the entertainment district to nearby subdivisions and "vintage lighting" would make the area more walkable.[35]

New Urbanism in Small Towns

As the trend of New Urbanism spread through the US (and beyond), it was inevitable that some small towns themselves would begin to consider how they could rethink (re)development. While it may seem odd that small towns would work to incorporate what was essentially small-town design into their existing planning codes, they didn't see it that way. Instead, they saw this approach as, for growing towns, guiding new growth and, for declining towns, promoting value in and propping up existing infrastructure. In one of the stranger stories I've encountered about this policy transfer, small town planners and developers from Steamboat Springs traveled to Denver to see and learn from a New Urbanist development. The project, Stapleton, was the redevelopment of the city's old airport as a mixed-use, high-density neighborhood. They also visited Lowry, another New Urbanist neighborhood. The idea was that any new development in Steamboat Springs (a small town) should follow this model (which mimicked small towns). So, planners from Steamboat Springs took a three-hour bus ride over the Rocky Mountains to tour Stapleton and learn more about how to build a small town.[36]

Here in Ohio, Fairmount Properties has excelled at building faux main streets, including two that parallel real main streets: one in Hudson (a Cleveland suburb known for its high property values and "good schools") and

Figure 3.4. Downtown Hudson, OH. Photo by author.

another in Kent. The Hudson project, First & Main, was built in 2004. It could easily be mistaken for the town's real main street as no expense was spared in mimicking the town's original architecture of classic multistory brick retail (Figure 3.4). Even the street is (new) cobblestone. Windows and architectural details abound here, along with classic small-town features: a gazebo, a park, benches facing the sidewalk, and American flags flying from the buildings. The developer's website makes clear the attraction for new tenants: "It serves a well-established marketplace which blends prosperous long-term residents with new young families, who have abundant disposable incomes that average more than $130,000."[37]

Not long after the Hudson development, Fairmount started on another main-street-style downtown development, this one in Kent. This development spanned several blocks and phases and included a complex network of developers and funding mechanisms. In all, it was $110 million project centered around New Urbanist thinking: multistory mixed-use buildings, a combination bus station / parking garage / bike parking transit center, park benches, street trees, and a pocket park, all built within the existing urban fabric of

Figure 3.5. Dan Smith Community Park in downtown Kent, OH. Photo by author.

downtown Kent (Figure 3.5). The new construction replaced mostly parking lots and single-story 1960s-era buildings. Equally important to the project, Kent State University, the city of Kent, and the state of Ohio worked together to create a walking path that made it easy to walk from campus to downtown, reestablishing a pedestrian connection that had been fenced off in 1975. The new development brought more than a dozen new businesses and jobs downtown and has earned the affection of (most) locals as a place to shop, eat, and go to the many festivals sponsored by our local Main Street program.

Not all small towns welcome a New Urbanist redesign, though, particularly when it feels forced upon them. In Plattsburgh, New York, where I lived and taught as a visiting professor for two years, what seemed like a winning (and well-funded) urban transformation did not go smoothly. The drama began just after I left town. It centered on a parking lot in the heart of downtown. Like a lot of small towns, the parking lot used to be a multistory building, but a fire left a vacant lot. The parking lot was popular among students living downtown, as it was basically unregulated, and at the back was a building that housed the city's farmers market. Just beyond the edge of the parking lot, nearly forgotten and hidden by trees, is the Saranac River.

In 2016, the city was awarded $10 million as part of New York State's Downtown Revitalization Initiative. The funds were based on a New Urbanist–style proposal that was centered around a mixed-use building that would preserve the three hundred parking spots at the site but add a multistory building with housing and retail.[38] It originally proposed recentering the lot on the river, creating an event lawn and farmers market as well as river access at the site (in plans shared after 2000, this space disappeared).[39] But as soon as the grant was awarded, opposition mounted, in part due to the lack of public input on the proposal, but also because some felt the money would be better spent elsewhere, like repaving roads and filling potholes. Then mayoral candidate Colin Read won the election based in part on this viewpoint. "This city is only as good as its weakest elements," he told reporters. "If our foundations are crumbling, it's not—it doesn't make an awful lot of sense to build a mansion on it." Supporters rolled their eyes at this perspective, noting that the state awarded the grant specifically to build the project as designed.[40] In the end, the parking lot is still a parking lot. The multistory building was never built. Lawsuits further stalled the project, and in March 2022, a county judge agreed with opponents that the city should have evaluated the project's effect on the environment, specifically the common loon habitat along the Saranac River.[41]

Balancing New Urbanist Dreams and Outcomes

My own assessment of New Urbanism is colored by my first introduction to the concept as a reporter for *The Saratogian* in Saratoga Springs, New York.[42] A developer was proposing a mixed-use development for a corner of the city abutting the interstate—prime real estate, and a parcel that been proposed as a Home Depot not long before. This proposal failed in part due to opposition by the very people who were now supporting this New Urbanist plan. They proposed a hotel, some retail, and apartments on fifty-four acres. Open space advocates were skeptical: Weren't New Urbanist projects supposed to be walkable? This was more than two miles from the city center and looked to me more like a close subdivision than a walkable neighborhood.

Nearly twenty years later, a drive around Excelsior Park shows a hotel, apartments, an empty lot ("available"), and little else. The promised coffee shops, hair salons, and grocery stores never materialized. The developer recently amended their special use permit to use the pledged twenty-seven-acre preserve to add another hotel and more housing. The project stalled because in 2022 residents sued to stop what is primarily "workforce" (affordable) housing from being added to their neighborhood because it adds more units than approved in the 2002 permit. They also expressed opposition to a planned domestic violence shelter and childcare center planned for the neighborhood.[43]

The slow and compromised roll-out of a New Urbanist development in Saratoga Springs is not how all these plans turn out. Certainly, there are many examples of success. But the very nature of combining the complex patchwork of cities with large-scale planned developments makes this type of development challenging. Small-town land use and street networks grew and evolved over decades, whereas these communities transition from planning to construction to completion in only a few years. Changes in where we work during the COVID-19 pandemic and beyond suggest that New Urbanism could either provide a panacea (becoming the true live/work/play community it promises) or further expand sprawl.[44]

I have mixed feelings about New Urbanism. I think a lot of us who inhabit and study cities do. The idea of the good parts of small towns (their walkability, density, and sense of community) being mixed with the best of cities (economic and racial diversity, efficient public transit, and retail options) sounds downright utopic. But at the same time, it all seems a bit too good to be true. *The Truman Show* captured one aspect of this, but also one wonders whether these new-old cities can escape from the structural trappings of all cities: gentrification, segregation, and affordability issues. After all, small towns are not immune from these problems; how would they *not* transfer to reproductions of small towns (whether as suburbs or neighborhoods in larger cities)? These are essential questions as we examine the experiences of small towns in the early twenty-first century.

CHAPTER 4

SMALL TOWNS AND THE RISE OF DONALD TRUMP

Most Americans live outside of small towns, so how do we learn more about these places? While film, television, and fiction are clearly part of this, nonfiction plays a role as well. National news media coverage of small towns is an essential component of understanding both actual events and cultural perceptions of these places. But what we read about small towns in the newspaper, that we can believe, right? Well, sometimes. This is not a story of alternative facts so much as it's a complicated interaction between cultural expectations and the actual lived experiences and events in these places. Understanding how the real and the ideal feed each other is of particular importance when examining how the news media covered small towns immediately after the 2016 election. Election outcomes in 2020 further illustrate that small towns should not be equated with rural places in American politics.

In 2016, analysts, many of whom predicted a win by Hillary Clinton, hung their heads and admitted that they must have missed the sentiments of the "average American in small towns" (overlooking that the average American doesn't live in a small town anymore). As Eugene Robinson wrote in the *Washington Post* the day after the 2016 election. " [Trump] stunned the world by energizing and mobilizing legions of 'forgotten men and women' . . . white, working-class Americans living in small towns and rural areas across the nation—who bought into his pledge to 'make America great again.'"[1]

This support in the (seemingly) inseparable "small towns and rural areas" was taken as a given. It was explained by a narrative that predated Trump:

a story of towns past their heyday where isolation and economic stagnation led to mass exodus. Certainly, there is some truth in this narrative, but small towns are not a monolith, and in fact my research at the precinct level shows them to be less red than surrounding rural areas, with some supporting Clinton in 2016 or Biden in 2020.[2] County-level research, although more granular in its approach, also shows small-town (micropolitan) counties to be less likely to vote Republican than purely rural counties. Analysis by Florida et al., for example, finds that counties that include small towns and mid-size cities voted overall less Republican than rural areas, and voted 3 percentage points more Democratic from 2016 to 2020.[3] To understand this disconnect, it's important to look back in media coverage of small towns well before the 2016 election, to the 2008 election and even further. This coverage mourned a "lost America" and focused attention on only one kind of small town, the downtrodden, declining, and devalued one, crafting an identity for all small towns around this narrative.

To explore the intersection of small-town trends and how these trends are narrated for a national audience, I looked at ten years of national media coverage, from May 1, 2012, to May 1, 2022. I was particularly interested in how media described the 2016 victory of Donald Trump in relationship to small towns, but I also looked at other small-town narratives they supported leading up to and after the 2016 and 2020 elections. To do this, I chose to use the term "small towns," plural, as this phrase was more likely to produce articles generalizing about small towns, rather than referring to events in a single "small town." I searched ten major national publications and filtered for general news articles about the United States.[4]

This search produced 1,341 articles, which I further pared down to eliminate those that used the phrase "small towns" but were not focused on this type of settlement (for example, "from small towns to big cities, everyone . . ."). These exclusions produced a final selection of 734 articles, which I used along with my own fieldwork and experiences to better understand the emergence of the "Trump offers hope to dying small towns" narrative over the past ten years and how media has refocused their attention after President Trump lost in 2020.

Focusing on Decline

A moving story of decline and abandonment is woven through media coverage of US small towns in the late twentieth century. Like gold rush ghost towns of the previous century, imagery of these places reflects a loss of their core economic driver: not gold, but now coal, timber, and the family farm. Without these major employers, the story goes, there's a mass exodus of young people, leaving behind only those who cannot afford to leave. Unlike the classic ghost towns, these departures and decline are slow, as jobs and people leave in dribs and drabs. Sporadic false hopes appear, new industries make promises, but a "new economy" never seems to materialize.

Beyond the decline of individual towns, this narrative is also portrayed as collective. After all, American small towns declined in terms of their share of the total population for more than a century. Mechanization and economies of scale took their toll on everything from farming to candy-making as large corporations in large cities increasingly dominate the economic landscape. In the 1990s and 2000s, as New Urbanists deified small towns, most news media coverage mourned their loss. While not all small towns are losing population, one type that is clearly in decline is that based on economies of extraction. These towns were built because of nearby resources: coal, timber, silver, copper. These are all time-limited resources, and when they were depleted (or became too expensive to extract), companies left and jobs disappeared. Many small towns like this were heavily dependent on a sole industry and struggled, losing residents and, with them, businesses and their tax base.

Of the small towns I've spent time in, Anaconda, Montana, was the saddest. Its earlier success was entirely dependent on the copper mined in nearby Butte, as it housed the smelter needed to process it. So, when the smelter closed in 1982, it absolutely devastated the town, and its riches, from its four-story hotel to its copper-gilded county courthouse, began to disintegrate or were dismantled and sold for parts. The smelting work left behind hundreds of unemployed workers, front yards riddled with arsenic and other poisons, and a massive hill of black slag.

I lived in Anaconda in May 2008 (early spring in Montana), staying in a $125-a-week flophouse above an Irish bar, with cigarette-singed shag carpeting, a hotplate, and a mini-fridge that froze everything. Cell reception was spotty there, but I'd hold my phone close whenever the neighbors fought or mistakenly pounded on my door. During the day, though, the people of Anaconda were upbeat and excited to share their experiences. Fay from the local motel invited me for tea, and Connie from the planning department took me on a tour around the city. When I visited the local history museum, Jerry (who spoke with an Irish accent and prided himself on being the "Last Smelterman on the Hill"[5]) told me stories from before the smelter closed. There was a sense of pride among those I spoke with in Anaconda—in their town's history and in that they'd stayed and were in it for the long haul—but also a deep sense of loss and a recognition that a future here would be an uphill climb

Figure 4.1. Remaining slag behind the county courthouse in Anaconda, MT. Photo by author.

out of a deep hole of population decline, job loss, and environmental devastation (Figure 4.1).

Every few years a new revitalization scheme is proposed in Anaconda. Many of the projects revolve around slag, a byproduct of copper smelting that is heaped in large piles looming over Anaconda. It looks like black dirt and is composed of iron and silica with just enough arsenic and lead to make it unusable for most purposes. Perhaps the most visible attempt to repurpose the slag is its use as "sand" in the Old Works Golf Course, which opened in 1997 (Figure 4.2). The golf course used only a small amount; 130 acres (55 million tons) remain. Others suggested making bricks out of slag or using it in the fracking process. "Every huckster and promoter in the western United States showed up in Anaconda [after the smelter shutdown] with the theme song, 'We can do this we can do that,'" said local lawmaker John Fitzpatrick. "Every single one of them was a bust."[6] Despite fitting the narrative of a downtrodden Trump-supporting town, Biden won Anaconda's eight core precincts with nearly 60 percent of the vote.

I saw similar economic decline in Lyon Mountain in New York's Adirondack Mountains where I was recruited to help organize and map photos for their railroad and mining museum when I worked at nearby SUNY Plattsburgh. To get

Figure 4.2. View of Anaconda and Old Works Golf Course. Photo by author.

to Lyon Mountain, you navigate a road that feels like it's going nearly straight up for half an hour (from nearly sea level at Lake Champlain to 2,000 feet), past the infamous Dannemora state prison. The surface of the town was first scraped bare of trees for homes, then mined until the last of the iron ore was too difficult to access. The mine closed in 1967, and the city's population declined from more than 1,053 in 1950 to 287 in 2020. Along the way, the local high school was shuttered. When New York State offered in 1985 to make the high school into a prison, it was hard to say no. It brought jobs back to the town. But that didn't last, either; it closed twenty-five years later, one of several prison closings in upstate New York. When I visited in 2011, the only job there was guarding the vacant building—a job held by my student's cousin, who snuck us in to give us a tour. The building was beautiful, but it couldn't handle unheated Adirondack winters, and the beautiful wood floors in the gym had begun to crack and buckle. In 2013 the building was bought by a Canadian businessman, ostensibly to become an ore-processing site, but when that deal fell through it was abandoned.[7]

Small towns built around resource extraction are like this: coal towns, iron ore towns, and timber towns. Across the US they were established with one purpose: extract as much of a resource from the earth as possible and enrich the companies that owned the mines or forests. People moved to these towns because the jobs paid moderately well, and others moved there to provide services to the folks in those jobs. They invested in infrastructure, beautiful architecture, parks, and schools, and these were successful towns until they weren't anymore. In some cases like Anaconda, it was a rapid decline with an immediate 1,500-person layoff. In others, it was slow, with always more promises of reopening or that those few last jobs would never go away. The cause wasn't always globalization, either. For many mining towns, they'd simply extracted all that there was to extract: The well had run dry.

Appalachian coal towns, like Windber, Pennsylvania, where my grandfather, great-uncles, and great-grandfather were coal miners, are no longer sustainable. In recent decades, demand for coal declined as natural gas prices dropped and environmental regulations increased. To meet the remaining demand, small underground coal mines cannot compete with large surface mines in the West. In 2015, 45 percent of the coal produced in the US came from only sixteen mines in Montana and Wyoming.[8] But these open mines require less labor, so there are more coal jobs in Appalachia: 18,071 in 2020, compared to 2,642 in the West. So, it's no surprise that Appalachian towns remain the face of coal mining in the US even though coal production there decreased dramatically in the past decades.[9] Coal production in Appalachia declined 45 percent between 2005 and 2015, and another 20 percent from 2019 to 2020.[10]

For timber towns, it's a bit more complicated. In the Northwest, forests grow slowly and logging them resembles an extractive industry, like coal or copper mining. But in the Southeast, pines grow more quickly and can be farmed.[11] Northwest towns are more dependent on management practices, as much of their land is federally owned, whereas Southeastern forests are mostly privately owned. Many forestry-dependent towns were also home to processing plants: paper mills or furniture factories. An increasingly globalized economy hit these, too, as outsourcing labor and materials made factories elsewhere more attractive. In the Pacific Northwest particularly, there was also a backlash against environmental impacts. This set up a battle between city and country dwellers. "What I hate is that urbanites refuse to recognize their role in this," Ann Goos of Forks, Washington, told a researcher. "Why would these loggers work so hard and put their lives on the line to harvest trees if no one wanted them? There's a timber industry because there's a demand for the products."[12]

Postmortems in the media can also be found for towns in the manufacturing areas of the Northeast and Midwest. In the Rust Belt "many of the industrial towns that once served as the country's economic heartbeat are now on life support."[13] Economies of scale led to the consolidation not just of extraction industries but of manufacturing and services as small companies consolidated or failed to compete with larger ones. Meanwhile, freer trade allowed companies to outsource labor to places with cheaper workers and fewer environmental regulations. This affected not only large cities like Detroit that had once been manufacturing powerhouses but also small railroad towns with a large percentage of residents employed in making things and shipping them out to the world. And while some Southern towns benefitted from companies that moved to states that made unionization difficult, most were coping with their own manufacturing declines in textiles, furniture, and cotton.

With declining populations in small towns and rural areas, services also consolidated in larger cities. Schools were shuttered, post office closures were threatened, and hospitals closed. This is a trend that started in the Great Plains during the Dust Bowl but intensified elsewhere in recent decades. There is an unwillingness to subsidize services that cost more to offer in rural places. In 2012, the threat of post office closures led to a backlash from customers and the federal government backing off. Veterans' services are also being lost from these places, as are schools, which close as populations dwindle.[14] Private services are also declining as customers grow fewer and poorer. Grocery stores are consolidating into suburban superstores, and dollar stores are moving in.[15] Between 2005 and 2023, 195 rural hospitals closed, many in small towns.[16] Many of these closures have as much to do with the economies of scale as they do with population decline in some small towns. Retail and services are cheaper to provide if done in bulk in a centralized location, even if they hurt quality of life in smaller places. And as quality of life declines, those who can afford to leave, leave.

Meanwhile, media reports focused on other small-town struggles: Dozens of articles focused on the effects of the opioid crisis, particularly in coal towns and the Rust Belt. The rise in mortality rate due to drug overdoses during the 2000s and 2010s is frequently discussed as part of the "deaths of despair" trend described by Case and Deaton.[17] However, McGranahan and Parker investigated these claims and found that the first wave of the crisis was more strongly connected to physical disability than to economic distress.[18] They also discovered that while the first wave of deaths was concentrated in West Virginia and Kentucky, and while books like *Dreamland*[19] and *Dopesick*[20] are focused on Appalachia, recent deaths due to opioid overdoses were more common in the Northeast.

Overall, it was true that globalization hit some small towns hard. Towns that were dependent on a single industry struggled to pivot when companies outsourced manufacturing jobs or found new and cheaper sources of raw materials in other countries. The financialization of what were once community-held resources was one of many factors that made rural areas less resilient in the late twentieth and early twenty-first centuries.[21] But within this narrative is a misguided focus on modernism and "progress," a straight-line story that suggested that for every big-city success there must be a small-town failure. There are indeed small towns in serious decline, but there are also small towns that are stagnant or transitioning and others that are economically resilient and growing.

But a more nuanced description of small towns, one that includes growth as well as decline, did not fit well with the story the media was trying to tell. Because of the strong image of the small town in the American imagination, the easiest and most effective way to cover small towns was as a single unit. In this case, the media painted a picture of all small towns (and rural areas) as dying. More broadly, rural America perceives itself perhaps not as dying, but as culturally disrespected and abandoned by urban America, not represented equally in political decision-making, and not getting their "fair share" of a government funding.[22] This may also be partially true in small towns, and certainly the *perception* of decline and resentment of urban elites by small-town America led the media to cast Donald Trump as their savior.

Trump and the "Small-Town Voter"

The urban/rural divide isn't new to analyses of American politics. But Trump's victory inspired a doubling down on this narrative. As Hardy writes, "Trump paints a darker picture of a limping nation in need of more radical change. That's a message that seems tailor-made for rural America. In small towns throughout the heartland, people reminisce about better days."[23] In 1920 the United States switched from being majority rural to being majority urban. Since the 1968 election until 2020 (and likely beyond), most people living in large cities voted for Democrats and most people living in rural areas voted for Republicans. In 2012, Mitt Romney won 83 percent of rural counties. In both the 2016 and 2020 elections, Donald Trump won 90 percent of these counties.[24]

The 2016 election was not the first time this narrative emerged in a presidential election. I spent July 4, 2008, in Wellington, Colorado, a northern exurb of Fort Collins and Denver that in four months would vote marginally for John McCain. Their Fourth of July parade (Figure 4.3) had just wrapped up,

Figure 4.3. Fourth of July parade in Wellington, CO. Photo by author.

and I was walking through the carnival that followed when I was introduced to a councilman by another one of the local politicians I had interviewed. "Oh, you like small towns, huh," he said. "I guess you aren't voting for Obama." It was only a few months earlier that Barack Obama had been criticized for saying people in small towns "cling to guns or religion or antipathy to people who aren't like them,"[25] and the folks in Wellington hadn't forgotten.

With Obama painted as a big-city community organizer by Republicans, John McCain's running mate, Sarah Palin, worked to stretch her credentials as a "small-town mayor." Wasilla is more of a suburb of Anchorage, but that didn't stop Palin, who played up her folksy side, from claiming small towns as her people.[26] She famously referred to small towns as "the Real America." Just like Obama's negative comments, Palin's comments led to a backlash—in the other direction. Critiquing the use of the phrase "real America," English professor Dennis Baron noted that there are twice as many *World of Warcraft* players than farmers in the country and argued:

> Republican semanticists like Palin define Real America as the small town rural refuge where you go to get away from the thoroughly fake America of cities like Boston (one of the oldest American cities, but not real), New York

(America's financial center, not real unless you've checked the balance in your retirement account lately), Philadelphia (America's first capital, home of the Liberty Bell, not real—have you heard it ring lately?), Washington (the unreal seat of the unreal federal government), San Francisco (that 1906 earthquake? wasn't real, unless it was meant as a warning against gay marriage), and Los Angeles (like a dream factory could ever be real?), cities that also happen to vote Democratic.[27]

The idea that small towns are somehow the *most* real or average America is not new. Think about John Mellencamp's 1985 hit that said small towns are "good enough for me," a framing that suggests those who wish to leave or improve small towns are elitist urbanists.[28] Particularly since the 2016 election, this has resounded as an argument from Republican candidates. And then in the summer of 2023, Jason Aldean released "Try That in a Small Town" and everything blew up (again). While Aldean said the song was about people in small towns watching out for each other, critics saw it as supporting vigilantism ("Got a gun that my granddad gave me / They say one day they're gonna round up / Well, that shit might fly in the city / Good luck / Try that in a small town"). When a music video featuring clips of urban protests interspersed with the site of a lynching followed up the song release, pushback got even stronger.[29] In the end, the video was quietly cleaned up, but the episode reflected how deeply ideas about small towns are rooted in the American imagination.

In the 2012 election, Rick Santorum worked to sell himself as the small-town candidate in the GOP primary, in opposition to the more cosmopolitan (and moderate) Mitt Romney. In a similar fashion to Donald Trump (and many other candidates, Democratic and Republican), Santorum promised to bring back manufacturing jobs to struggling small towns in the Rust Belt and beyond: "Government policy is strangling small-town America . . . We're going to give small-town America a chance to come back."[30]

After winning the Republican primary, Romney, despite his wealthy suburban background, tried to take on the reins of small-town champion by running a bus tour through small towns in the swing states of New Hampshire, Pennsylvania, Ohio, Iowa, Wisconsin, and Michigan, calling these towns "the backbone of America." In announcing his candidacy, he spoke explicitly about the perceived divide between the urban Democrats and rural Republicans: "The president seems to take his inspiration not from the small towns and villages of New Hampshire but from the capitals of Europe."[31]

In 2016, it was quickly clear to political pundits that small towns were no Clinton strongholds: Brooklyn-born Bernie Sanders had a better shot, given his folksy communication style and Vermont credentials. One article describe a Sanders commercial shown in Iowa, to the tune of Paul Simon's "America" ("Kathy, I said as we boarded a Greyhound in Pittsburgh / Michigan seems like a dream to me, now / It took me four days to hitchhike from Saginaw / I've gone to look for America"), which featured small towns and small townsfolk prominently.[32] Another article recognized that Sanders's successes were based in small towns and rural areas (Democratic primary data shows this to be a more complicated situation).[33]

Despite being an New York City urbanite with a mansion in suburban Florida, Donald Trump was immediately pegged as someone who would win over those in small towns. And, it should be noted, this was an accurate prediction for rural areas. Small towns are a bit more complex. While there was surprise that these rural and small-town voters were able to put Trump over the top in electoral college votes, this was not a refrain new to post-election analysis. Before the election, political pundits repeated the mantra that these were Trump territory. "What we're seeing across the country is that Trump is just outperforming other recent Republican candidates in a lot of these smaller, rural areas, and in small towns—in some areas that were once Democratic," political scientist Alan Abramowitz told the *Wall Street Journal*.[34]

"American Carnage"

For the "Trump saves small-town USA" narrative to work, though, the towns must be threatened, declining, or dead. After all, his promise was to "Make America Great Again." At his 2017 inauguration, Trump focused his attention on America's failures: its closed factories, drugs, and crime: "This American carnage stops right here and stops right now," he said. *Vox* called it "doomsday rhetoric".[35] *The Guardian* called it a "sinister view of the U.S."[36] And the *Los Angeles Times* described it as "raw, angry and aggrieved."[37] The examples that Trump gave of US decline were mostly (fact-checkers agreed) hyperbole and exaggeration. But the perception of decline—particularly by white men who felt threatened by changing economic and social structures—was what mattered. And a large part of this narrative involved the decline of the American small town. The speech struck a chord for some who mourned the small towns they remembered from their childhood: "Hearing the phrase 'American carnage,' I thought about small towns in Ohio, near where I'm from, that used to be flourishing and now are half-deserted and boarded up. The *Rand McNally Road Atlas*, that founding document of American optimism, includes who knows how many small towns across the country that exist today in name only," writes Ian Frazier.[38]

In their memoir, presidential advisors Corey Lewandowski and David Bossie explain that "American carnage" referred to towns like Monessen, just outside of Pittsburgh: "It was a place where the American dream had been dead for years and there was almost no hope of getting it back."[39] The last steel mill closed there in 1987. Trump visited Monessen on the campaign trail in 2016 and said fixing it was "very simple" and all that was needed was the "right thinking."[40] This pessimistic view of small towns was highlighted by J. D. Vance in *Hillbilly Elegy*, a timely book that was used by Democrats and Republicans alike to explain Trump's 2016 victory. In his book, Vance painted gloomy pictures of both Appalachia and the Rust Belt, claiming their abandonment by the political system.[41] Vance grew up in rural Kentucky and a small city in Ohio, something he wrote about and then touted in his 2022 US Senate and 2024 vice-presidential bids.

In the last decade, pessimism sells, and Americans are buying.[42] In 2018 Pew Research found that few Americans believed that families would be better off in the future.[43] The COVID-19 pandemic and subsequent economic uncertainly likely did not help improve their outlook. Little surprise then that the media focuses on the one segment of small towns that are losing population and jobs. In looking at this pessimism and its role in a narrow view of small towns, it is important to consider the role of race, demographic change, and manufactured fears of "white replacement." The narrative is that small-town residents fear obscurity.

And yet the stereotype that small towns are racially and ethnically homogenous is a flawed one. Research on small-town demographics illustrates that in fact, many (particularly those outside of the Midwest) are looking more like large cities in their demographics.[44] Lee and Sharp used RUCA codes to examine the assumption that small towns are mostly white and found that small urban areas in non-metro counties are in fact more likely to be non-white than small metro areas.[45] In my own research I've found that on average small towns are well representative of national diversity. But these data can be misleading since while some towns are truly diverse, others are majority minority: In the Southeast, many small towns in agricultural regions have long been majority Black due to a history of slavery, sharecropping, segregation. In the Southwest, many towns are primarily Latino, a trend that has spread northward throughout the West, particularly in California's Central Valley and Central Washington.

In keeping with the theme of "American carnage," many argued that throughout Trump's presidency, a focus on crime in cities was a reminder to his core voters that their (white) towns were safe . . . for now. He warned of crime from the cities reaching the suburbs and small towns—a warning that many saw as a racial dog whistle. A closer look at crime statistics shows that since the 1990s overall crime rates are down, but there was a spike in 2020. This increase (+30 percent in homicide rates) affected large cities, but crime in small cities and rural areas also increased (+25 percent) during this period. Authorities blamed the stress and social disconnections caused by the COVID-19 pandemic.[46]

But of course, Trump's use of crime as a political talking point dated back well before 2020. Kelly added, "The audience he's trying to get is constantly agitated and upset. He always has a nose for white victimhood."[47] In addition to stoking fear of African Americans in big cities, Trump also spent time encouraging fear of Latino immigrants. Perhaps most famously in 2016 he said: "They're bringing drugs. They're bringing crime. They're rapists. And some, I assume, are good people."[48]

Many small towns in the US saw an increase in Hispanic residents over the past twenty years. In particular, meatpacking jobs in the Midwest and agricultural work in Central Washington State attract nonwhite workers. In some towns the demographic change is particularly large. Quincy, Washington, for example, was one town I spent time in 2008 and visited again in 2016. Its Hispanic population grew from 37 percent in 1990 to 65 percent in 2000 to 78 percent in 2020. The white population of the town stayed around 1,700, but the Hispanic population grew from 3,362 in 2000 to 5,845 in 2020. Interviews with white local officials (in 2008 and 2022, only one of seven councilmembers are nonwhite) suggested a cultural divide and, at times, outright racism.

In 2008, the (white) mayor seemed disgruntled about the Latino influence on food in town: "There's a lot of Mexican restaurants, but not a lot of restaurants where you can just sit down and have a regular dinner." At a prominent corner in downtown Quincy are two variety shops with many handwritten signs in Spanish. One resident said there were concerns about this change on Main Street: "[Their shops] don't look the same as ours, they look transplanted from Mexico." One councilman thought this shift could be an asset to Quincy, that downtown could be transformed into a "Little Mexico," but this idea never came to pass, he said, because "we've got a lot of people who aren't into that."

While Quincy is experiencing measurable demographic change, other small towns have had smaller increases in diversity. But even these small increases in nonwhite residents can cause concern among white, politically homogenous residents. "In rural areas, or small towns, where everyone speaks the same language, or practices the same customs, life can be simpler, more predictable, less frictional," Lane assesses. "Economists call these 'compositional amenities,' and many people value them above the benefits of diversity—even above economic gains."[49]

But despite the "friction" of recognizing difference and the hardships caused by structural racism, the reality of being targeted by simply existing as a Black or Latino or Asian person in America was never *not* a small-town issue. Sundown towns existed across the United States from 1890 to 1968, using ordinances, deed restrictions, signs at the edge of town, and threats of violence to prevent Blacks and other nonwhite groups from remaining in the town after dark. While many southern towns in Jim Crow America were segregated, these towns in the West, Midwest, and Northeast purposefully excluded nonwhite residents. While now illegal, the demographics of sundown towns persist.[50] My own hometown, Schuylerville, had zero Black and zero Hispanic residents in 1990, and still no Black residents and only thirty-five Hispanic and eight mixed-race residents in 2022, according to the U.S. Census Bureau.

The 2020 murder of George Floyd briefly raised attention to issues of race in small towns, as protests took place across the country. The response in small towns was noticeable enough to capture media attention. "I am shocked. I am amazed by what I have seen," sociology professor Jack Bloom told the *Washington Post*.[51] Two weeks after Floyd's murder, the *Washington Post* estimated at least 4,700 protests across the county.[52] These protests reached well beyond large cities to include small towns and rural areas, which are diversifying: many adding more nonwhite residents than white residents every year.[53]

While politicians like Sarah Palin may see small towns as their territory, in terms of winning elections, they often ignore the diversity that actually exists in these towns. In particular, majority-minority towns and neighborhoods tend to vote Democratic. In Quincy, the city voted 54 percent for Biden in the 2020 election[54]—this despite the city being in the middle of very red rural Washington State.

My research at the precinct scale in Ohio, Pennsylvania, and Wisconsin showed that small towns voted on average 8–10 percentage points more Democratic than rural areas in the same county in each of these three states.[55] While Biden did not win most small towns, and certainly not at the levels of large cities in the same states, there was a clear distinction between settlement types by population density. Small towns do not vote the same as nearby rural places.[56] Among the three states I looked at, the greatest difference between small towns and rural areas was in the reddest state, Ohio. There are 130 small towns in Ohio, comprising 901 precincts. Ohio includes rural and small-town Appalachia, Rust Belt cities and small towns, and rural farming communities. A population dot map of Ohio (Figure 4.4) illustrates the 50/50 split of the

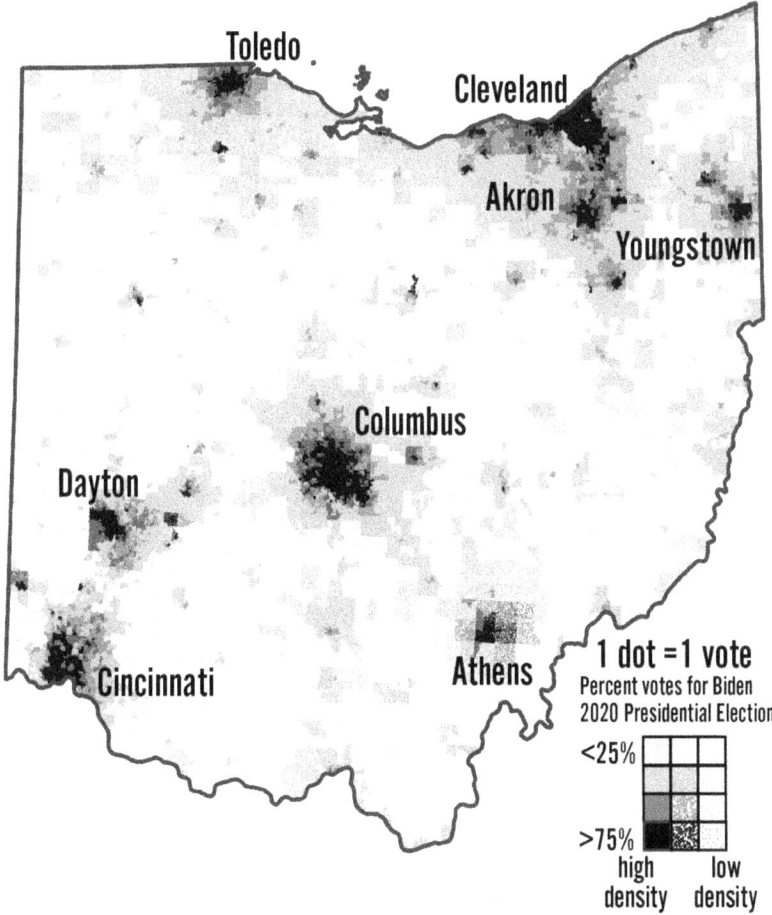

Figure 4.4. Democratic-majority and Democratic-leaning precincts in Ohio's 2020 presidential election. Map by author.

suburbs, which make up 43.9 percent of the voters in the state, the deep (but dispersed) red of rural areas, and the high density of Democratic votes in large cities. In nearly all counties, small towns leaned more Democratic than rural areas. Some of the counties with the largest differences included college towns, but not all, as counties with college towns also tended to have rural areas that voted more Democratic. Exceptions to the small town / rural gap were typically suburban counties where the rural areas, while less dense, were closer to large cities and their suburbs and so voted more Democratic than more distant small towns. Biden won small towns in four counties in Pennsylvania, six in Ohio, and fourteen in Wisconsin.

It is important to address the role of college towns in the broader political landscape of small towns. As we may expect due to their demographics, college towns certainly play a role in small towns voting more Democratic on average. In Ohio, the top five counties in terms of difference between small towns and surrounding rural areas are home to a college town (Oxford, Cedarville, Bowling Green, Athens, and Oberlin).[57] Even removing all ten college town–influenced counties in Ohio, the difference between small towns and rural areas in the remaining 63 counties is on average 7.7 percentage points (compared to 9.5 percent if college towns are included). Even so, it is important not to asterisk-out college towns: They are, after all, one type of small town, just as much as exurbs, farm towns, coal towns, and other types of places are also small towns worthy of inclusion in drawing conclusions about these places.

College towns and the racial diversity of some towns are not the only reasons small towns tend to lean further to the left than surrounding rural areas. The very same political preferences cited as causing the red/blue divide can also influence the political geography of small towns. These places are younger and more diverse than rural areas. They are denser and thus more attractive to liberals who are more likely to look for homes in walkable communities.[58] Returning to Rodden's (2019) analysis of the roots of the urban/rural divide, perhaps it should not be surprising to see these places as more Democratic than their rural counterparts.[59] They are former hubs of manufacturing and railroad towns, and now some (though not all) are increasingly destinations for knowledge workers untethered from large cities by increased broadband connectivity.[60]

Small Towns and National Politics: Looking Ahead

Small towns are not a large portion of the US population, but in tight elections, they should not be overlooked. While suburbs are often seen as purple battlegrounds for presidential candidates, certainly there are also votes to be won in small towns—by either party. And this is an essential point: despite media narratives, small towns are not homogenous in their political leanings, nor do they always follow their rural neighbors.

In 2002, Judis and Teixeira argued that there is less a big city/small city divide and more an industrial/postindustrial divide that would decide our political future.[61] They saw the emerging Democratic majority as coming from large and small postindustrial cities and suburbs, "ideopolises" that refocused their economies on new technologies and twenty-first-century services. The transformational vote in these places, they argue, is the white working class, the same group that pundits ceded to Trump after the 2016 election. In 2020, Teixeira doubled down on his belief that this group will make the difference in future elections (thus an argument to focus on a moderate agenda). He noted that while demographics (growth of a college-educated, more diverse electorate) are in Democrats' favor, this is quickly counterbalanced by reliability of non-college-educated white voters to choose Republicans.[62]

There is an important distinction to be made when talking about small towns, white working-class voters, and Trump support. The entire idea of "American carnage" and white working-class resentment assumes that the rural poor are Trump's base. Edelman (2021) goes so far as to call most of rural and small-town America economic "sacrifice zones" where poverty and disinvestment feed an attraction to Trump's authoritarian populism.[63] But Carnes and Lupu (2017) use the demographics of Trump voters to dispel this myth, finding that most were not working class.[64] While certainly rural, two-thirds of Trump voters were above the nation's median income (a number that becomes even more meaningful when we consider the low cost of living in most rural areas). Additionally, while 69 percent of Trump voters in 2016 did not have a college degree, 60 percent of these voters were above the median national income of $50,000.

So, while the media are quick to buy into a narrative of Trump making promises of revival to dying, white, poor small towns, the reality is more complicated. First, not all small towns are poor or white. Second, not all Trump supporters are resentful of blue state success because they are themselves successful. The false urban/rural dichotomy is at the heart of this misrepresentation, which fails to acknowledge diversity in rural places and their contributions to the national prosperity.[65]

It's a dichotomy that continues in part because it is helpful to Republicans if they can sell voters on the victimhood of rural places but at the same time on their moral superiority to large cities. Many Democrats, meanwhile, buy into this narrative because their target audience lives primarily in cities and suburbs. In the *National Review*, Kevin Williamson was critical of people and towns who can't keep up with the new economy: "The truth about these dysfunctional, downscale communities is that they deserve to die. Economically, they are negative assets. Morally, they are indefensible. Forget all your cheap theatrical Bruce Springsteen crap. . . . The white American underclass is in thrall to a vicious, selfish culture whose main products are misery and used heroin needles. Donald Trump's speeches make them feel good."[66] Some Democrats, though, worry a focus on large cities is "not sustainable" and that they're ignoring white small-town voters at their peril. "For a party that predicates itself on inclusivity," Representative Dean Phillips told the *New York Times*, "I'm afraid we're acting awfully exclusive."[67]

The "left behind" narrative exudes victimhood, and the *Hillbilly Elegy* narrative centers selfishness. My interest, in talking to people in small towns and learning stories of struggle and success, was in looking beyond these narratives. I asked many of those I interviewed about their place in this world, about structure and agency: To what extent do they feel like their town has control over its own future? What is the role of outside forces—national and global—in that future? The answers to these questions, discussed over the next two chapters, illustrate why these towns are politically diverse and remind us that they should not be assumed to fit the mold that either Republicans or Democrats set for them.

CHAPTER 5

DREAMING BIG IN SMALL TOWNS

For large cities, size is (nearly) everything. Population growth, and certainly economic expansion, are seen as near-universal signs of success. More people living in a city means more customers, more taxpayers, and more volunteers. Higher demand for housing and services means higher costs, higher incomes, and higher tax revenue. This brings in more funds to maintain and improve infrastructure: There's regular maintenance of roads; schools are rehabbed; trails and parks are added. Growth is both a tool and a measure of economic development.[1] Meeting a minimum population threshold (particularly if those residents are wealthy) means that a city reaches critical mass for basic services (a grocery store, schools, competing banks, specialty retail, etc.) or can attract new types of services that in turn attract more residents and provide more (and better-paying) jobs. Meanwhile, population decline can reduce demand and cause businesses to close and services (both public and private) to dwindle. So understandably, media and academia alike work under the premise that a growing city is a successful city.

This assumption presents a dilemma for small towns: If these towns grow, they become less small, and at some point they stop being small towns. Big-city-ness is both a goal and a possibility of erasure of their identity. Their smallness is often one of their selling points, with a strong sense of community, mom-and-pop businesses, and compact walkability that often (but not always) is found in the American small town. In sprawling, booming small towns, these desirable qualities seem distant. Instead, they must contend with the same problems as large growing cities—traffic congestion, gentrification, unaffordable housing, overflowing classrooms—and they also must navigate the difficulties of an identity crisis brought on by being a small town becoming a large(r) city.

This chapter examines why some small towns are booming, with a focus on the role of decades of amenity migration, a trend accelerated by COVID-19. In looking more closely at examples of growing small towns, I consider how this growth presents challenges to urban sustainability and how small towns respond. From an economic development perspective, it's important to think about small towns as urban places at both the local and the regional scales. As cities, small towns with a wide range of population trends can offer lessons and warnings in how we can achieve sustainable urban development. Density is at the heart of many prescriptions for environmental threats posed by human habitation. A denser settlement can reduce energy use and allow for more efficiency in the use of auto alternatives like walking, biking, and public transit. Population growth, on the other hand, is seen as a threat to the small-town "way of life." This contradiction in growing small towns makes them places that can offer insights into how other cities can be both successful and sustainable.

Why Small Towns Grow

Do cities "decide" to grow? For some, this is not even an option. They may adopt a slogan of "open for business," keep taxes low, and eliminate restrictions on housing development. But in the end, if pull factors aren't there, their populations will remain stagnant or decline. These are the towns that we heard about so often in the media narratives about those left behind. Looking at the US small towns described in chapter 1, about half of them lost population between 2010 and 2020. But that leaves another half of towns that are growing in population—some quite rapidly. Success comes from a variety of factors, but amenities, broadly defined, are a common factor. More than just natural beauty, these towns also offer cultural resources, economic and ethnic diversity, and a small-town "look" that outcompetes nearby suburbs.

The desire for growth starts out with the bare minimum: drawing in businesses to decrease unemployment and attracting residents to fill vacant houses and shop at stores and restaurants. For some cities, just stemming the tide of outmigration is enough to call it a win. Many towns offer incentives to businesses through enterprise zones and similar targeted policies to increase jobs and tax revenue. Others invest in parks or subsidize new retail to attract (wealthier) residents.

There's a growing industry in coaching small towns to succeed: organizations like Strong Towns, the Main Street America program, and paid consultants like Richard Florida all contribute to a belief that small cities can grow; they just need to follow certain rules. While these approaches can certainly help shift the tide, my research suggests that proximity to larger successful cities, natural amenities, and a strong cultural economy are the primary drivers of population growth in small towns. While literature on population growth in urban and rural areas tends to separate these three drivers, and I'll describe them as distinct forces below, I also argue here that these three forces are most effective when intertwined.

Amenity Migration

Fifty years ago, demographers tracked counterurbanization in the US—movement from the city to the country. Writing in 1980, geographer Brian Berry saw this trend as "a clean break with the past" and predicted a future of decentralization in the US. Growth in non-metro areas outpacing growth in cities was an extension of the anti-urban bias that led to the "white flight" of the 1950s with a bit of back-to-the-land movement thrown in, pushing participants beyond suburban areas into the countryside.[2] As Berry noted, there were also improvements in transportation and communication and increased occupational mobility. Interest in leaving the city coincided with and was in part caused by economic restructuring as manufacturing jobs declined and service jobs boomed.[3] The geographic range of employment opportunities expanded, and focused on places with natural amenities like mountains, lakes, and oceans as well as National Park "gateway towns" like Jackson, Wyoming; Moab, Utah; and Aspen, Colorado.[4]

In Steamboat Springs, Colorado, an eccentric named Mason Rumney predicted the effects of amenity migration in the 1980s: "Rumney envisions Steamboat Springs as a 'mountain home for the on-line world,' a place where people with computers can live and work and connect with jobs and ideas all over the world." The *Denver Post* article about Rumney's predictions, which many laughed off, was part of a series about Steamboat Springs as its small ski area grew and it became better known. The article went on to explain Rumney's theory about "using inexpensive Radio Shack computers and telephone lines. Brains would flow out from electronic cottages in Steamboat, and money would flow in. No industry, no traffic, and a cadre of bright, affluent neighbors."[5] While the reporter (and critics at the time) reacted skeptically, in hindsight, Rumney saw the future that we're all now living in, one where city size no longer determines its attractiveness to even the most cosmopolitan of potential residents and businesses.

The telecommuting trend of the 1980s turned out to be just a precursor to the early 2000s, when changes in technology led to even greater mobility not just for employees but for entire companies.[6] Infrastructure improvements from interstates to airports also allowed for easier travel between large cities and once-isolated areas. Small towns and rural areas were transformed by amenity migration, creating tension between longtime residents and newcomers, and "changing the essential character and flavor of that community."[7] Migrants also created opportunity, bringing new wealth to these places and creating jobs that allowed those who may have left to remain in their hometowns.

My introduction to Steamboat Springs was the *New York Times* article "Off to Resorts, and Carrying Their Careers," which illustrated the opportunities and challenges of an increasingly mobile job market. High-speed internet was making it possible for newly "location-neutral migrants" to move to rural areas and small towns where they once just had second homes. This shift in migration patterns brought with it a very different crowd: rather than retirees, entire families were arriving and becoming active in the community as customers, volunteers, and voters.[8]

Steamboat Springs grew steadily over the past twenty years, increasing in population from 9,815 in 2000 to 13,048 in 2020, a number that would be higher except for an urban growth boundary and topography that curtails new housing. As a resort town, Steamboat Springs is dominated by the tourist industry, with high home values (median was $1.1 million in 2020) and above-average income. The growing population is driven by those who can afford to move there. Like other towns that were once only seasonal destinations, Steamboat Springs now attracts year-round visitors, as well as new residents and businesses.

Steamboat Springs began as a small ranching community, but within ten years of the 1908 establishment of the city's railroad depot, it became the busiest cattle shipping center in the West, according to a timeline in the chamber of commerce. Coal mining in the late nineteenth century also supported a small population in the area, and springs deemed therapeutic attracted some tourists in the summer months. In 1913, Carl Howelsen arrived in Steamboat Springs via Chicago from Norway. Howelsen brought skiing to Steamboat Springs, building ski jumps and facilities, and organizing races and a winter sports club. Skiing, while a local obsession in the following years, did not become a national draw until the 1960s, when the Storm Mountain Ski Corporation opened a ski resort in the mountains at the edge of town. As the ski resort changed hands, millions of dollars in improvements were made and marketing increased. In 1973, the city annexed the "mountain village," the resort's commercial/residential base, located two and a half miles from downtown Steamboat Springs.

Figure 5.1. A man-made stream and beach in Steamboat Springs, CO, built for summer tourists near the ski resort.

In recent years, Steamboat Springs has shifted from being a winter holiday destination to being a popular choice for second homeowners and others looking for an amenity-rich escape from cities and suburbs. While there is still a boom in population at winter holidays, there has been an increase in both year-round residents and summer tourists (Figure 5.1). In a survey of Routt County residents, residents who felt they "got their town back" during the summer expressed concerns about ongoing events like Triple Crown Baseball Academy, an annual baseball camp.[9] In addition, several media reports and studies of the town found an increase in "location-neutral" business owners moving to Steamboat Springs for its quality of life. Former mayor of Steamboat Springs Towny Anderson told me that the city was irrevocably changed in 2007 by the acquisition of the resort by the Canadian development-oriented company Intrawest, now part of Alterra, which owns resorts across the world, including Vermont, Hawaii, Mexico, and France. Most debates in the city (and there are many) are about how and where the city will grow, not *if* it should grow.

Towns like Steamboat Springs are extreme examples of amenity migration, like Moab, Utah; Vail, Colorado; and other well-known small towns in the West. But there are also lesser-known small towns affected by migration: exurbs, artsy college towns, and places of COVID-19-created exile. These towns also have dramatically increased home values, population growth, and fierce debates over development as their popularity and populations grow.

Exurban Growth

Part of the urban hierarchy, yet separated from it by low-density rural areas, exurbs are at the very edge of commuting range, beyond the traditional suburbs. These towns and subdivisions would be far smaller without nearby cities yet, at the same time, consider themselves independent from them. Taylor describes exurbia as a "city-connected, city-rejecting, form of settlement," arguing that "exurbia is more than a geographic zone; it is a way of life with multiple social, economic, political and environmental interconnections."[10] For Mitchell, the move to exurban areas is not just about moving *to* the countryside, but about moving *away* from the city, while others are driven by a pastoral ideal.[11]

Exurbs are part of urban sprawl, pushing development further and further beyond the city, leapfrogging over rural areas. While the term *exurban* can be applied to any commuter-driven settlement on the urban fringe, my interest is in small towns that were once independent and are now bedroom communities for larger cities. These cities are growing rapidly in population and becoming wealthier, with home values soaring and populations staying or becoming more white and less racially and economically diverse.

From an economic growth perspective, the demand for land and housing is a plus. New residents draw entrepreneurs to fill empty businesses, fix up homes that are in disrepair, and add to the tax base. But not everyone is excited about the newcomers, who also bring changes to city character and increased traffic: housing developments replace farm fields, and mom-and-pop stores may be pushed out of business. My research shows that exurbs aren't just around large cities. Smaller cities like Bend, Oregon (population 103,686) are pricing out new residents, sending them to surrounding small towns (Prineville, Madras, and Redmond) to look for housing. Zoning restrictions and urban growth boundaries can cause development to skip over surrounding rural land and into the nearest already established town.

Wellington, Colorado, is one of these cities. It's more than an hour from Denver, and while some residents commute there, many others work in Fort Collins (population 168,972). Signs at Wellington's border announce that it is "a great place to grow." And if growth is a sign of success, surely Wellington is a model city. With only 2,672 residents in 2000, in 2020 its population was 8,651. In the last twenty years, dozens of housing developments were built around the city's tiny downtown as the city again and again expanded the areas targeted for growth under Colorado's required urban growth boundaries.

Retail has shifted from serving farmers to catering to suburbanites. In 2008, the town's comprehensive plan described their desire to be "user-friendly" for developers: "This plan is vastly different from other Colorado communities who are attempting to limit growth."[12]

When I spoke with him in 2008, Wellington's then mayor, Larry Noel, said that while there are physical and legal constraints in some directions, "our biggest growth here is north, we can go a long way, all the way to the Wyoming border" (twenty-five miles away). Their most recent plan removes this comparison but includes the first two goals: "Develop a diverse, healthy and vibrant economy by encouraging businesses that add to the tax base and provide jobs for local residents" and "develop efficient processes for those desiring to develop land or start businesses in the Town of Wellington."[13] Later goals hedge this primary goal with notes about ensuring growth does not compromise infrastructure, community amenities, and "a wide range of housing opportunities."

In 2022, as real estate values soared, Wellington was the only town in Larimer County where the median home value remained below $500,000.[14] Median household income in 2020 was $89,100, nearly $20,000 more than in Fort Collins, where the median home value was $20,000 higher. As an exurb, Wellington was not surprisingly less diverse than Fort Collins (86.5 percent non-Hispanic white compared to 79 percent). Both Fort Collins and Wellington were less than 2 percent African American, compared to 10 percent Black residents in Denver.

College Towns and Creative Cities

A third category of relatively successful small towns is made up of those that managed to leverage cultural amenities to draw new employers and attract new residents. Most of these are college towns. College towns are growing more slowly than exurbs or amenity-driven small towns, at a rate of about 3.5 percent over the last ten years. But they've shown sustained economic success in part because of the stability of education as a local industry. They also offer a variety of cultural amenities—museums, music venues, art galleries, and festivals—that may not be available in other towns.

In the early 2000s, Richard Florida predicted and heralded a new urban reality where the demands of the "creative class" was central to cities' success.[15] Florida's controversial ideas were both predictive and prescriptive, and the popularity of *The Rise of the Creative Class* meant that planners, city managers, and economic development directors were taking his ideas and trying to find ways to become creative cities.[16] Goals became focused on attracting the creative class through cultural amenities: a healthy downtown full of coffee shops and bookstores, recreational opportunities, an active nightlife, and a strong gay-friendly atmosphere.

When I lived in Ellensburg, Washington, for six months in 2008 as part of my dissertation research (and to avoid Los Angeles rents), I found a thriving town that was part college students but also part creative professionals. Ellensburg Downtown Association director Tim Bishop said that one aspect of this success stemmed from keeping college students in town after they graduated. Many of them provided services to the university, and others worked to use the proximity of Seattle (two hours west) and the affordability of Ellensburg to their advantage. Bishop credited the college town culture for keeping these students in town, as well as in attracting new folks from Seattle who were looking for a more affordable—but still urban—place to live.

About 5 percent of the towns that I studied are college towns. In addition to the amplified presence of young adults and cultural amenities, these places also have unique economic differences. Education, of course, is often the number one employer, but many universities and colleges also attract STEM employers. Business incubators in Florence, South Carolina, and Beckley, West Virginia, are home to numerous startups and attract investors and researchers with local college connections.[17] Global connections to the knowledge economy due to university locations are found not only in large cities but in smaller college towns as well.[18]

The Best of All Worlds: Proximity, Amenities, and Working from Home

A new round of urban-to-rural (and small town) migration was well documented during the COVID-19 shutdown.[19] Between July 1, 2020, and July 1, 2021, the US Census showed decline in the largest US cities and growth in the smaller metro areas, as well as non-metro parts of the US. Overall growth in the US during this period was nearly nonexistent due to more deaths and reduced immigration, leading any increase in population to suggest domestic migration.[20] These data reflected a late 2020 Gallup survey that showed an increased interest among Americans in living in small towns and rural areas (48 percent) versus cities (25 percent). Interest in moving to the suburbs dropped for the first time since the survey began in 2001.[21]

When schools and businesses closed during the pandemic, city residents who could afford to headed for rural areas and small towns outside of New York City and other urban areas. Some left for second homes, others rented long-term Airbnbs, and still others took the opportunity to buy a new house in the country. Some migrations went well beyond exurban moves, as workers that were now footloose headed to "Zoom Towns" in isolated rural areas.[22]

The checklist for pandemic migrants was much like those of people who had already left to work from home: cultural amenities, urban downtown "feel," natural recreation areas, and not *too* far from their previous home so they can still meet up with friends. These similarities meant that many of the most popular COVID-19-era destinations had already experienced growth in the last few decades as high-speed internet service expanded. These factors, Florida and Kotkin argue, "will outlast the virus . . . the pandemic worsened the new urban crisis of rampant gentrification, high living costs, and class and racial division." They predicted while some remote workers will return to the cities, up to 20 percent would retain this lifestyle.[23] To see the future of where these workers might live, I look back to my own past.

The move to more isolated, amenity-rich small towns is something I first noticed as a newspaper reporter in the early 2000s in Saratoga Springs, New York. Saratoga Springs (pop. 28,056) is one of the fastest-growing cities in New York State. It's also by nearly all measures a small-town success story. I watched the city change rapidly from the 1990s, when I was a student at a nearby high school, to the early 2000s, when I was a newspaper reporter there and lived downtown. Today, twenty years later, parts of Saratoga are nearly unrecognizable: the density of downtown increased tremendously as multi-story apartment buildings replaced parking lots and single-story retail from the 1970s and '80s. My former newspaper office (built in 1905) was lost to the declining print media industry, its presses were sold, and it is now a brewery and coffee shop.

While most resort towns are built around natural resources like skiing or national parks, Saratoga Springs' amenity infrastructure is its architecture and overall urban design. Despite some significant destruction by urban renewal programs, its main street, Broadway, and seventeen-acre downtown park survived nearly intact and ready to attract urban nostalgists of the twenty-first century. Even more valuable, its historic racetrack and wooden grandstand also survived and held to its late summer racing season, bringing in nearly 50,000 more people to the city in July and August. These visitors bring additional revenue for the city and local businesses, resulting in improved infrastructure and a wider variety of stores than might be expected in a small town.

Saratoga Springs was the summer destination of the new rich from New York City from the 1870s to the 1950s. Photos of the time show women with parasols and men in fine suits walking up and down its main street, to see and be seen. The crowd today, especially in the summer, and especially in August when the racetrack is open, is much the same. The summer streets bustle late into the night. To see Saratoga Springs today, you would never guess that in the 1970s and '80s many gave up on its success. The city even changed the traffic light schedule to slow down traffic, hoping drivers would see a business they liked and stop. Long stretches of once glamourous homes fell into disrepair, particularly in the city's working-class West Side. Glamorous hotels from the Victorian era were torn down, and urban renewal left its mark there as it had in many other cities with downtown strip malls and parking lots. A suburban shopping mall and new interstate drew shoppers and commuters out of its downtown core.

By the time I started working as a newspaper reporter at *The Saratogian* in 2000, the city was already on an upswing. I first started to suspect something was happening in Saratoga Springs that spoke to broader trends during the early days of the internet. In my first year as a reporter, I visited the just-opened Masie Center, run by online-learning pioneer Elliott Masie, who'd moved to Saratoga from Boston because the internet allowed for him to live anywhere, and he wanted to live *there*. A year later, on 9/11, we reported on our city's single death (dad, hockey coach, and banker Don Krauth) and many near-misses for those who regularly worked in the Twin Towers, including our county supervisor. These were commuters who took on the four-hour drive or train commute so they could live the small-town life in Saratoga Springs on the weekends. The internet made this possible. For the three years that I was a reporter in Saratoga Springs, even though it was the early days of the internet, the city was changing in subtle ways. The relative isolation of the city became less important as its connections increased, and its green spaces, Victorian architecture, and horse farms became more attractive to those with more residential flexibility.

Today Saratoga Springs is vibrant and dense (or, pessimistically: expensive and congested) (Figure 5.2). Population growth in the city has been stable, but development just outside municipal boundaries is growing rapidly. While the natural features—spring waters and baths—that drew visitors are less vital to the city's economy today, today a sense of place in the form of old Victorian buildings, a rich nightlife, an all-season music scene, and proximity to the Adirondacks is the real draw. Being only three and a half hours by train to New York City just sweetens the deal. This overlap of attractions, along with the COVID-19-era leap forward in remote work suggests that Saratoga Springs may be the future of many other amenity-rich small towns. But it also predicts some of the forthcoming challenges.

Figure 5.2. New and old multistory, mixed-use buildings in downtown Saratoga Springs, NY. Photo by author.

What Happens When Towns "Boom"?

Growing small towns have many of the same problems that growing large cities do, and then other challenges on top of this. As in many cities, if the supply of housing cannot keep up with demand, residents face an affordability crisis. More than this, the increase in costs can push out the city's most vulnerable residents—renters—as landlords seize on the new success to increase prices. New residents, particularly those with higher incomes, can shift the nature of retail in cities. Longtime storeowners facing increased rents may move outside the city or close up shop entirely. The type of stores that are successful may change, bringing in a yoga studio where there once was a bodega, for example. A final change I'll discuss here is more particular to small towns: a change in character. While certainly urban neighborhoods can expect this as populations grow, small towns can find this particularly dismaying because part of their identity is wrapped up in their *smallness*. So as more and more residents move into town, longer-term residents may grow disgruntled, or they may just leave.

In the big-city sense, gentrification involves "competition for urban space" and the resulting displacement of residents who are unable to afford rising prices for rent or mortgages.[24] These residents are frequently low income and are often Black or Hispanic. The process of gentrification is not just private decisions to come or go, but also involves attempts by local officials to increase revenue and/or reduce crime.[25] In promoting increased property values, cities must be willing to compete with other potential spaces of investment and be prepared to transform their natural and built environment to "lure wealthy investors, residents, and tourists to town."[26] Small-town gentrifiers are attracted to an idealized countryside but at the same time seek out cosmopolitan small towns so as not to completely lose urban amenities.[27] Hines describes these newcomers as the "post-industrial middle class" in search of rural experiences.[28] They move to small places with the hope of experiencing an "authentic" experience there, but create both intended and unintended changes in these places through middle-class consumer demands ("I love it here, but what would really be great is a yoga studio where that feed and grain store is . . .").[29]

Loss of Affordable Housing
The influx of wealthy residents and increased demand for places to live reduces the availability of housing. Steamboat Springs is one of the most extreme examples of this trend in small towns, making housing unaffordable for all but the wealthiest. While the resort town has long included many temporary service jobs, in recent years, particularly with the influx of new amenity migrants, the division has become more noticeable. "For a long time here, we didn't know how much people were worth," said Vision 2030 project manager Tammie Delaney. "It didn't matter if they were living in a cabin up at Hahn's Peak or they were building a mountain mansion up at Dakota Ridge." She adds that a survey by the Vision 2030 committee showed concern about "social stratification."

One survey respondent wrote, "People moved here because of the flat social structure. I grew up here and never realized there was such a thing as social structure, until I went out into the real world. At the county, regional level people are starting to feel this have/have not [divide]." Many low-income workers in Steamboat Springs must find homes in other towns and commute due to the high cost of rent. On Route 40 just west of Hayden, a sign suggested that residents "Save gas, move from Craig to Hayden." At the other end of the housing spectrum, wealthy residents build "McMansions" at the rural edge of town.

In Steamboat Springs, and increasingly in other towns as well, "solutions" to this division have included government support and regulation of affordable housing. But, said Noreen Moore, business resource director of Routt County Economic Development Cooperative, there are still several residents who see this as "charity." A 1999 community survey found that 51 percent of those surveyed agreed that affordable housing is the "most important" issue to "ensure that the local community is preserved." But 22.5 percent disagreed with this statement. Vision 2030's survey showed that while residents believed that affordable housing was "threatened," most did not consider the issue to be as "important" as other issues such as open space preservation.

This disconnect is illustrated through numerous failed attempts to bring affordable housing, or even moderately-priced housing, into town. One of the more telling battles was over the development of a parcel best known as Steamboat 700. This project was planned for one of the few developable areas adjacent to the city, on its west side. It would have built seven hundred homes on 536 acres, but residents called for a yes/no vote on the city plan to annex the property due to concerns about the project affecting the city's character. The vote to annex failed, and over the next decade, other proposals for developing the land fell through. In 2021, an anonymous donor provided the $24 million needed by the Yampa Valley Housing Authority to purchase the land and build affordable housing.[30] The next year, the Housing Authority proposed building 2,300 units (mostly apartments) on the land, now named Brown Ranch (Figure 5.3). While some residents continued to voice concerns, the Housing Authority moved forward, counting on state funding and a short-term rental tax to pay for construction. Housing costs at Brown Ranch would be capped at 30 percent of residents' income, and only local workers or retirees would be eligible to live there.[31] While the city voted to approve the annexation in 2023, opponents (again) forced a referendum and (again) voted against the planned development the following spring. Concerns involved the size of the project and "a different group of people" who would live there ("I know it sounds horrible," the concerned resident clarified at a city council meeting).[32]

In some ways Steamboat Springs is exceptional: Home values and income far exceed most other small towns (or large cities). But it's also indicative of a problem facing many small towns, if in a far less dramatic fashion: the challenge of providing affordable homes even as demand increases, while reducing sprawl and preserving the open space that attracts new residents there in the first place. Gentrification and speculation aren't just problems in the wealthiest small towns. These processes also affect towns with lower incomes where even moderate increases in home values can displace longtime residents.

The home construction boom in Quincy, Washington, was a combination of meeting a long-ignored need for middle-class housing and speculation on

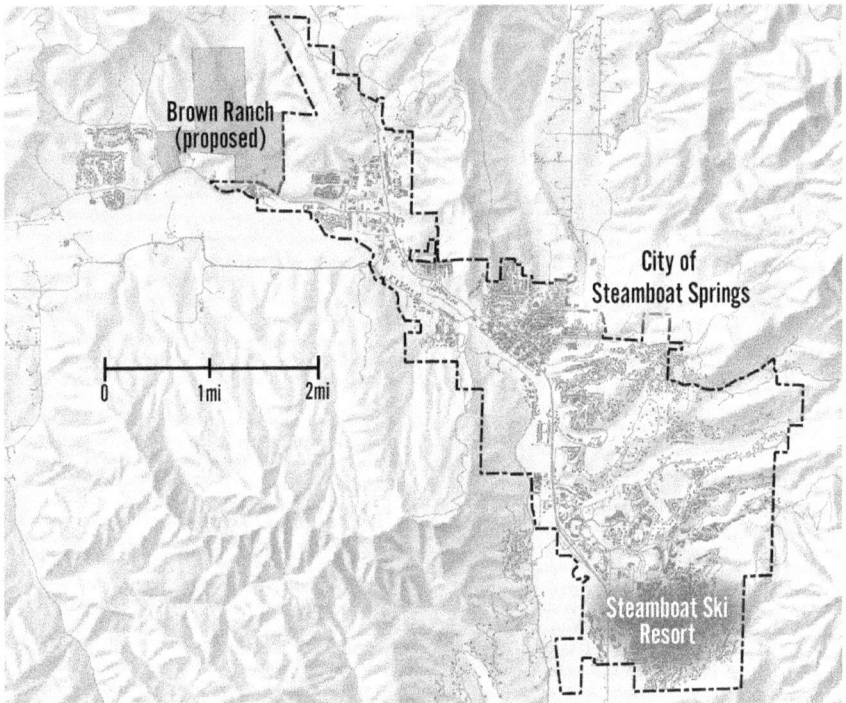

Figure 5.3. Map of Brown Ranch proposed for Steamboat Springs, CO. Adapted from Yampa Valley Housing Authority. Map by author.

the need for upper-class housing. As the town grew, several new developments offered middle-class homes, priced in the mid-$100,000s, which sold easily to local agriculture workers. In the mid-2000s, Microsoft and Yahoo! announced plans to build server farms in the town, taking advantage of affordable electricity (2.6 cents per kilowatt-hour) from the nearby Grand Coulee Dam. As local officials tell the story, just the idea of high-tech jobs was enough to prompt out-of-town developers to build expensive homes in a development just south of town. Only a few of the $450,000 homes were built before the developers realized that few employees were needed to operate the tech facilities, and many lots still sit as vacant reminders of the jobs that never came (Figure 5.4). In the end, each data center brought only about fifty jobs; many of these were low-wage, entry-level positions. Of 132 homes planned in Serenata, only 28 were built, and today many of the lots are still empty, sandwiched between the city's original housing stock to the north and more modest new homes (1,000 square feet) to the south. While the housing demand never materialized, the city profited greatly from sales tax, and residents saw an estimated $200 decrease in

Figure 5.4. Serenata $500,000 home in front of an older Quincy, WA, home. Photo by author.

property taxes. However, with their property value assessments also increased, it seems unlikely that residents saw much of this profit. Instead, councilman Jose Saldana said, they saw only an increase in housing costs while their wages remained stable.

Loss of Character

The influx of new residents can also change the character of the local community. Much like big-city gentrification, residents with more cosmopolitan tastes (and more disposable income) bring yoga studios, art galleries, and bistros into towns more used to diners and dive bars. Farmland and open space are plowed under to make room for new homes and strip malls. Historic buildings are renovated or torn down as new homes and businesses arrive. All of these changes can result in long-term residents pushing back on the idea that growth is a necessary part of small-town success.

Many respondents to the Vision 2030 survey saw Steamboat Springs' sense of community as threatened. Some saw it as disappearing or gone. One respondent wrote: "When your main street is filled with galleries and real estate offices, you have lost the community." But overall, most respondents wrote that "sense of community" (although often left undefined) is one of Steamboat Springs' most valuable assets, distinguishing it from larger cities and other resort towns.

In Steamboat Springs, a debate over whether to allow a Walmart at the edge of town revealed that most voters wanted a cheaper place to shop. Downtown Steamboat Springs has few clothing stores aimed at residents; expensive outdoor clothing shops are the norm, and so a new big box store was welcomed as it brought more options for shoppers. In Quincy and other towns, the divide between rich and poor can be seen in debates about discount stores. What is "classy" to some is "unaffordable" to others. When I spoke with him in 2008, Quincy councilman Jose Saldana was frustrated with what he sees as the local marking-up of household necessities, and said he and many of his constituents would welcome a Walmart. In Ellensburg, Washington, an advertisement promoting the addition of regional retail quoted a resident who felt that the county needs more affordable stores: "So many people think they speak for every citizen of the county . . . not all of the citizens can afford to shop at specialty stores."

When I lived there, Ellensburg was in the middle of hard-fought battle between those who wanted to bring more larger retail stores to the area and those who wanted to support local stores and prevent sprawl. Unlike in any small town I've lived in before, there are five supermarkets walking distance from downtown, including a superstore, Fred Meyer. But "The Fred" is still small compared to Walmart and Target, and those on the big-box side of the debate said they wanted a wider variety of shopping options. Zoning restrictions kept stores from sprawling into the types of large lots these stores required. In the end, the city council approved rezoning but Walmart never came. The recession stalled retail hopes, and today the commercial strip on the edge of town has a Hampton Inn, an IHOP restaurant, and not much else.

The concern in Ellensburg was not just about a change in retail or hurting local business; it was also a broader concern about the loss of the city's character. Calls for growth are typically couched in assurances that growth will be "managed" and will be the "right kind." So, when residents in Ellensburg pushed for the development of a new retail development at the interstate, they insisted that the goal was to bring in Costco, Macy's, and Victoria's Secret—not Walmart.[33] But of course Walmart is one of the few (possibly the only) large-scale retailers interested in locating in small towns.

Opinions about Walmart are also mixed in Quincy. While local historian Harriet Weber said, "People don't want big-boxes here . . . we will do anything to keep a Walmart out of Quincy. It's not what we want for Quincy. It's not what Quincy is," most town officials seemed open to or enthusiastic about the idea. But Saldana said, "We want people to shop locally, but the thing is, it's expensive . . . I don't have anything against Walmart because I'm a consumer."

Port of Quincy commissioner Curt Morris saw the town's recent attraction of data centers as a draw for franchises: "I think it's going to be dynamite for Quincy," he said. "It's bringing things we've never had." Hindsight is 20/20, but by 2023, neither a Walmart nor any franchise besides McDonald's and Pita Pit had come to town.

"Getting a Walmart" or "getting a Chipotle" are seen by many town officials as small-town success stories. To attract a franchise means that your town is growing, expanding, that it has economic promise and is a worthy investment. Ellensburg's tumultuous relationship with its downtown and the threat/promise of big-box stores is indicative of the forces promoting (and preventing) commercial sprawl, forces that have been at work for nearly a hundred years, a culture that most townspeople grew up with. For thirty years, Ellensburg held off major commercial development on its fringe. "Because we were stagnant, we didn't get the seventies-style urban renewal, and we didn't get the Chipotle franchises," said then head of Ellensburg Downtown Association Tim Bishop in 2008. "The challenge now is not to succumb to the idea that this is the only sign of economic development." Nostalgic re-creations and protection of open space and historic buildings are constructed not just to answer the calls of residents. A reassertion of the small-town identity is also profitable: as Towny Anderson, former mayor of Steamboat Springs and executive director of Historic Routt County, noted: "Places that will be prosperous are those that preserve their cultural heritage. People don't come here for Walmart."

Sense of place is also connected to a sense of history. More often than not, this is a past that connects an increasingly mobile and globally connected society to *the land*. We can see this in a closer look at how small towns market their connection to the "Old West." At the same time, nostalgia for a time of rural isolation disconnects the small town from the urban hierarchy: While increasingly connected, small towns also celebrate their isolation. Rather than supporting the adage of newer-better-bigger, towns have increasingly promoted (if not succeeded in preserving) their rural, agricultural heritage. In some ways, this celebration of the Old West is not new. This image has long been marketed regionally. But I found that this history has taken on a greater importance: one that moves beyond themed hotels and gift shops. It also comes at a time when the reality of small towns—their economic and social base—is moving further and further from their historic roots. This division both intensifies the attraction to the past and forces an inauthentic recreation of a disappearing landscape.

In Steamboat Springs, residents see the city's agricultural heritage as an important part of its small-town character. "Take the resort away from us and it's still a cow town," wrote the *Steamboat Pilot*'s editorial staff in support of the local cattlemen. "Take Steamboat's cowboy image away from the resort and it's just another ski area—and an out of the way one at that." In Steamboat Springs' chamber of commerce, a timeline notes that the city ended the annual cattle drive down the main street in the 1970s: It was deemed "unsuitable for Steamboat's image and tourism." But in 2001, the chamber decided to bring back the cattle drive. Sureva Towler, a local writer and critic of the "new" Steamboat Springs, describes the event in a *Denver Post* column: "Last summer the town ran a herd of cows down Main Street in tribute to the Good Old Days. A handful of tourists and a dozen failing ranchers, paid $100 by the chamber of commerce, ran 100 head of cattle down Main. It was high noon and high heat, 98 by one guestimate, so they didn't actually run. They sank into liquid asphalt . . . a few tourists and two poodles gawked as the cows lumbered out of trucks, plodded down three blocks and struggled back into trucks."[34]

Ellensburg also has a rodeo, but only once a year. The rodeo is a regional event more than a local one, timed to coincide with the county fair. Town residents, particularly the newer ones, often left (or claimed to have left) town for the weekend of the rodeo to avoid traffic and cowboy-hat wearing visitors who waited in lines outside local restaurants. But even for those who are not participants, the rodeo is important to the town's image. It is featured throughout promotional literature and on billboards and building façades throughout town.

Quincy, too, while focusing on a high-tech future, promotes its past (and present) through agricultural imagery. "Farming is the heart and soul of Quincy. It's the heritage of farming here in the valley," said historian Harriet Weber. On vacant storefronts, the town has painted old farming equipment, and at street corners, it has placed old, rusted farm equipment. Councilman Scott Lybbert said this was his idea, the "avenue of ag-tiques" to promote and celebrate the town's past. At the town's main intersection, a vacant building has been painted with scenes from the 1950s, the town's boom days after irrigation brought water to its farmland. Along a small commercial strip about half a mile from the center of town is a restored farmhouse, which has been turned into museum.

No one equated the advance of time and growth (or loss) of population with an increased sense of community. Nearly all see a sense of community as important but threatened. "It is a difficult thing to balance progress versus keeping the soul of a community," said Quincy historian Harriet Weber. Having more people, and particularly more new people, was seen as decreasing the connections between residents and decreasing the shared experience of the small town. Most residents—rightly or wrongly—saw newcomers (people as well as businesses and industries) as somehow "different" or "disconnected" from a shared sense of place and history.

In recent years, the city was bolstered by increasing numbers of new Latino residents, many of whom work for the commercial farms. The demographic shift from 37 percent Hispanic in 1990 to 78 percent in 2020 resulted in noticeable resentment from some local white residents as more and more businesses and schools become predominately Hispanic. Several Quincy residents suggested that they hoped an influx of workers and money associated with the server farm industry would shift the "balance of culture," so to speak, away from the Hispanic-dominated agriculture industry. "It's always been a Hispanic industry, and that's good, it's diversified," said one councilman. "Thank heavens we've got these technology industries that have come in and diversified us even more." Other racial "concerns" came from residents who spoke about going to the grocery store or post office and not knowing anyone. "You don't have that small-town feel like you did before," the mayor told me. "Part of that is due to growth; part of it is demographics. There's a huge Hispanic population in the city, and the cultures don't mix too much."

In Wellington, which, until recently, was also focused on agriculture, the percentage of Hispanic residents was smaller. As in other exurban small towns, its white population grew as wealthy folks from large cities moved beyond the traditional suburbs to buy homes. One town trustee told me that she was glad her kids didn't "have to deal with racial conflict" in school. She claimed that the town's downtown market, run by a Hispanic family, didn't carry basics like milk and bread and sent an advertising flyer out in Spanish. This didn't go over well with local (white) families, she said. Few interviewees in any of the towns I visited acknowledged any racism or racial conflict. In Quincy, however, newspaper editor Chuck Allen did note that "there's a little bit of fear that way; there's a perception that Hispanics bring in crime and that Anglos are going to have to provide them with things." But, he said, "sometimes people want to make it into a race thing, but what they're really complaining about is poor people."

In Quincy, there is a clear connection between an increasing Hispanic population and an increasing population overall (an indicator, for some, of economic success). In other small towns across the country an influx of (Latino) immigrants may make the difference between a stable population and a declining population. While research shows immigrants have an overall positive impact on a community's economic health, they are not always well received. Carr et al. compare the hostile response of Hazelton, Pennsylvania, with a more welcoming attitude in St. James, Minnesota, finding that the rate of change combined with long-standing political labor divisions can make a difference in reception of new workers. They suggest that small towns with long-term population loss may be more receptive to newcomers than places that only recently have experienced decline.[35]

Thinking Small in a Nation of "Big"

Population growth in the United States, as viewed by most Americans, is seen as a success: more jobs, more people, more income, more income tax, better schools, which then draw in more people, and so on. Even if we're uncertain about celebrating population growth, then we know for sure that what we don't want is population decline. Population decline in the US, particularly in the Great Plains and the Rust Belt, is a cause for concern. Rotting barns in the countryside, abandoned schoolhouses, and vacant lots and factories in cities all are signs of decline and decay. Are these an inherent effect of population loss in small towns and rural areas? Or can cities stay small while staying vibrant and relevant? Growing small towns face similar challenges to growing neighborhoods in cities gaining population. There are limits to a city's ability to control its growth. It has more control over *how* it grows.

The Slow City movement offers one approach to retaking control over how a city grows and changes. The movement is primarily European, with only two cities in the United States certified as Slow Cities (Sebastopol and Sonoma, California) of 272 cities worldwide.[36] Cities that sign on to be Slow Cities are committing to protecting environmental resources and promoting local production and consumption. More specifically, Mayer and Knox argue that the movement focuses on a community economic development approach that works to be more equitable, place-appropriate, and authentic. They found that the multiple goals of the Slow City movement help draw in a wide variety of stakeholders from across the three *E*'s of sustainability (environmental health, social equity, and economic success) to provide support for these goals.[37] American small towns may benefit from this approach to economic development. The next chapter offers some examples of how small towns integrate the sustainability principles of slow cities into their plans for the future.

CHAPTER 6

SUSTAINABLE FUTURES FOR ORDINARY CITIES

Small towns play a strong role in our imagination, politics, and urban design. But how will they fare in the future? Predictions for the future of small towns range from erasure because of depopulation to stagnation to erasure of their character due to *over*population. To sustain small towns at a level where they remain viable as small, dense, affordable places is to fulfill the small-town ideal firmly rooted in American culture. Is this feasible? If so, how? Identifying a path forward for the places that Jennifer Robinson called "ordinary cities"—those that don't sit at the top of the global city hierarchy—can help us find a way forward for all human settlements.[1]

There's a path to the future if these places can maintain a careful balance between isolation and globalization, between integration and independence, between embracing change and valuing a sense of place and history. This balance can produce sustainable small towns and offer lessons for larger cities. Sustainability means providing for the three *E*'s: environmental health, social equity, and economic success, in both the present and the future.[2] By including time as a factor, sustainability advocates are saying you can't be so focused on success in the present that you burn out before you get to the future, but also you can't be so worried about preparing for the future that you forget about those who need help right now. The future for small towns requires attention to sustainability and, with it, other careful balancing acts. They are wrapped up in a world that is constantly shifting; their viability depends on their ability to globalize but still isolate, to maintain a steady identity but remain economically and culturally flexible. This is not an easy task, and so we can learn from those that adapt more easily to new social, economic, and environmental realities.

Balancing Isolation and Globalization, Independence and Integration

The very definition of small towns requires some isolation from larger cities. There is value in this, in remaining distinct from other places, not close enough to be subsumed by sprawl, and independent enough to make decisions that benefit their own community. Technology and infrastructure have certainly narrowed these gaps over time. Small towns vary in the degree to which they remain distinct from nearby cities. For some, their economic and cultural distinctiveness is clear. Others have become bedroom communities, dependent on other cities for everything from retail to a historic identity. In the 1990s, Jim Kunstler was already discouraged about my hometown, Schuylerville. The jobs at the local textile mill along the canal were long gone and local stores soon followed, replaced by regional and national chains. "You cannot have a community without a local economy," he wrote. "To buy things made far away, sold by merchants who also live far away, is to be a colony."[3] Of course, while Kunstler and others romanticize preindustrial (and postapocalyptic) isolation, the reality is that outside influence on all places in the world is inevitable and oftentimes beneficial.[4]

In an answer to a question about "sense of community" conducted by Routt County, Colorado, one resident said, "When we moved here, the sense of community came partly from our proud ability to survive what we did not have here."[5] But times have changed in Routt County, and today thanks to high-speed internet, Amazon, increased air service, and national retailers, material goods and services are easy to find, even more than three hours from Denver. In today's small towns, what once made these places special—isolation and "doing without"—is lessening. Our sense of small towns as isolated is, of course, misguided in the twenty-first century. Global capital and the internet have seen to that. And while some, like this resident, would argue that connectivity is hurting small towns, others say that it is improving their quality of life.

Globalization and any number of economies of scale transitions (like the success of Walmart) are top-down influences on life in small towns. And there's only so much that can be done about the changes it brings. In my dissertation research, in addition to "What is changing?" I asked research participants, "What control do you have over these changes?" One Steamboat Springs–based Vision 2030 citizens' committee member said she was concerned that despite her efforts, the town was changing: "Though on one hand, I'm committed to preserving the things that I value here, there's part of me that thinks that's out of my control."

In many municipalities, there is a divide between the assessment of statistics measuring socioeconomic and demographic change and the creation of planning documents describing how communities will deal with this change. One assumes dependence, the other independence. Of course, in a world of grays, neither of these tells the whole story of how small towns function in a constant renegotiation of space between the local and the global. Often, the everyday lives of residents are the result of interdependence between individuals, neighborhoods, cities, the nation, and the world.

Three hours from Tucson and two and a half hours from El Paso, Silver City, New Mexico, is physically isolated from other large cities. Residents pride themselves on their independence: They have a small college, an independent radio station, some basic retail, and vibrant arts and food scenes. It's a town that is increasingly home to mostly retirees and artists, but it also profits from being a retail center for surrounding rural communities. While the nearby copper mine continues to be the largest employer in the county, local officials noted that they didn't expect this to last and that they're focusing their attention on other economic strategies for the future. The town created both a cultural plan and a sustainability plan to guide its path forward in a post-mining economy.

While isolation may be valuable to small towns, there's also value in being increasingly connected to places around the globe, especially other cities. The small towns in my dissertation research were all at least two hours from a larger city: Seattle, Denver, and Tucson. For most cities this connection is heavily intertwined with local economies. There is, in some cases, great dependence of the smaller city on the larger city, for employment and amenities like more specialized retail stores and services, for example. However, the relationship between these cities is not simply hierarchical. It is a relationship of interdependence, too, rather than a smaller community needing a larger city. Steamboat Springs, Colorado, for example, relies on the city of Fort Collins as a distant shopping center but also provides an outlet for Fort Collins–based restaurants to open a branch in Steamboat Springs, expanding their business and increasing their profits.

It's an economic balancing act for small towns in particular to keep profits in-house by supporting locally owned businesses but at the same time to stay relevant by offering national retail choices to residents. The same goes for jobs, of course: National retail and global manufacturing and resource extraction siphon money out of the community, but they can also make a huge difference in the number of jobs available for residents. And given the nature of capitalism, there's often little that local officials can do even if they prefer local companies to outsiders.

The New Coal (Copper, Iron Ore, Timber) Town

The origin story of many small towns is their location near natural resources. Given the limited nature of these resources and increasing attention to their environmental impacts, they are undependable as mechanisms for long-term economic development. Some towns adapt to the loss of original types of employment better than others: They transition to other jobs, many of which are healthier for the local environment. But other small towns struggle, particularly if the shutdown of their main employer was rapid and unexpected. These are cities that in many cases have never known any other type of major employment. Their entire town culture, not just jobs, but the arts and nonprofits, and parks, all of it revolves around a single industry. Change in these towns is slow and difficult.

In Anaconda, Montana, locals talk sadly about Black Monday: September 29, 1980, when Atlantic Richfield Co. ended copper smelting operations. Until 1980, Anaconda paired with the extraction of copper at Butte had been the center of the regional economy. Jobs in 1948 paid nearly $240 a day (in 2022 dollars) as a starting wage, which gave plenty of reason to live in this isolated city that was still cold and snowy when I first visited in early summer. The wealth from the copper mine and its employees funded parks and an art deco movie theater; copper was lavishly used around the city to adorn buildings and the roof of the county building at the center of town. In addition to losing more than a thousand jobs, the town lost its major philanthropist.

The idea that somehow people in cities that have lost their economic base should "just move" to find new jobs is lampooned by Roger Moore in *Roger & Me* (how do you leave a place where your house is worth $10,000 to go to a place where homes cost $200,000?) and what was true for residents of Flint, Michigan was also true for Anacondans. On an emotional level, this was their home, their families lived here. On a practical level, homes in places with few jobs are far less valuable than homes in place with more, better-paying jobs. And in Anaconda, there are additional concerns of lead and arsenic poisoning in yards and playgrounds. If Anaconda got relief from anywhere, it was from the attraction of Montana's wilderness and its ability to draw tourists, but larger cities like Butte and Helena, and more scenic towns like Philipsburg tend to siphon off visitors and migrants to Anaconda.

Coal towns in Appalachia and iron ore towns in the Great Lakes region and Adirondacks face similar challenges. Unlike Anaconda, there was not one single day when surprised workers were told they were no longer needed. Coal production is slowly declining and there are fewer and fewer coal mining jobs. Coal is getting harder and more expensive to reach, public outcry against techniques like mountaintop removal is getting louder, and, most importantly, our political will to lower greenhouse gas emissions is getting closer to matching our scientific understanding of its impacts and the economic benefits of switching to a more plentiful resource.

One of the earliest places in the US to transition away from coal is Colorado, where in 2019 a state climate bill set dramatic greenhouse gas goals: a 90 percent reduction in emissions by 2050. Electric companies were pushed to move away from coal and toward solar and wind energy. This means closing mines and coal-fired power plants that provide hundreds of jobs in each town. In Craig, Colorado, the Trapper Mine is set to close by 2030 at a cost of four hundred jobs and decades of cultural integration with a coal-driven economy. Residents of Craig "felt like they were being set adrift," said Kristan Uhlenbrock, host of a podcast about the transition. "How would you feel if part of your identity was to go away?" While many in Craig were angry about the decision to close the mine, some noted that they were lucky to be given nearly a decade to plan what comes next. People support the coal mine because they need to feed their families, Jennifer Holloway, executive director of Craig's Chamber of Commerce, told Uhlenbrock, "We're not the bad guys." They're just used to the broader community being supported financially by the power plant. "It's a dependency relationship as well that we have to wean ourselves from," she said.[6]

While some states are pushing electricity companies away from coal and natural gas, in others natural resources remain a boom/bust economy. I visited Safford, Arizona, during a boom in the late 2000s. All around me, hotels were being built, primarily for the construction workers building the first open-pit copper mine in the US in thirty years. I couldn't find any open hotel rooms except at the local bed and breakfast. In the years after I visited, the fortunes of Safford's mine went up and down. When I returned eight years later, hotel rooms were cheap and easy to come by. The city had invested in its downtown, which now had brick sidewalks, trees, and flowers, but the businesses were just as empty as before.

The small town has long had a role of providing natural resources—both agricultural and mineral—to global and national companies. This boom-and-bust economy, particularly in the West, has shown small towns to be at the mercy of global trends. In Safford, Freeport-McMoRan Copper & Gold spokesman Kimball Hansen predicted a bright future for the local mines, and possibly even a new larger mine to come, but only three months after we talked, six hundred mine workers were laid off after copper prices dropped from $4 a pound in mid-2006 to $1.67 a pound in November 2008.[7] Prices dipped again and there were furloughs in 2020, but by the end of 2022, prices were back to $4. Mining in Safford is predicted to continue until 2041.[8]

Anaconda similarly is affected by global trends, as Phelps Dodge found they could extract copper more cheaply in Chile than in the United States. The environmental devastation left behind by the smelting process means that even without Phelps Dodge as an employer, the town's redevelopment remains dependent upon Superfund negotiations with the global corporation. Superfund investigation and cleanup documents fill shelf after shelf at the local library; negotiations have been ongoing for twenty-five years, and local officials seem resigned to this process. At a county commissioners' meeting, an outside planner hired to help the county said, "The most important news is there appears to be a plan about the Superfund plan that has lasted longer than one month." This was in 2008. In 2022, forty-two years after the smelter closed, Atlantic Richfield (now a subsidiary of British Petroleum) finally signed an $83 million consent decree to cover the remaining costs of remediating pollution in the town's creeks, pastures, commercial areas, front and back yards, and open spaces.[9]

The New Farm Town

"In the American imagination, at least, the family farm still exists as it does on holiday greeting cards: as a picturesque, modestly prosperous expanse that wholesomely fills the space between the urban centers where most of us live," writes Semuels in a gloomy assessment of the American small farm in the twenty-first century.[10]

While farm towns are often at the heart of our imagined views of small towns, commercialized large-scale agriculture has greatly changed the role of small towns in this traditional economic sector. Suburban and exurban sprawl into the countryside has altered the priorities of landowners, as have new uses of land in small towns and their surrounding areas. But some of the earliest industrial successes of the United States were in agriculture, leading to nostalgia for the small towns that served farmers during this time. The wide expanse of land between the coasts lent itself to small places in between wide expanses of farm fields and grazing lands. Our relationship with the agricultural hinterlands is one of false disconnect, Cronon writes in *Nature's Metropolis*.

"Americans have long tended to see city and country as separate places," he writes, "more isolated from each other than connected."[11]

Towns dependent on agriculture are similarly dependent on the whims of global and national economic trends. Many small towns in the United States were built on farming, but with urbanization and the rise of commercial agriculture, there's been nearly a century of change and uncertainty. Farms making under $300,000 a year dropped from half of US food production in 1991 to a quarter in 2017.[12] Yet even as agricultural data shows the decline of the traditional family farm, and food comes from farther and farther afield, agriculture as a *culture* is still central to many small towns in the United States.

Journalist Grady Clay names my hometown of Schuylerville, New York, as an example of an "abandoned farm/area/town," noting James Howard Kunstler's estimate of farms as having declined from 100 to "20 of any consequence."[13] I always thought that I grew up in a farm town; our only high school electives were in operating farm equipment and the business of farming. But Schuylerville hasn't been a true farm town for more than a century. Farming came early to the Hudson Valley and New England, but it left early, too. Stone walls hidden among forests hint at a history long since overgrown or washed away. Instead, Schuylerville was more of a canal town to move goods up and down the Hudson River; then a textile mill town; then, when Kunstler and I both lived there, a hollowed-out factory town; and today, a relatively successful bedroom community of Saratoga Springs. The farms that remained pushed back against the tide of history with conservation easements and right-to-farm laws. Despite our fears, the farmland around my childhood home at the edge of a 1970s subdivision was never sold to a real estate developer. It's still a mix of hay, feed corn, and alfalfa surrounded by county-owned forest land, as is most of the land between my rural home and Schuylerville's downtown.

For the farms that remain, popular culture is helping to root them in place: In this "abandoned farm" landscape, new farm-based businesses seek to meet the demands of suburbanites. These are not your grandparents' farms. Nine Miles East, for example, sells boxed salads, lunches, and pizzas. They deliver to the surrounding county, south to Albany, and even to Boston. This farm partners with another "abandoned farm," one that Kunstler specifically bemoans the decline of in his Schuylerville article: what was known for years as Bullard's Orchard. While the farm (now called Saratoga Apple) is no longer in the hands of its Revolutionary-era family, its new owners successfully transformed it into a cider mill and brewery on a hill overlooking the Hudson River just outside Schuylerville. Next door, you can visit another farm that offers a corn maze in the fall and still another that has revived bottled milk delivery. Schuylerville's farm economy, small as it is, remains secure for the moment.

These newcomers to Schuylerville's retail landscape are part of a much broader trend of value-added agriculture that promotes production and marketing traditional farm products in a way that allows them to sell at a higher price point. Approaches range from being certified organic to producing more artisanal-oriented products to offering crops as part of an experience (such as pick-your-own).[14] Marketing locally produced products through farmers markets and other direct-to-consumer sales offers another way for farmers to raise profits beyond just an increase in quantity of goods produced. Depending on the scale of the operation, these farms and markets can help change the retail landscape of nearby small towns, returning them to their traditional role as farm-to-market centers.[15]

Farming is not a hidden industry; its aesthetics remain an important part of how we understand the places we live. Small towns thrive on this and nostalgia for the family farm remains strong. So when farming shifts elsewhere or consolidates into larger enterprises, what becomes of the land and infrastructure left behind? Wellington, outside of Fort Collins, Colorado, was once a mostly agricultural community. But in the past few decades, much of its farmland has been developed as single-family homes. The Wellington West development, built in 1992 at what was then the town's western fringe, on the state road leading to Fort Collins, doubled the size of the town. The development was marketed to families "tired of the traffic noise, crime, and overall lack of privacy where they currently live . . . wanting to move to a small town." The success of Wellington West attracted more developers: Four building permits were issued in 1990 and one hundred in 1995; the town expanded by two hundred acres between 1992 and 1996.[16]

Boundaries in Wellington continued to expand as the town's population grew from 2,751 to 11,722 in 2021. Farmland is disappearing rapidly, replaced with housing developments to the north and south of the town. A new elementary school was built at the southern edge of town, and commercial and industrial growth is slowly following residential development. The town, long dependent on Fort Collins's shopping centers, recently opened a new supermarket and hardware store. Wellington continues to encourage this growth—the town's master plan includes a quote from William Jennings Bryan: "Destiny is not a matter of chance, it's a matter of choice. It is not a thing to be waited for, it is a thing to be achieved."[17]

There remain some reminders of Wellington's past. Just outside the city limits, the Bee Family Centennial Farm Museum is what is left of the 115-year-old

Figure 6.1. The interior of the Old Colorado Brewery highlights the original wooden walls of the old grain elevator in Wellington, CO. Photo by author.

farm. The family sold ten acres of the farm to a developer, placed a conservation easement on 140 acres and sold them to Colorado State University, and retained the other ten acres for the museum centered around the original farmhouse. In town, meanwhile, another artifact was preserved and integrated into the cultural landscape: the town's grain elevator. In operation since 1922, the elevator sat unused from 1998 to 2016. Renovations exposed and sanded down the thick wooden walls and added a Plexiglas cover to allow visitors to look up into the seventy-five-foot-tall elevator (Figure 6.1). Today the brewery is run as the Old Colorado Brewing Company, which moved to Wellington in 2016 after operating as the first microbrewery in Fort Collins.[18]

In other examples of capitalizing on farming heritage, the Ellensburg Rodeo has come to be both a local celebration of ranching and agriculture and a vehicle for attracting tourists. While the rodeo is only one weekend a year, it is advertised prominently throughout the town. In events like the annual Western Art Show, Ellensburg seeks to unite heritage tourism with cultural tourism. A brochure aimed at those traveling between Seattle and Spokane ("We're on the way to anywhere") advertises downtown Ellensburg as a destination: "featuring many beautiful brick buildings dating back to 1889, gives a feeling of entering another, more relaxed era."

The New Factory Town

From my office window at Kent State, I can see the colorful international flags flying on the roof of one of the new downtown office buildings (Figure 6.2). When geographers visit, I'm always sure to point these out. There are flags from Brazil, Mexico, China and a half dozen other countries. These aren't just randomly chosen flags; they're the countries where Amatek, the business housed there, has "international branches"—that is to say, they are a celebration of places where manufacturing jobs were outsourced. Manufacturing jobs have been bleeding from Kent for decades. Even before the May 4, 1970, shooting, the loss of these jobs even as the college boomed was a source of bitterness between town and gown. But in 2012, when Kent redeveloped its downtown, Amatek was one of the first companies to sign up for the new space. This move brought ninety office workers downtown, supporting restaurants and shops. And a few years later, when the city was looking for a company to sponsor their free downtown skating rink, Amatek again volunteered.

Even in manufacturing towns where companies have departed, the factories they left behind are being repurposed for a new economy. North Adams, Massachusetts, was a particularly hard-hit town, with 2,300 jobs cut in November 1970 by the town's main employer, Sprague Electric. On top of this, the city's government had taken a wide swing of the urban renewal wrecking

Figure 6.2. Flags of Amatek manufacturing and offices around the world, on top of downtown Kent, OH, headquarters. Photo by author.

ball, destroying an entire side of Main Street in the late 1960s. What was left behind was a city with less than half its peak population, high poverty, and low high school graduation rates. But it was the town's empty space that brought value: The director of the Williams College Museum of Art saw a large-scale art exhibit in an abandoned factory in Cologne and suggested using the Sprague Electric factory building as a way of expanding the college's collection.[19]

Sociologist Sharon Zukin was not optimistic: "when the last factories have closed their gates and neither business nor government offers a different scenario, ordinary men and women can be persuaded that their city is ready to enter the symbolic economy."[20] She points out that the project was sold differently to locals versus the art world: as an economic development project versus an independent internationally valuable institution. "In a fragile economy, making that community financially and emotionally dependent on a transnational museum adds irony to tragedy," Zukin argued, expressing concern about how an avant-garde art museum would be able to integrate in a working-class small town.[21] Serious questions were raised by Zukin as well as the *New York Times* and *Boston Globe* regarding funding and the appropriateness of outsiders bringing a museum into a town, but in the end the museum was built and opened in 1999.[22]

Not only did the Mass MOCA deal not fall apart; it exceeded expectations both as a museum and especially as a tool for economic development in North Adams. Research finds that creative ventures in small towns can benefit from the "smallness" of these places as they focus in on what makes them unique and benefit from the quality-of-life features provided to those who move from larger cities. At the same time, small-town officials can be reluctant to invest in the large-scale changes needed to promote a cultural economy.[23]

Today, former factory towns across the country—from the Rust Belt to the textile and furniture towns of the South—are looking toward the North Adams model for reviving declining towns. These towns suffer under a vast number of vacant lots and polluted brownfields, and so particularly for small towns, finding a new use for even a single building that had a negative impact on their tax base could make a big difference. This space can be used for almost anything: In Portsmouth, Ohio, a factory became an addiction treatment center.[24] In Cleveland, there's an indoor mountain biking park. In Rocky Mount, North Carolina, a large old factory was made into a lofty cooperative workspace.[25] In Old Town, Maine, an old paper mill was bought by a Chinese cardboard recycling company.[26] Here in Kent, a former women's dress manufacturing factory along the Cuyahoga River became a water bottling operation.

Large old factories and industrial buildings in small towns make great craft breweries, as they have space for bulky equipment and taprooms. A brewery provides a third space for people to meet up with others in their community, reviving long-stagnant neighborhoods.[27] The number of breweries in the US grew from 124 in 1986 to 5,301 in 2016; more than 3,000 of these are microbreweries, and many of them in small towns.[28] *Atlantic* writer James Fallows, who traveled to small towns looking for markers of success, always mentions breweries when he talks about these places: "The existence of craft brews really is a marker of a town that's on the rise. It employs hundreds of thousands of people across the country, so it's a real business that's making a real difference locally."[29]

In the South, the proximity of cotton gin factories to downtowns makes them excellent candidates for redevelopment. One of the largest and most celebrated projects is in Prattville, Alabama, a company town built around a cotton factory that is now a 73 percent white exurb of Montgomery. This is a $37 million, seven-year project. The factory operated from 1848 until 2012, when it was bought and shuttered by a company that manufactures fully automated cotton gins. The factory sat vacant for a decade but is now 127 loft apartments, which city officials say will help revitalize their downtown just across the Autauga Creek. At its peak the factory was the largest in the world and relied on more than a hundred enslaved people to keep it operating.[30] The apartments rent for $1,390 to $2,125 a month.

Cotton mills across the country (and the world) are being redeveloped as textile manufacturing becomes more automated and is outsourced to other countries. These mills are often at the center of small towns and cities and have the benefit of currently popular brick walls and large wooden beams to attract buyers. Even in Yazoo City, Mississippi, which demolished its cotton press building, there is still hope that the site, which is adjacent to city's downtown and train station, will be redeveloped.[31]

The New Tourist Town

Tourism as a force in small-town economies is not, for most locales, new. It has long been an important part of resort towns, like Steamboat Springs, college towns like Ellensburg, and arts towns like Silver City. However, as the economy shifts away from traditional employment like manufacturing, agriculture, and resource extraction, towns' reliance on tourism increases. Many of the small towns I visited included tourism as part of their development plan. In the towns I researched, I found three types of tourist marketing, many of which overlapped. Heritage tourism focuses on the town's past, in mining or agriculture. Cultural tourism includes the creation of "art walks" and other events along with the advertisement of art galleries and other destinations. Natural tourism promotes the natural features of a town and its surrounding rural areas both for aesthetic purposes and for outdoor sports. These three types of tourist promotions relied upon the towns' "small-town feel" to support the local economy.

As a source of revenue, Anaconda, Montana, has perhaps moved the furthest toward attracting tourists. In its smelting days, Anaconda had no need for tourists. As a rough-around-the-edges industrial town, it attracted few. But after the smelters closed in the early 1980s, Anaconda needed a new source of employment and revenue. As Bryson points out, Anaconda has sought to revive its lost smelter, if not physically then through a surge of nostalgia.[32] The Anaconda Local Development Corporation advertises itself as "reinvesting our past to shape our future today" in the local visitor's guide. The last remaining piece of the smelter, a 585-foot tall smokestack (built in 1919), was preserved by local activists and is now the focus of a state park (although, ironically, inaccessible due to pollution concerns).

While not all of Anaconda's tourism promotion plans have been successful, the town has been able to draw some tourists through a golf course designed by Jack Nicklaus, which includes sand traps filled with slag (a dubiously safe byproduct of the smelting process). The course was named best course in America with under $50 greens fees, according to its promotional brochure. A hotel that was supposed to accompany the golf course never materialized, much to the dismay of local officials, who had provided numerous financial incentives for the complex.[33]

Other towns also combine historic buildings with a more modern attention to arts events. Silver City, while not statistically growing or prospering, has been hugely successful in marketing its sense of place and artistic offerings. A town brochure boasts: "Year after year, Silver City is consistently rated one of the best small towns in America, one of the nation's best places to visit, live, and retire." Among the honors it lists are best small town, best mining town, best small art town, healthiest to live and retire, top retirement spot, best towns for art and music lovers, and "outstanding community." In addition to selling Silver City as a thriving art community, the town's chamber of commerce also markets Silver City as a "gateway to 3.3 million acres of solitude," and promotes its proximity to the Gila Wilderness.

Safford, two hours west of Silver City in Arizona, advertises connections to the Gila River and other natural areas. On the cover of the Graham County tourist brochure, a photo of a man fishing with his daughters advertises

"Life the way it ought to be." Safford's advertising includes several themes common to small towns. It is part of a food-themed driving tour, the Salsa Trail, which runs through small towns of Arizona and includes farm stands and Mexican restaurants. The "Old West Trail" also runs through several small towns in Arizona, including Safford, with "600 years of Western history along a route steeped in legend."

While most articles in *National Geographic Adventure* magazine are aimed at outdoor tourism, they also offer advice to amenity migrants. Each year, the magazine lists its top fifty best places to live: "A change of address can bring instant gratification. You could wake up tomorrow in Missoula and kayak off your own deck at dawn, sneak in singletrack at lunch in Chattanooga—or choose your own adventure in any one of the country's best base camps. But a move is a long-term investment. So, this year we selected 50 innovative towns that aren't just prime relocation spots right now, but smart choices for the future. Not only do they have the action. They've got a plan."[34]

The magazine offers a connection between tourism and migration: an attraction to "authenticity" and to proximity to rural areas. It lists Silver City as one of these towns, noting that it is "what Santa Fe was before trustafarians took over," a place with trails adjacent to town and connections to regional wilderness areas, mountains, and the Continental Divide Trail. This connection is increasingly being made by those who study amenity migration and its effects on towns that were once just tourist destinations.

Yampa Valley Partners' indicator report found that many migrants to northwestern Colorado are coming from the Denver suburbs, Phoenix, and Los Angeles.[35] Jonathan Schechter, who studies the growth of resort towns, said in an interview, "people are moving to these places because they want to, because they love these places in a deeply personal way, and because they can." Thus while increased mobility is universal, the effects of this mobility are inherently geographic. Noreen Moore, business resource director of Routt County Economic Development Cooperative, agrees: "These people shop around for a community." Moore said that to newcomers, Steamboat Springs represents a "real community": "They're not here to be Lone Eagles; they clearly picked this community so they could be part of it." Advertisements by developers support this: Many advertise the sense of community and small-town feel offered by Steamboat Springs. In Steamboat Springs' early tourism days, they advertised an authentic "Old West" experience; a 1975 advertisement boasted: "Steamboat is the West . . . it's something we don't manufacture. It's here. . . .You walk into the hardware store, and the talk is more likely to be about fences and cattle than downhill skiing."

Yet, in the last thirty years, the ranch town has been edged out by the ski town. I thought of this transition when I spoke with the city council president's office: named Old Town Real Estate, it was not in the old town (downtown), but instead at the Walmart plaza, across the street from a preserved historic barn that is now at the center of a housing development. True tourist towns (not those just *promoting* tourism as one aspect of their economy) are in this very odd place at the edge of working hard to preserve authenticity but losing it through their success. Western ski towns (Telluride, Jackson Hole, Vail, Lake Tahoe) are perhaps some of the best examples of this, but there are also New England towns like Nantucket, Martha's Vineyard, and Bar Harbor, or Southwest towns like Sonoma, Taos, and Moab.[36] Whether they are focused on history or nature, or both, these towns' success is at odds with the preservation of these valuable features. The same is true for their sense of community as gentrification pushes out longtime residents and attracts newcomers, second-home owners, and Airbnbs.

While for towns like Steamboat Springs, which developed a tourism-based economy before the increased mobility of the past ten years, amenity migration may be an unintended (if nevertheless profitable) side effect of place promotion, other towns are now proactively seeking migrants. Their advertising campaigns often use the same promotion techniques used to attract tourists. Anaconda and Wellington's comprehensive plans, which express a desire to grow in population, suggest the importance of using small-town qualities to attract new residents and industries.[37]

Silver City's Gila Resources Information Project executive director Allyson Siwik said that investing in downtown is key to attracting new residents, those who "want to come to a town that's real." She said that while longtime residents tend to take their vibrant downtown for granted, "I think people who come from elsewhere, who have lost a downtown, they see it." Ellensburg's attraction of pre-retirees suggests another type of migration, one that combines both flexible work plans with the desire of baby-boom retirees to find affordable, attractive places to live.

Around the same time that new residents came looking for jobs in small towns, "location-neutral" CEOs and lower-key leaders were finding that in a digitally enhanced world, they no longer needed to live in large cities to run productive companies. Location-neutral businesses follow their owners to places they choose for lifestyle reasons. The term was coined by Moore, who said that area leaders are reluctant to see these newcomers as an important part of the economy. A report by Moore surveyed sixty-one location-neutral business owners and employees, and she believes that there are many more who are benefitting the local economy.[38] "We're used to a place-based economy," she said. "It has been a one-horse town, mining, or ranching, or tourism."

Tim Bishop, executive director of Ellensburg's Main Street Program, said that he sees an opportunity for the town to retain college students who might otherwise seek jobs in Seattle and other "West Side" suburbs. "At the same time that businesses are becoming location neutral, entrepreneurs are becoming increasingly location-specific," he said. "They're thinking, 'I really want this quality of life' and that's where they're opening their business." He suggested that the city needs to work on a plan for supporting networks of independent contractors who are based in Ellensburg but use the internet to work with national and international clients.

In Safford, Sheldon Miller, executive director of the Graham County Chamber of Commerce, noted that "everybody has to be a visitor before they become an investor." Similarly, Silver City MainStreet program director Frank Milan said that the program's goal was to create a "climate of opportunity" downtown to encourage businesses to open in a town with a strong sense of place, which can attract both tourists and locals to patronize these businesses.

Think Locally, Act Locally: Value in the Environment

In some US small towns, environmental changes brought about by humans are easy to ignore. In others, it's impossible. In 2018, Paradise, California, was mostly destroyed by wildfire. In New England, ski towns are getting less snow, and in the Southwest, towns dependent on the Colorado River are running out of water to drink and irrigate crops. In northern New York, the logging season is shortened as roads thaw into mud earlier.[39] Climate change and other environmental disasters are increasingly issues of concern in small towns. Reliance on natural resources as industry or amenities makes small towns particularly vulnerable to the environmental changes brought by climate change. And the small land areas of these places means that a natural disaster can affect the entirety of the town at once, not just one neighborhood. Many small towns are increasingly reliant on the aesthetic value of a healthy ecosystem, green spaces, and other amenities due to efforts to attract tourists and residents. This makes resilience to natural disasters, pollution, and other environmental resources particularly important in small towns.

The need for preparation for and response to environmental harms is not limited to rich or poor, environmentalists or businesspeople. When I worked on Routt County, Colorado's Vision 2030 project, I looked closely at survey data from more than a thousand residents. I found that in a town dependent on amenity migration, residents valued environmental resources, although for different reasons. New residents moved there looking for beautiful open spaces to view from their large new ranch houses. Multigenerational residents valued beauty, but many also came from ranching backgrounds and so valued the history in agricultural open spaces. Business owners recognized that the river and trees and open spaces brought tourists. While values differed, most residents found a common goal in protecting the county's open spaces.

In Silver City, a town sustainability plan focuses on responses to inevitable changes in temperature and precipitation. It included a vulnerability and risk assessment focused on promoting town resilience. Concerns particular to Silver City included drought, flooding due to extreme rain events, and wildfires. The report also focuses on the town's infrastructure: the ability of police and fire crews to respond to emergencies: "Climate variability poses a threat to existing community priorities and affects a local government's ability to deliver on its existing commitments."[40] Sustainability efforts by the city include contracting with a solar company to install solar panels at their wastewater facility, saving the city $70,000 a year and reducing the use of fossil fuels to process municipal water.[41] The city also opened a sustainability office in an old gas station downtown.

The small city is a particularly important scale to focus on enacting change: large enough to make policy, but small enough to not get tied up in large-scale bureaucracy (although politics—that's another story). Small towns also need not reinvent the wheel to find changes that will help reduce their environmental impacts. Discussing the place of ordinary cities in responding to climate change, Haupt et al. write that large cities often implement place-specific solutions, whereas in smaller cities they often enact changes that can be transferred to hundreds or thousands of others. Large-city policies have value in scale, but small-city policies have a value in scaling up.[42]

There is an urgency among cities, large and small, to get involved in changing environmental policy through an increase in membership in organizations recognizing a commitment to fighting climate change. Encouraged by Agenda 21, a United Nations–authored proposal for how local change can help to achieve their sustainable development goals, many cities have made policy changes to reduce environmental impacts, even as their national governments fail to act. There was also a movement after President Donald Trump rejected the Paris Agreement climate accord for cities to sign on themselves to the same goals, but at the city scale. For carbon emissions in particular, International Council for Local Environmental Initiatives (ICLEI) offers a toolkit for towns to measure emissions and identify the most impactful opportunities to make changes. In the US, 155 cities under 50,000 population are members of ICLEI.[43]

Both in terms of greenhouse gas emissions and other environmental impacts, small towns can be at a disadvantage (in impacts and in ability to act) due to their reliance on single industries. Tourism is one example of an industry threatened by environmental hazards created or amplified by human activities. Research describes and predicts impacts of climate change including warmer temperatures in already warm locales, reduced snow at ski resorts, wildfires, and extreme weather.[44] For small towns, this can be particularly devastating to homogenous tourism-based economies. In June 2022, Gardiner, Montana, heavy rains washed away the road connecting the town to Yellowstone National Park. This immediately severed economic connections as well, as tourists could no longer go through Gardiner on the way to the park, and tour guides could no longer use the town as a home base.[45]

In addition to being vulnerable to environmental impacts of human activities, the reliance on a single industry for economic viability can also lead to resistance against attempts to prevent these impacts. Quincy, Washington, is a farming town that transitioned into commercial agriculture with the help of irrigation from the nearby Columbia River. In 1950, the city's population was 804, and they were still waiting for water from the Grand Coulee Dam to arrive, but by later that decade, Quincy was becoming a food processing center for ConAgra, among others. This industry has dominated the town in the past fifty years. In 2001, *Seattle Times* reporter Duff Wilson published *Fateful Harvest*, which described his investigation into the dangers of agricultural pollution in Quincy. With the encouragement of Patty Martin, the city's mayor at the time, Wilson investigated the recycling of industrial by-products by Cenex into fertilizers, finding harm to crops, farm animals, and people in the town. To Martin, this was an environmental justice issue: The pollution was bankrupting farmers and harming children in a high-poverty, majority-Hispanic city. To Wilson, to stop the practice of recycling waste as fertilizer was a particularly small-town challenge: "It's true what they say about small towns, the closeness, the community. It comes out in good ways when somebody needs help or somebody dies and people gather round . . . But it can come out in bad ways, too. I think about the courage it takes to challenge a power structure like the fertilizer industry in a farm town."[46]

While attempts to recover damages from the fertilizer industry mostly failed, the investigations by Martin, Wilson, and others led to state laws requiring the reporting of fertilizer contents, and many products were taken off the shelves.[47]

Toward a Transformative Economy: Balancing Change and History

To survive—and certainly to thrive—small towns need to be flexible and to change as the world changes around them. Whether it's social, environmental, or economic change, improving adaptive capacity is an essential part of success for small towns. So, while residents have little ability to control global and national forces from their small town, they do have the ability to prepare for and respond to these changes.

Small towns as pockets of population density in the countryside owe their existence to specific economic factors: They were central places, settlements that arose where services were provided for those living in surrounding rural areas. Today, the ability of a small town to sustain itself without outside contributions is less clear. Transition is inevitable, and the struggles of larger Rust Belt cities like Detroit that placed all their bets on a single economic sector is also evident in small towns. For some, the increased efficiency of agricultural technology means consolidation: a landscape of winners and losers. For others, the one-two punch of efficiency and outsourcing led to the decline of factories and the towns themselves. We often talk about the postindustrial era in terms of steel and auto manufacturing, but the water-powered technology of cities along fall lines from Maine to Georgia became outdated far earlier (and long before the North American Free Trade Agreement) as electricity replaced hydropower and factories could move elsewhere. For many towns, most of their history takes place well after these industries are gone: punctuated by the *almost*s of a possible new factory or revival of an old one; the promise of tourism and the reality that this is rarely enough to create well-paying jobs. It's important to see economic sustainability as fluid. Which is to say, death is not always permanent. And it is rarely death. In some towns, it's a slow stagnation. In other cases, death is creative destruction, a new phoenix rising from the ashes of the old economy.

Successful towns also recognize the intangible value of aesthetics, history, and nostalgia.[48] Tourism relies on these factors, but there can also be a broader lure for new residents, meaning new taxpayers, meaning new money. Small-town decision-makers realize that to escape the boom/bust cycle of a single-source economy, one economic resource cannot be at the same time destroying another. A *High Country News* article describes the resistance of Superior, Arizona, to the return of the mining industry. As Thompson writes: "There was a time when Western mining towns would have loudly welcomed the return of the industry. But things have changed since the last bust, and like a jilted lover being courted anew by a long-lost ex, the old mining towns are wondering if they still have room for mining in their new cultures and economies." Towns like Superior, he argues, are torn between encouraging the more stable growth that comes with an amenity-based economy and supporting the return of mining, which, while unstable, helps to preserve the character of their town.[49]

Small towns won't succeed or thrive because they are somehow better places with better people or a stronger sense of community; they aren't the real America any more than any other place in the US. They also won't fail if they're missing specific, quantifiable characteristics like mountains or a university.[50] The success of most small towns is instead dependent on their ability to react to change. To their benefit, they do have less bulk, so when they need to pivot they can do so quickly. This doesn't mean they will, of course. But towns that can see change coming and respond are stronger in the long term and thus more sustainable.

CONCLUSION
Transforming the American Small Town

The small town of the American imagination is both independent and isolated, but this was never really true, and it certainly isn't true today. The US small town of the twenty-first century is part of a global system of an increasingly connected economy that permits rapid shifts to places with lower costs of labor and materials, immigration, and a warming climate that is playing out right in our backyards with wildfires, drought, and floods. Nationally, small towns are affected by our interconnections through the internet, political divisions, and economic ups and downs.

Many who write on globalization argue that it is, in essence, a homogenizing force. But even if this is true, it's not necessarily a flattening. After all, there are winners and losers in the globalizing world, and a bit of distance from these changes could mean less winning, but it could also mean less losing. On top of this, economic and social marginalization is not necessarily specific to geography; as Doreen Massey points out, this disconnect can also be tied to identity in the forms of gender, race, and class. There are layers to this unevenness that can come into play in cities both large and small. Additionally, the effects of globalization are not necessarily unidirectional. Globalization does not just mean change that is enforced from large places to small; it can also mean small places affecting large ones. Places cannot simply become "globalized" (i.e., homogenized), since they are part of a complex web of identities affected not just by grand events but by everyday actions.[1]

When I spoke with her at the very beginning of my research on small towns, Ellensburg, Washington, mayor Nancy Lillquist said that locals need to be realistic about what the American small town can be, given both individual decision-making and broader constraints: "My ideal, if I controlled everything, we would have a small town with all the different services you could ever want, locally grown, locally made, small cottage industries that provide the goods and services that we need and we'd all be this self-sustaining ecosystem. That would be lovely. We all can still work toward that, toward that ideal, and find a way to make that work, but at the same time the rest of the world goes on around us."

In American culture, existing small towns and neighborhoods are prized as "self-sustaining," or at least possessing the possibility of independence from other suburbs and cities. New Urbanist neighborhoods promoted as "sustainable" offer the promise of local employment, mixed-use development, and a compact, walkable urban core. Alternatively, the unidirectional concept of dependence is thought to be a necessity of suburbia wherein the suburb needs a city. The suburban lifestyle of connectivity, primarily through the automobile, suggests a lack of independence from larger cities and national and global trends. Suburbia, according to this narrative, erases the essence of the individual and relies on group decisions rather than singular ones. So as the antisuburbia, there is a suggestion, if not an outright statement, that the ideal small town can function independently from cities and suburbs. And yet small towns cannot be easily defined as either dependent or independent of outside forces or individual choices. As with larger cities, small towns are interdependent as multiple scales of agency interact to create the contemporary landscape and experiences of those who live there.

While national and global forces act upon small towns, it does not mean that in a world of big cities, small towns don't matter. I don't see them "pushed away to counterculture marginality" (as Manuel Castells predicted) anytime soon.[2] Being affected by outside influences also does not mean that small towns do not have the ability to enact change of their own. Small towns matter, and small towns can change the world. Here's why.

Small towns provide a dense urban environment that can, as part of a sustainable regional system, contribute to the reduction of carbon emissions and other negative consequences of suburban sprawl. In fact, it's at the regional scale where small towns can start to make important changes. It's at this fuzzy point between rural and urban where we (the residents, officials, decision-makers, businesspeople) can indeed make a difference in local/regional/national/global sustainability, as it's here where we can choose to either sprawl across rural areas or build densely and make choices that follow through on this design. One small piece of demographic data stood out to me when I separated small towns from larger cities and rural areas: While their car use was, sadly, higher than other settlement times, their commute time was far lower: nearly half of people living in small towns had a commute of less than fifteen minutes.

This suggests that while the reality of a more sustainable lifestyle is not in place yet, the potential for the reduction in automobile use for daily transportation is tantalizingly close.

In *Nature's Metropolis*, William Cronon refutes the dichotomy between rural and urban in which urban is destructive, consumptive, and part of the world, and rural is serene, self-sustaining, and isolated. He writes: "Americans have long tended to see city and country as separate places, more isolated from each other than connected. We carefully partition our national landscape into urban places, rural places, and wilderness . . . we rarely reflect on how tightly bound together they really are."[3] Cronon establishes a connection of production and consumption between Chicago's urban center and the small towns and rural places of the Midwest. My research on small towns shows similar connections between large cities, small towns, and rural areas, although now set in an economy where knowledge and service industries are increasingly edging out traditional industrial and agricultural activities. There is no simple hierarchy based on population size, and, as Cronon shows, there never was.

In eastern Washington State, the work of the Cascade Agenda, now known as Forterra, highlighted the big-picture importance of preserving or restoring the compact nature of small towns. In 2008, I was at a city council meeting where Ellensburg voted to become a member city of the Cascade Agenda, "a collective 100-year vision for conserving Washington's remarkable landscapes in the face of a growing population and a changing economic base."[4] The program makes important connections between desire for a sustainable metropolitan region, preserved open space, and small cities beyond the borders of the Seattle-Tacoma metro area. It encourages cities to join (for free) as member cities to express a commitment for "complete, compact, and connected" urban design, and offers staff assistance and educational programs toward this goal. They also provide a guide to the Washington State planning process to encourage individual support of these urban design goals.

In Northeast Ohio, the Western Reserve Land Conservancy (WRLC) does similar work, promoting development in cities and working with property owners to conserve rural land. Unique to the Rust Belt, the WRLC promotes development in dense urban areas by creating land banks that consolidate small vacant land parcels into larger pieces of land that are easier to sell to developers. Both organizations, and many others across the country, support the ideas behind the urban-to-rural transect. This model illustrates how our settlements function best when rural is rural and urban is urban—that is to say, avoid creating population density in rural areas, but also avoid placing large plots or single-family homes in high-density urban areas. This reduces development in greenfields and encourages development (and remediation) of previously polluted brownfields and development that will support retail, services, and public transportation within cities.

What can we learn from small towns? We know that many (but certainly not all) people want to live there, or at least in what they think of as a small town. Small towns are dependent on outside influences that create/destroy jobs, support/defeat environmental protection, and enhance/reduce social equity. Small towns have agency and can promote—or derail—sustainable development at the local level. At the same time, New Urbanism shows us that there is a market for the form and aesthetic of small towns. When you're working at the regional scale (and above), the most valuable role of small cities is to provide dense, walkable places. Preserving open space at the city level is important, but only if the demands of the urban place are not just moved into the surrounding countryside. To return to chapter 1, to be urban, small towns require the same density as large cities. This density establishes the possibility of car-free (or car-lite?) living by creating a critical mass for stores, employers, and schools. But a possibility is only a possibility until it is be acted on by the city and its residents.[5]

At the same time, the rest of the world goes on around us. This thought from the Ellensburg mayor stayed with me as I visited and talked with folks in towns across the country over the next few months and then revisited them a decade later, as well as built a life in my own small town. The world has never felt so near as when I was driving empty streets to do curbside grocery pickup during the early days of the pandemic or talking on Zoom with a colleague across the globe. And it has never felt so narrow as when I run into friend after friend at the farmers market or reading through close-minded comments section on the local Facebook page.

At the intersection of urban and rural, globalized and isolated, tight-knit and close-minded, small towns offer above all *opportunity* for change. There's an opportunity in these places to embody so many of the ideals that our fictional and architectural visions of what a small town should be afford to them. Unfortunately, just because there's opportunity doesn't mean they will be successful or sustainable. It doesn't mean that everyone in these towns will benefit as they should. But so many of the towns I visited had at least small success stories, even those that looked incredibly challenged on paper: They had small wins, and every one of the towns had kind people who were proud of their town and stayed to fight for it even in the bleakest of times. And some towns? Some towns I never wanted to leave.

I first met Tammie Delaney because I was studying Steamboat Springs, where she grew up, and was running a community visioning project for Routt County. Tammie said that Steamboat Springs was nice, but the place I really needed to see was Hayden, 20 minutes to the west. This is a town that at 2,000 people doesn't have enough people to be a small town by Census standards (although it's growing quickly), and when I first visited it didn't really have much going on. But Tammie lived there, in an historic ranch house overlooking the Yampa River, and she was convinced that it could *be* somewhere: a place that people would want to live, work in, and visit. I came back to Routt County many times after I stayed in the Steamboat Campground for three weeks in 2008. In January 2009, Tammie and her husband, Patrick, took me on a tour of their new project: They'd bought a grain elevator.

The grain elevator in Hayden, as in a lot of towns in the West, was a landmark in the center of town. It wasn't used for much anymore, just a feed and grain store and (this is what the Delaneys knew was important) a place where people would stop to chat. This role is what Oldenburg calls a "third place," one that is not work or home but a place to build connections and community.[6] And building community was exactly the goal of the Delaneys. During one visit about ten years ago, Tammie laid out her ideas to me, and I sketched them out as a map of the complex of buildings surrounding the grain elevator: a coffee shop, artists' lofts, housing, and a large space that could host community functions like weddings and barn dances. This was their dream. They started slowly, changing the feed and grain store into a coffee shop in 2013. Patrick (an amazing baker) gets up at 5 a.m. to bake bread and pastries to sell before heading over to his property management job in Steamboat Springs. Tammie runs the shop in the mornings, greeting the customers and making the lattes. When I visited five years later, it was a bustling shop with several baristas, and they rotated through several partners selling antiques and flower baskets in the back.

It's the last five years that really changed the town, though. The Delaneys began working with a Steamboat Springs–based investor and built several Airbnb units in front. They started offering wine tastings in the back breezeway of the complex and partnered with a wood-fired pizza maker to use the coffee shop for dinners at night (Figures C.1 and C.2). The Yampa Valley Brewing Company built a tap house next door, added a large outdoor patio, and brought in daily food trucks. When I visited in 2022, it was always busy, a mix of tourists and locals (and their dogs). Hayden now has its third place.

But maintaining and enhancing the granary wasn't the only thing the Delaneys were doing in Hayden over the past decade. Tammie joined the school board and was elected president. She helped write grants to fund a new

Figure C.1. The breezeway area of the Granary complex in Hayden, CO. Photo by author.

Figure C.2. The Granary in Hayden, CO, at dusk. Photo by author.

elementary school and a large new town playground. Patrick was elected to the Yampa Valley Electric Association board—an important role as one of Hayden's historic employers, a coal-fired power plant, winds down its operations and transitions to clean energy. The Delaneys of course are not the only folks working to build community in Hayden; there are many more. But their work shows what can be done by a few dedicated individuals to help transition a town to the new economy—even as the world goes on around them.[7]

ACKNOWLEDGMENTS

This book came together with the support and contributions of residents and leaders in small towns across the US who took the time to meet with me and share insights about their homes, in particular, Tammie and Patrick Delaney, who inspired me to a life of building community. I am grateful to Kent State University and our chapter of AAUP for supporting the Non-Tenure Track Professional Development Excellence Pool that funded a return visit to my study sites. Thanks also to the reviewers of this book, who provided important suggestions for revisions and additions that improved and clarified its content. I appreciate the insights of Dr. Chris Willer, who as a PhD student took interest in the issues of small-town classification and helped talk through and enrich the material of chapter 1. The women's writing group at Kent State kept this work moving along (especially during my non-tenure and early mom years). Alongside them, it was Andy and Teddy and my life away from work that kept me sane: much love to my family and my village for their support.

NOTES

Introduction

1. Throughout the book I use the term "American small town" to refer to US small towns. While I recognize that this narrow definition of America is problematic (as America includes all countries in North and South America), when this term is used along with "small town," it typically refers to those in the United States. The "American small town" reflects those of both reality and imagination, so I thought it was important to keep the phrase intact.
2. Kunstler, "Schuylerville Stands Still," 412.
3. Kunstler, *The Geography of Nowhere*, 186.
4. "Top 20 Urban Planning Books (of All Time)."
5. Duany and Plater-Zyberk, "The Second Coming of the American Small Town."
6. Duany and Plater-Zyberk, "The Second Coming of the American Small Town."
7. Wuthnow, *The Left Behind*.
8. Zito, "How Trump Made Small-Town America Matter Again."
9. See Mapes, "Using Big Data to Study Small Places"; Perry, Meko, and Uhrmacher, "Small Towns Don't Vote Like Other Rural Areas"; Rodden, "'Red' America Is an Illusion."
10. Marsh, "Continuity and Decline in the Anthracite Towns of Pennsylvania."
11. Massey, "A Global Sense of Place."

Chapter I

1. See Aiken, *The Cotton Plantation South since the Civil War*; Lichter et al., "Municipal Underbounding"; Aiken, "Race as a Factor in Municipal Underbounding."
2. "Community Development Block Grant Program."
3. Reynnells, "Rural Resources and Funding."
4. Pipa and Geismar, "The New 'Rural'?"
5. Brennan, Hackler, and Hoene, "Demographic Change in Small Cities."
6. Knox and Mayer, *Small Town Sustainability*.
7. Pipa and Geismar, "The New 'Rural'?"; D. L. Brown, Cromartie, and Kulcsar, "Micropolitan Areas and the Measurement of American Urbanization."
8. Cromartie, "Documentation."
9. Morrill, Cromartie, and Hart, "Metropolitan, Urban, and Rural Commuting Areas."
10. Cromartie, "Documentation."
11. Pesaresi et al., "Operating Procedure for the Production of the Global Human Settlement Layer."
12. Mapes, "Urban Revolution."

13 Ratcliffe, "A Century of Delineating a Changing Landscape."
14 "Proposed Urban Area Criteria for the 2010 Census."
15 "Urban Area Criteria for the 2020 Census—Final Criteria."
16 "Global Human Settlement Layers."
17 Gumprecht, *The American College Town*.
18 Even with these issues, though, of the 31,909 census-designated places (CDPs) identified in 2020, 12,129 of these have a population density of over 1,000 people per square mile, only 853 of which have a population of over 50,000 (6,587 between 2,500 and 50,000). A higher threshold of 2,000 people per square mile, there are 5,570 CDPs.
19 M. Woods, *Rural*.
20 B. Berry and Garrison, "The Functional Bases of Central Place Hierarchy."
21 P. Lewis, "Small Town in Pennsylvania."
22 To compare cities, suburbs, small towns, and rural areas, I used the 2020 definition of urban area, and identified small towns as all cities under 50,000 population. The remaining large cities include suburban areas, so to separate these, I identified the primary city or cities of the urban area by the name used by the Census Bureau, and used the CDP of this name to separate out the central city from its suburbs using GIS. So all CDPs within the large urban areas but not within the central cities were designated as suburbs. All non-urban areas were designated as rural. Population, race, and ethnicity data is from the 2020 census, and the remaining data is from the 2017–2021 American Community Survey.
23 For the cluster analysis, small towns were identified by their location within a 2010 urban cluster, due to major changes in the 2020 data release. Data is from 2020 and the 2017–2021 American Community Survey, using CDPs matched to the name of the primary city identified by the Census Bureau (some urban clusters connect a small CDP to a larger city).
24 Blau, "Manchester"; Rau, "After Sellout, Bonnaroo Navigates Tenuous Relationship with Coffee County."
25 Tan, "A Record 2010 Vermonters Died of an Opioid Overdose Last Year"; "Rutland, Vermont: Time to Shine."
26 Keck, "Rutland Honors Two Men Who Died in Tropical Storm Irene."
27 Claro, "The Incredible Comeback of Laurel, Mississippi."
28 Key, "Laurel, Mississippi: A Historical Perspective," 82–84.
29 Odell, "Returning to Laurel."
30 Hathorn, "'My Hometown Too'"; "Laurel High School."
31 Hancock, "The Anonymous Town That Was the Model of Desegregation in the Civil Rights Era"; Kleiner, "Race Relations in Yazoo City, Mississippi"; Mann and Rogers, "Segregation Now, Segregation Tomorrow, Segregation Forever?"
32 Grabar, "The Real Story of the Affordable Housing Development that Dave Chappelle Helped Kill."
33 Gumprecht, "College Towns in the United States: Table 1."
34 Broom, "Fast-Growing Snoqualmie: Two Tales of One City."

Chapter 2

1 Hubbard, "Space/Place."
2 Lefebvre, *The Production of Space*.
3 Hummon, *Commonplaces*.
4 Lynch, *Image of the City*; Buttimer and Seamon, *The Human Experience of Space and Place*.
5 Tuan, *Topophilia*, 99.

6   Lowenthall, "Past Time, Present Place."
7   Marsh, "Continuity and Decline in the Anthracite Towns of Pennsylvania"; Lowenthall, "Past Time, Present Place."
8   Halbwachs, *On Collective Memory*; Said, "Invention, Memory, and Place."
9   Gould and White, *Mental Maps*.
10 Paradis, "The Transformation of Place"; Egan, "Vanishing Point"; Marsh, "Continuity and Decline in the Anthracite Towns of Pennsylvania."
11 Russo, *American Towns*.
12 Krieger, *City on a Hill*.
13 Lingeman, *Small Town America*.
14 Herron, *The Small Town in American Literature*.
15 Herron, *The Small Town in American Literature*.
16 Russo, *American Towns*.
17 Lingeman, *Small Town America*; Russo, *American Towns*.
18 Adicks, "The Small Town"; Holbling, "From Main Street to Lake Wobegon and Half-Way Back"; Brederoo, "Capra's Small Town."
19 Cronon, *Nature's Metropolis*.
20 Russo, *American Towns*.
21 Jakle, *The American Small Town*.
22 Francaviglia, *Main Street Revisited*; Jakle, *The American Small Town*.
23 Jakle and Wilson, *Derelict Landscapes*.
24 Fuguitt, Brown, and Beall, *Rural and Small Town America*; Jakle and Wilson, *Derelict Landscapes*; Egan, "Vanishing Point."
25 Olson and Lyson, *Under the Blade*.
26 Jakle, *The American Small Town*.
27 P. Lewis, "Small Town in Pennsylvania," 344.
28 Fuguitt, Brown, and Beall, *Rural and Small Town America*.
29 Swanson, Cohen, and Swanson, *Small Towns and Small Towners*, 17.
30 Hart, "Small Towns and Manufacturing."
31 Paradis, "The Transformation of Place"; Lew, "Authenticity and Sense of Place."
32 Russo, *American Towns*, 297.
33 Meinig, "Symbolic Landscapes." See also G. D. Nelson, "The Town Was Us."
34 Hummon, *Commonplaces*; Jakle, "America's Small Town/Big City Dialectic."
35 Brederoo, "Capra's Small Town."
36 Levy, *Small-Town America in Film*.
37 Francaviglia, *Main Street Revisited*.
38 Sanders, "Norman Rockwell."
39 Lingeman, *Small Town America*, 33.
40 Barker, "Order and Image in the American Small Town."
41 S. Lewis, *Main Street*.
42 Van Doren, *Contemporary American Novelists*.
43 Expanded upon by Hilfer, *The Revolt from the Village*.
44 Van Doren's description encapsulates the traditional small-town writings and their critique: "The village seemed too cozy a microcosm to be disturbed. There it lay in the mind's eye, neat, compact, organized, traditional: the white church with tapering spire, the sober schoolhouse, the smithy of the ringing anvil, the corner grocery, the cluster of friendly houses; the venerable parson, the wise physician, the canny squire, the grasping landlord softened or outwitted in the end; the village belle, gossip, atheist, idiot; jovial fathers, gentle mothers, merry children; cool parlors, shining kitchens, spacious barns, lavish gardens, fragrant summer dawns, and comfortable winter evenings. These were elements not to be discarded lightly, even by those who perceived that time was discarding many of them as the industrial

revolution went on planting ugly factories alongside the prettiest brooks, bringing in droves of aliens who used unfamiliar tongues and customs, and fouling the atmosphere with smoke and gasoline." Van Doren, *Contemporary American Novelists*, 147.
45 Lingeman, *Small Town America*.
46 Tournier, "Small Towns at the Crossroads."
47 Motamayor, "Twin Peaks Inspired a Lasting Legacy of Smalltown Weirdness in Television."
48 MacKenzie, "What Home Means to David Lynch."
49 Lutz, "Up and Down Main Street."
50 Weber, "Richard Russo, Happily at Home in Winesburg East."
51 Crampton, *The 100 Best Small Towns in America*; Urbanska and Levering, *Moving to a Small Town*.
52 Swanson, Cohen, and Swanson, *Small Towns and Small-Towners*; Villani, *The 100 Best Art Towns in America*; Dickson, *In Search of Mayberry*; Juran, *Find Your Small-Town Paradise*; Clayton, *Small Town Bound*; Schultz, *Boom Town USA*.
53 Grudowski, "Outside's Best Towns 2004"; "Best Places to Live: Top 100"; Thomas, "Study: Small Cities in the West Tops for Best Quality of Life."
54 Crampton, *The 100 Best Small Towns in America*.
55 Juran, *Find Your Small-Town Paradise*.
56 Munsell, "Small Town."
57 Clayton, *Small Town Bound*.
58 K. Campbell, "Stuck on Small-Town TV Shows."
59 Fries, "'Ed' Rolls a Strike," 32.
60 Franklin, "Western Exposure"; Garron, "Everwood"; Speier, "Everwood"; Tucker, "Widower's Peak."
61 Neuhaus and Neuhaus, "'Sometimes It Feels More Like a Commune Than a Town.'"
62 Lenker, "Romance Author Robyn Carr on Bringing Her Virgin River Series to Life with Netflix."
63 Stevens, "'Parks and Recreation.'"
64 Yuko, "The Three Subversive Messages of 'Schitt's Creek.'"
65 Fraser, "How 2018's TV Shows Explored the Horror of Misplaced Nostalgia."
66 Fisher, "Horror and Small Towns."
67 Burno, "HBO's 'Lovecraft Country' Explores 'Sundown' Towns In Massachusetts."
68 Romano, "Gilmore Girls' Final Words Change Everything."
69 St. James, "Gilmore Girls: A Year in the Life Takes Place in a Beautiful, Perfect Bubble."
70 "Ideal Community Type"; "For Nearly Half of America."
71 Newport, "Americans Big on Idea of Living in the Country."
72 Van Green, "Majority of Americans Prefer a Community."
73 DeSilver, "How the Most Ideological Polarized Americans Live Different Lives."
74 Van Green, "Majority of Americans Prefer a Community with Big Houses." See also D. Cox et al., "Hopes and Challenges for Community and Civic Life."
75 Newport, "Americans Big on Idea of Living in the Country."
76 P. Lewis, "Small Town in Pennsylvania," 349.
77 Duany and Plater-Zyberk, "The Second Coming of the American Small Town," 28.

Chapter 3

1 Duany and Plater-Zyberk, "The Second Coming of the American Small Town."
2 In opposition to the "Nowhere" described by Kunstler and "Placelessness" described by Relph.

3 Blackerby, "Picket-Fence America"; Davis, "Visions of Seaside."
4 Delgadillo, "The 'New Urbanism' Movement Might be Dead."
5 Quammen, "A Drink of Death."
6 "The Plan of Chicago."
7 Stephenson, "The Roots of the New Urbanism."
8 Fluck, "*Euclid v. Ambler*: A Retrospective."
9 Appler, "Changing the Scale of Analysis for Urban Renewal Research"; R. Nelson and Ayers, "Renewing Inequality."
10 L. Woods, "Lost Newburgh."
11 Zipp, "The Roots and Routes of Urban Renewal."
12 Willer, "Towards a 'National' Main Street."
13 S. Berry and Russell, *Built to Last*, ii.
14 S. Berry and Russell, *Built to Last*, iv.
15 "Growth Policy Statement of Vision," xix, 1–5.
16 "Safford Downtown Vision Plan."
17 "Ellensburg Comprehensive Plan."
18 Redmon, "The Man Who Reinvented the City."
19 Fulton, "The New Urbanism."
20 Katz, *The New Urbanism*; Zak, "Rep. Matt Gaetz Wants You to Know Who He Is."
21 Gao et al., "Locating New Urbanism Developments in the U.S."
22 "HUD Hope IV."
23 "Housing with Dignity."
24 Trudeau, "A Typology of New Urbanism Neighborhoods."
25 Roberts, "New Urbanism Is Just Growth by Another Name."
26 Turner, "Green New Urbanism."
27 Falconer Al-Hindi and Staddon, "The Hidden Histories and Geographies of Neotraditional Town Planning."
28 Blum, "The Mall Goes Undercover."
29 Sorenson, "Location Analysis of Lifestyle Centers."
30 Drukker and Jabuka, "Steps towards a New Suburbia."
31 Cope, Freimuth, and Miller, "Reviews and Reflections on Planned Communities."
32 Christman, "Ohio's Crocker Park Offers a Glimpse."
33 "What Carmel, Indiana, Can Teach America about Urbanism"; Van Allen, "Carmel Grows Up."
34 "City Center Stow Request for Proposals."
35 DiAlesandro, "Downtown Brimfield Entertainment District?"
36 Gee, "City Sees Future West of Town."
37 "First & Main."
38 LoTemplio, "Napoli: Plattsburgh 'Looking Real Good.'"
39 "Durkee Site Development."
40 Hirsch, "Plattsburgh Mayoral Candidates Battle over $10 Million Grant."
41 Alba, "Durkee Street Plans Snubbed in Court."
42 Mapes, "Developing Excelsior Park."
43 Thurston, "Planning Ready on Excelsior Park"; Liberatore, "Residents Sue over Saratoga Excelsior Park."
44 S. Moore and Trudeau, "New Urbanism."

Chapter 4

1 E. Robinson, "What Happens When President Trump Has to Face Reality?"
2 Mapes, "Using Big Data to Study Small Places."

3   Florida, Patino, and Dottle, "How Suburbs Swung the 2020 Election."
4   Using the Factiva database, I selected ten major national publications, with a focus on broad scope and regional diversity (*The Boston Globe*, *Chicago Sun-Times*, *The Christian Science Monitor*, *The Denver Post*, *Forbes*, *The Atlantic*, *Los Angeles Times*, *The New York Times*, *The Washington Post*, *The Wall Street Journal*, *Houston Chronicle*, *The Plain Dealer*, and *USA Today*). I filtered stories to political and general news and excluded entertainment, travel, lifestyle, and opinion. I also excluded non-US references to small towns.
5   "Gerald 'Jerry' Hansen."
6   Bryan, "Slag."
7   Hajela, "Film Studio, Tech Park, Yoga Retreat."
8   Berkowitz and Meko, "Appalachia Comes Up Small in Era of Giant Coal Mines."
9   "Annual Coal Report."
10 Bowen et al., "An Overview of the Coal Economy in Appalachia."
11 Norton, Howze, and Robinson, "Regional Comparisons of Timber Dependency."
12 S. Hines, "Trouble in Timber Town."
13 M. Y. H. Lee, "Donald Trump's False Comments Connecting Mexican Immigrants and Crime."
14 Dao, "Review Urges Defense Dept. to Broaden P.T.S.D. Help"; Cushman and Nixon, "Postal Service Drops Plan to Cut Rural Offices."
15 Goodnough, "Vermont Towns Have an Image."
16 Alexander, "America's Rural Hospitals Are Dangerously Fragile"; S. R. Johnson, "States with the Most Rural Hospital Closures."
17 Case and Deaton, *Deaths of Despair and the Future of Capitalism*.
18 McGranahan and Parker, "The Opioid Epidemic."
19 Quinones, *Dreamland*.
20 Macy, *Dopesick*.
21 Edelman, "How Capitalism Underdeveloped Rural America." See also Edelman, "Hollowed Out Heartland, USA."
22 Cramer, *The Politics of Resentment*; Currid-Halkett, *The Overlooked Americans*.
23 Hardy, "Rural America Yearns to Get Glory Days Back."
24 Benzow, "Rural America Is Not All Trump Country."
25 Gura, "Guns and God."
26 Bradley and Katz, "A Small-Town or Metro Nation?"
27 Baron, "The Semantics of Politics."
28 "John Mellencamp: My Life in 15 Songs."
29 Martinez, "Jason Aldean's 'Small Town' Is Part of a Long Legacy."
30 Murray, "Election 2012," A5.
31 Viser, "Officially in, Romney All about the Economy," A1.
32 Corasaniti, "Bernie Sanders, and Simon and Garfunkel."
33 A. Cox, Parlapiano, and Watkins, "Iowa's Democratic Caucus Results."
34 Zitner and Overberg, "Rural Vote Fuels Trump."
35 Mattson, "President Trump's 'American Carnage' Speech."
36 Pilkington, "'American Carnage.'"
37 Barabak, "Raw, Angry, and Aggrieved."
38 Frazier, "Rural America Could Stand Remembering."
39 Bossie and Lewandowski, *Trump*.
40 Palmer, "Trade 'Disaster' Worsens Under Trump."
41 Lucey, "JD Vance Accepts VP Nomination for Vice President."
42 Montlake, "Politics of Pessimism."
43 Parker, Morin, and Horowitz, "Looking to the Future, Public Sees an America in Decline."

44 For example, Slack and Jensen, "The Changing Demography of Rural and Small-Town America"; K. M. Johnson, "Demographic Trends in Rural and Small Town America"; Carr, Lichter, and Kefalas, "Can Immigration Save Small-Town America?"; Lichter, "Immigration and the New Racial Diversity in Rural America"; L. Nelson and Hiemstra, "Latino Immigrants and the Renegotiation of Place and Belonging in Small Town America"; Bose, "Refugees and the Transforming Landscapes of Small Cities in the US."
45 B. A. Lee and Sharp, "Ethnoracial Diversity across the Rural-Urban Continuum."
46 Frosch, Maher, and Elinson, "Murder Rates Soar in Rural America."
47 Montanaro, "Trump Escalates Racist Rhetoric."
48 M. Y. H. Lee, "Donald Trump's False Comments Connecting Mexican Immigrants and Crime."
49 Lane, "What Will It Take for Democrats to Woo the White Working Class?"; Crowley and Ebert, "New Rural Immigrant Destinations"; Lichter, "Immigration and the New Racial Diversity in Rural America"; B. A. Lee and Sharp, "Ethnoracial Diversity across the Rural-Urban Continuum."
50 Loewen, *Sundown Towns: A Hidden Dimension of American Racism.*
51 Williams, "Reaction Goes beyond Major Cities."
52 Dvorak, "Protests in the Rural U.S. Do Small Towns Justice."
53 Logan, *Diversity and Disparities*; Robertson, "Protests against Racism Reveal Hidden Diversity."
54 Park et al., "An Extremely Detailed Map of the 2020 Election."
55 "Presidential Precinct Data for the 2020 General Election."
56 My research was also replicated in conversation with the *Washington Post* using a slightly different methodology, with similar findings. See Perry, Meko, and Uhrmacher, "Small Towns Don't Vote Like Other Rural Areas."
57 Gumprecht defines college towns as those with student enrollments making up 20 percent or more of a town's total population.
58 "Ideal Community Type."
59 Rodden, *Why Cities Lose.*
60 Mapes, "Urban Revolution."
61 Judis and Teixeira, *The Emerging Democratic Majority.*
62 Teixeira, "Demography Is Not Destiny."
63 Edelman, "Hollowed Out Heartland, USA."
64 Carnes and Lupu, "It's Time to Bust the Myth."
65 Love and Loh, "The 'Rural-Urban Divide' Furthers Myths about Race and Poverty."
66 Williamson, "The Father-Führer."
67 Herndon and Goldmacher, "In Rural Areas, Prospects Sink for Democrats."

Chapter 5

1   Molotch, "The City as a Growth Machine."
2   B. J. L. Berry, "Urbanization and Counterurbanization in the United States."
3   P. B. Nelson, "Geographic Perspective on Amenity Migration across the USA."
4   Stoker et al., "Planning and Development Challenges in Western Gateway Communities."
5   Carrier, "Computers in the Pines."
6   Gosnell and Abrams, "Amenity Migration."
7   Yagley et al., "They Paved Paradise."
8   Leland, "Off to Resorts, and Carrying Their Careers."
9   "Vision 2030: Heart and Soul of Our Community."
10 Taylor, "No Boundaries."

11 Mitchell, "Making Sense of Counterurbanization."
12 "Town of Wellington Comprehensive Plan," 2008.
13 "Town of Wellington Comprehensive Plan," 2014.
14 Ferrier, "Fort Collins Home Prices Continue to Soar."
15 Florida, *Cities and the Creative Class*.
16 Zimmerman, "From Brew Town to Cool Town."
17 Gumprecht, "The American College Town"; Sablik, "Growing Rural America through Startups."
18 Foote, "Beyond Studentification in United States College Towns," 1357.
19 For example, Gottsacker, "The Ramifications of Exploding Interests in Small-Town Living"; Ibbitson, "Rural America Is Now Experiencing 'Disaster Gentrification'"; "COVID-19 Is Pushing Americans Out of Cities and into the Country"; Sen, "Booming 'Zoom Towns' Should Ease City Housing Costs."
20 Frey, "New Census Data Shows a Huge Spike."
21 Saad, "Country Living Enjoys Renewed Appeal in U.S."
22 Sodja, "Boom Town."
23 Florida and Kotkin, "America's Post-Pandemic Geography."
24 Verlaan and Hochstenbach, "Gentrification through the Ages"; Wyly and Hammell, "Gentrification, Segregation, and Discrimination."
25 Verlaan and Hochstenbach, "Gentrification through the Ages."
26 Bryson, "The Nature of Gentrification," citing Harvey, " From Managerialism to Entrepreneurialism."
27 Ghose, "Big Sky or Big Sprawl?" 530–533.
28 J. D. Hines, "In Pursuit of Experience," 302.
29 Ghose, "Big Sky or Big Sprawl?"; J. D. Hines, "In Pursuit of Experience."
30 Anderson, "Housing Authority Closes on Steamboat 700 Land."
31 Semuels, "America Needs to End Its Love Affair."
32 Hesse, "Steamboat Voters Reject Plan to Annex Land"; Bastone, "Will Brown Ranch Save Steamboat Springs—or Ruin It?"
33 Llera, "The Need for Big Box Retailers in Ellensburg."
34 Towler, "Obituary of the Old Town."
35 Carr, Lichter, and Kefalas, "Can Immigration Save Small-Town America?"
36 Cittaslow, https://www.cittaslow.org.
37 Mayer and Knox, "Slow Cities."

Chapter 6

1 J. Robinson, *Ordinary Cities*; Haupt, Eckersley, and Kern, "How Can 'Ordinary' Cities Become Climate Pioneers?"
2 S. Campbell, "Green Cities, Growing Cities, Just Cities?"
3 Kunstler, "Schuylerville Stands Still."
4 *World Made by Hand* provides a fictional foray into Kunstler's views of a post-global society.
5 "Vision 2030: Heart and Soul of a Community."
6 Uhlenbrock, "You Knew."
7 Rudolf, "Copper's Every Dip is Felt in Arizona."
8 "Morenci Copper Mine, Arizona, USA."
9 "Atlantic Richfield Company Agrees to Complete Multimillion-Dollar Cleanup."
10 Semuels, "'They're Trying to Wipe Us Off the Map.'"
11 Cronon, *Nature's Metropolis*.
12 Semuels, "'They're Trying to Wipe Us Off the Map.'"

13 Clay, *Real Places*, 179.
14 Lu and Dudensing, "What Do We Mean by Value-Added Agriculture?"
15 Byrd, "Local Markets."
16 Ahlbrandt, *History of Wellington, Colorado*, 76.
17 "Town of Wellington Comprehensive Plan," 2008.
18 Garcia, "Wellington's First Brewery Opening Valentine's Day."
19 Oehler, Sheppard, and Benjamin, "Mill Town, Factory Town, Cultural Economic Engine."
20 Zukin, *The Cultures of Cities*, 79.
21 Zukin, *The Cultures of Cities*, 103.
22 Oehler, Sheppard, and Benjamin, "Mill Town, Factory Town, Cultural Economic Engine."
23 Jayne et al., "The Cultural Economy of Small Cities"; Lorentzen and van Heur, *Cultural Political Economy of Small Cities*.
24 Alfini, "Counseling Center to Convert Factory into Treatment Facility."
25 Abrams, "A Second Chance for North Carolina's Shuttered Factories."
26 Barry, "A Maine Paper Mill's Unexpected Savior."
27 Sisson, "Craft Beer's Big Impact on Small Towns and Forgotten Neighborhoods."
28 "Brewing Up a New Use for Old Buildings."
29 Cowan, "Small Town America in Renewal."
30 Reeves, "Alabama Cotton Gin Factory's Transformation Haunted by Slavery's Ghost"; Roney, "Crowd Gets Sneak Peek at Prattville's $37 Million 'Gin Shop' Project."
31 "Yazoo City Comprehensive Plan 2019."
32 Bryson, "The Nature of Gentrification."
33 Haffey, "Contractor Sues Developers for Non-Payment of Failed Hotel Project."
34 Tuff and Melville, "50 Best Places to Live."
35 Ford, Kramer, and Mapes, "Community Indicators."
36 See Rothman, *Devil's Bargains*.
37 "Anaconda-Deer Lodge County Growth Policy"; "Town of Wellington Comprehensive Plan 2008."
38 N. Moore and Ford, "Location-Neutral Businesses."
39 Thill, "Shorter Winters Chip Away at New York State Logging Town's Future."
40 "Town of Silver City Sustainability Plan 2030."
41 Heinrich, "Town of Silver City."
42 Haupt, Eckersley, and Kern, "How Can 'Ordinary' Cities Become Climate Pioneers?"
43 "Meet the ICLEI USA Network."
44 FitzPatrick, "Toxic Fertilizer"; Wilson, *Fateful Harvest;* Kaján and Saarinen, "Tourism, Climate Change and Adaptation."
45 Georges, Vitkovskaya, and Partlow, "Yellowstone Is This Town's Golden Ticket."
46 Wilson, *Fateful Harvest*, 3–4.
47 Wilson, *Fateful Harvest*.
48 Mapes, "Landscapes of Nostalgia."
49 Thompson, "Reluctant Boomtown."
50 Ingram, "I Called This Place 'America's Worst Place to Live.'"

Conclusion

1 Massey, *Space, Place, and Gender*; Flusty, *De-Coca-Colonization*.
2 Castells, *The Rise of the Network Society*. See also Sassen, "A New Geography of Centers and Margins," 73.
3 Cronon, *Nature's Metropolis*, xvi.

4 "The Cascade Agenda."
5 As Fishman writes in "New Urbanism": "The real challenge to planning lies in creating diversity, walkability, and sustainability throughout the metropolitan region in a network of carefully designed small communities that complements and supports the central city."
6 Oldenburg and Brissett, "The Third Place."
7 For more on the Delaneys and Hayden's transition, see J. Brown, "Here Comes Hayden," and Franz, "Life after Coal."

BIBLIOGRAPHY

Abrams, Amanda. "A Second Chance for North Carolina's Shuttered Factories." *New York Times*, June 15, 2021. https://www.nytimes.com/2021/06/15/business/north-carolina-factories-redevelopment.html.

Adicks, Richard. "The Small Town: Magnet and Storehouse." In *Change and Tradition in the American Small Town*, edited by Robert Craycroft and Michael Fazio, 49–57. Small Towns series. University Press of Mississippi, 1983.

Ahlbrandt, Arlene Briggs. *History of Wellington, Colorado and the Boxelder Valley, 1864–1996*. Vestige Press, 1999.

Aiken, Charles. *The Cotton Plantation South since the Civil War*. Johns Hopkins University Press, 2020. Chapter 11: New Settlement Patterns, pg. 307–339.

Aiken, Charles. "Race as a Factor in Municipal Underbounding." *Annals of the Association of American Geographers* 77 (1987): 564–579.

Alba, Fernando. "Durkee Street Plans Snubbed in Court." *(Plattsburgh) Press Republican*, March 3, 2022. https://www.pressrepublican.com/news/durkee-street-plans-snubbed-in-court/article_bbe71c18-9b76-11ec-9566-1f9cd0a92e42.html.

Alexander, Brian. "America's Rural Hospitals Are Dangerously Fragile." *The Atlantic*, January 2018. https://www.theatlantic.com/business/archive/2018/01/rural-hospitals/549050.

Alfini, Michelle. "Counseling Center to Convert Factory into Treatment Facility." Spectrum News 1, March 21, 2021. https://spectrumnews1.com/oh/columbus/news/2021/03/21/portsmouth-factory-to-become-addiction-treatment-center.

"Anaconda-Deer Lodge County Growth Policy." Anaconda-Deer Lodge County Planning Department, 2019. https://www.adlc.us/DocumentCenter/View/1554/Anaconda-Deer-Lodge-County-Growth-Policy-2019.

Anderson, Dylan. "Housing Authority Closes on Steamboat 700 Land." *Steamboat Pilot*, August 12, 2021. https://www.steamboatpilot.com/news/housing-authority-closes-on-steamboat-700-land-polis-says-project-is-good-candidate-for-state-support.

"Annual Coal Report." US Energy Information Administration, October 18, 2022. https://www.eia.gov/coal/annual/pdf/table18.pdf.

Appler, Douglas R. "Changing the Scale of Analysis for Urban Renewal Research: Small Cities, the State of Kentucky, and the 1974 Urban Renewal Directory." *Journal of Planning History* 16, no. 3 (2017): 200–221. https://doi.org/10.1177/1538513216657006.

"Atlantic Richfield Company Agrees to Complete Multimillion-Dollar Cleanup of the Anaconda Smelter Superfund Site." US Department of Justice, September 30, 2022. https://www.justice.gov/opa/pr/atlantic-richfield-company-agrees-complete-multimillion-dollar-cleanup-anaconda-smelter.

Barabak, Mark. "Raw, Angry, and Aggrieved, President Trump's Inaugural Speech Does Little to Heal Political Wounds." *Los Angeles Times*, January 20, 2017. https://www.latimes.com/politics/la-na-pol-trump-inauguration-speech-analysis-20170120-story.html.

Barker, James. 1981. "Order and Image in the American Small Town." In *Order and Image in the American Small Town*, edited by Michael Fazio and Peggy Whitman, 3–7. University Press of Mississippi, 1981.

Baron, Dennis. "The Semantics of Politics: Defining the Real 'Real' America." The Web of Language (blog), October 22, 2008. https://blogs.illinois.edu/view/25/5406.

Barry, Ellen. "A Maine Paper Mill's Unexpected Savior: China." *New York Times*, January 15, 2020. https://www.nytimes.com/2020/01/15/us/maine-mill-china.html.

Bastone, Kelly. "Will Brown Ranch Save Steamboat Spring—or Ruin It?" *5280: Denver's Mile High Magazine*. February 2024. https://www.5280.com/will-brown-ranch-save-steamboat-springs-or-ruin-it.

Benzow, August. "Rural America Is Not All Trump Country: A Closer Look at the Rural Counties That Biden Won." Economic Innovation Group, November 17, 2020. https://eig.org/rural-america-is-not-all-trump-country.

Berkowitz, Bonnie, and Tim Meko. "Appalachia Comes Up Small in Era of Giant Coal Mines." *Washington Post*, May 5, 2017. https://www.washingtonpost.com/graphics/national/coal-jobs-in-appalachia.

Berry, Brian J. L. "Urbanization and Counterurbanization in the United States." *Annals of the American Academy of Political and Social Science* 451, no. 1 (1980): 13–20.

Berry, Brian, and William Garrison. "The Functional Bases of the Central Place Hierarchy." *Economic Geography* 34, no. 2 (1958): 145–154.

Berry, Susan, and Sharman Apt Russell. *Built to Last: An Architectural History of Silver City, NM*. New Mexico Historic Preservation Division, 1986.

"Best Places to Live: Top 100." *Money Magazine*, 2007. https://money.cnn.com/magazines/moneymag/bplive/2007/top100.

Blackerby, Cheryl. 2016. "Picket-Fence America: 'New Urbanism' Flourishes in Seaside." *Palm Beach Daily News*, September 24, 2016. https://www.palmbeachdailynews.com/story/entertainment/society/2016/09/24/picket-fence-america-new-urbanism/9671749007.

Blau, Max. "Manchester: Rock City." *Bitter Southerner*. Accessed January 5, 2023. https://bittersoutherner.com/manchester-rock-city.

Blum, Andrew. "The Mall Goes Undercover: It Now Looks Like a City Street." *Slate*, April 6, 2005. https://slate.com/culture/2005/04/the-latest-incarnation-of-the-shopping-mall.html.

Bose, Pablo S. "Refugees and the Transforming Landscapes of Small Cities in the US." *Urban Geography* 42, no. 7 (2011): 958–978.

Bossie, David, and Corey Lewandowski. *Trump: America First: The President Succeeds Against All Odds*. Center Street, 2020.

Bowen, Eric, Christiadi, John Deskins, and Brian Lego. "An Overview of the Coal Economy in Appalachia." Appalachian Regional Commission, 2018. https://www.arc.gov/wp-content/uploads/2018/01/CIE1-OverviewofCoalEconomyinAppalachia-2.pdf.

Bradley, Jennifer, and Bruce Katz. "A Small-Town or Metro Nation?" Brookings Institute, October 8, 2008. https://www.brookings.edu/articles/a-small-town-or-metro-nation.

Brederoo, Nico J. "Capra's Small Town." In *The Small Town in America: A Multidisciplinary Revisit*, edited by Theo d'Haen, Johannes Willem Bertens, and Hans Bak, 184–196. European Contributions to American Studies. VU University Press Amsterdam, 1995.

Brennan, Christiana, Darrene Hackler, and Christopher Hoene. "Demographic Change in Small Cities, 1990 to 2000." *Urban Affairs Review* 40, no. 3 (2005): 342–361.

"Brewing Up a New Use for Old Buildings." National Association of Realtors, December 21, 2017. https://www.nar.realtor/on-common-ground/brewing-up-a-new-use-for-old-buildings.

Broom, Jack. "Fast-Growing Snoqualmie: Two Tales of One City." *Seattle Times*, February 27, 2011. https://www.seattletimes.com/seattle-news/fast-growing-snoqualmie-two-tales-of-one-city.

Brown, David L., John B. Cromartie, and Laszlo J. Kulcsar. "Micropolitan Areas and the Measurement of American Urbanization." *Population Research and Policy Review* 23, no. 4 (2004): 399–418.
Brown, Jennifer. "Here Comes Hayden: One of Colorado's Last Down-Valley Ski Towns to Pop Is Having Its Moment." *Colorado Sun*, August 13, 2021. https://coloradosun.com/2021/08/13/hayden-down-valley-skisteamboat.
Bryan, Zachariah. "Slag: An Economic Savior, or Another Disappointing Business Venture?" *Choteau Acantha*, April 19, 2018. http://www.choteauacantha.com/article_650f5298-4404-11e8-b6a0-733354da9b0c.html.
Bryson, Jeremy. "The Nature of Gentrification." *Geography Compass* 7, no. 8 (2013): 578–587.
Burno, Christian. "HBO's 'Lovecraft Country' Explores 'Sundown' Towns In Massachusetts." WBUR. https://www.wbur.org/news/2020/09/17/hbo-lovecraft-country-sundown-towns-massachusetts.
Buttimer, Anne, and David Seamon. *The Human Experience of Space and Place*. St. Martin's Press, 1980.
Byrd, Kaitland. "Local Markets: Value-Added Products at Farmers' Markets." In *Southern Craft Food Diversity*. Bristol University Press, 2021.
Campbell, Kim. "Stuck on Small-Town TV Shows." *Christian Science Monitor*, November 15, 2002. http://www.csmonitor.com/2002/1115/p15s02-altv.html.
Campbell, Scott. "Green Cities, Growing Cities, Just Cities? Urban Planning and the Contradictions of Sustainable Development." *Journal of the American Planning Association* 62, no. 3 (1996): 296–312.
Carnes, Nicholas, and Noam Lupu. "It's Time to Bust the Myth: Most Trump Voters Were Not Working Class." *Washington Post*, June 5, 2017. https://www.washingtonpost.com/news/monkey-cage/wp/2017/06/05/its-time-to-bust-the-myth-most-trump-voters-were-not-working-class.
Carr, Patrick J., Daniel T. Lichter, and Maria J. Kefalas. "Can Immigration Save Small-Town America? Hispanic Boomtowns and the Uneasy Path to Renewal." *Annals of the American Academy of Political and Social Science* 641, no. 1 (2012): 38–57. https://doi.org/10.1177/0002716211433445.
Carrier, Jim. "Computers in the Pines: It's a Spacey Idea for Resort Jobs." *Denver Post*, January 27, 1985.
"The Cascade Agenda: A 100-Year Vision for Pierce, King, Kittitas, and Snohomish Counties." Forterra: Land for Good, April 2015. http://web.archive.org/web/20231003165121/http://www.landscope.org/washington/partners/clc/.
Case, Anne, and Angus Deaton. "Deaths of Despair and the Future of Capitalism." In *Deaths of Despair and the Future of Capitalism*. Princeton University Press, 2020.
Castells, Manuel. 2000. *The Rise of the Network Society*, 2nd ed. Blackwell, 2000.
Christman, Samantha. "Ohio's Crocker Park Offers a Glimpse at What Eastern Hills Might Become." *Buffalo News*, March 2, 2018. https://buffalonews.com/business/local/ohios-crocker-park-offers-a-glimpse-at-what-eastern-hills-might-become/article_c75b3089-9bbc-54e6-be2d-26dabe2e8ac0.html.
"City Center Stow Request for Proposals." City of Stow (Ohio), September 2018. https://mikerasor.com/wp-content/uploads/2018/09/18-0917-Request-For-Proposals-Draft-wAppendix-1.pdf.
Claro, Danielle. "The Incredible Comeback of Laurel, Mississippi." *Southern Living*, October 1, 2022. https://www.southernliving.com/travel/mississippi/laurel-mississippi-comeback.
Clay, Grady. *Real Places: An Unconventional Guide to America's Generic Landscape*. University of Chicago Press, 1994.
Clayton, John. *Small Town Bound: Your Guide to Small-Town Living*. Career Press, 1996.

"Community Development Block Grant Program." Department of Housing and Urban Development. Accessed January 5, 2023. https://www.hud.gov/program_offices/comm_planning/cdbg.

Cope, Ronald S., Kimberly Freimuth, and Stephen R. Miller. "Reviews and Reflections on Planned Communities." *Urban Law* 49 (2017): 483.

Corasaniti, Nick. "Bernie Sanders, and Simon and Garfunkel, Put Focus on Voters." *New York Times*, January 21, 2016. https://www.nytimes.com/2016/01/22/us/politics/bernie-sanders-and-simon-and-garfunkel-put-focus-on-voters.html.

"COVID-19 Is Pushing Americans out of Cities and into the Country." World Economic Forum, January 19, 2021. https://www.weforum.org/agenda/2021/01/rural-life-cities-countryside-covid-coronavirus-united-states-us-usa-america.

Cowan, Lee. "Small Town America in Renewal." CBS News, May 6, 2018. https://www.cbsnews.com/news/a-small-town-america-in-renewal.

Cox, Amanda, Alicia Parlapiano, and Derek Watkins. "Iowa's Democratic Caucus Results: Precinct by Precinct." *New York Times*, October 3, 2020. https://www.nytimes.com/interactive/2016/02/01/us/iowa-caucus-democratic-precinct-results.html.

Cox, Daniel, Karlyn Bowman, and Jacqueline Clemence. "Hopes and Challenges for Community and Civic Life: Perspectives from the Nation and Indiana." Survey Center on American Life, November 18, 2020. https://www.americansurveycenter.org/research/hopes-and-challenges-for-community-and-civic-life-perspectives-from-the-nation-and-indiana.

Cramer, Katherine. *The Politics of Resentment: Rural Consciousness in Wisconsin and the Rise of Scott Walker*. University of Chicago Press, 2016.

Crampton, Norman. *The 100 Best Small Towns in America*. Prentice Hall, 1993.

Cromartie, John. "Documentation: 2010 Rural-Urban Commuting Area (RUCA) Codes." USDA, 2020. https://www.ers.usda.gov/data-products/rural-urban-commuting-area-codes/documentation.

Cronon, William. *Nature's Metropolis: Chicago and the Great West*. W. W. Norton, 1991.

Crowley, Martha, and Kim Ebert. "New Rural Immigrant Destinations: Research for the 2010s." *Rural America in a Globalizing World* (2014): 401–418.

Currid-Halkett Elizabeth. *The Overlooked Americans: The Resilience of Our Rural Towns and What It Means for Our Country*. Basic Books, 2023.

Cushman, John H., Jr., and Ron Nixon. "Postal Service Drops Plan to Cut Rural Offices: Agency Will Keep Locations Open with Fewer Hours." *Boston Globe*, May 10, 2012.

Dao, James. "Review Urges Defense Dept. to Broaden P.T.S.D. Help." *New York Times*, July 13, 2012. https://archive.nytimes.com/atwar.blogs.nytimes.com/2012/07/13/study-calls-for-better-assessment-of-government-p-t-s-d-programs.

Davis, Robert Smolian. "Visions of Seaside: 1946–2011." Seaside Research Portal, University of Notre Dame. https://seaside.library.nd.edu/essays/visions-of-seaside.

Delgadillo, Natalie. "The 'New Urbanism' Movement Might Be Dead." *Governing*, September 26, 2017. https://www.governing.com/archive/gov-new-urbanism.html.

DeSilver, Drew. "How the Most Ideological Polarized Americans Live Different Lives." Pew Research, June 13, 2014. https://www.pewresearch.org/short-reads/2014/06/13/big-houses-art-museums-and-in-laws-how-the-most-ideologically-polarized-americans-live-different-lives.

DiAlesandro, Wendy. "Downtown Brimfield Entertainment District? Trustees Say It's Possible." *The Portager*, September 21, 2022. https://theportager.com/a-downtown-brimfield-entertainment-district-trustees-say-its-possible.

Dickson, Scott. *In Search of Mayberry: A Guide to North Carolina's Favorite Small Towns*. Parkway Publishers, 2005.

Drukker, Colin, and Lisa Jabuka. "Steps towards a New Suburbia: The Benefits of Comprehensive Planning." *Focus* 4, no. 1 (2007): 8. https://core.ac.uk/download/pdf/19154788.pdf.

Duany, Andrés, and Elizabeth Plater-Zyberk. "The Second Coming of the American Small Town." *Wilson Quarterly* 16, Winter (1992): 19–50. http://archive.wilsonquarterly.com/sites/default/files/articles/WQ_VOL16_W_1992_Article_01_1.pdf.
"Durkee Site Development." City of Plattsburgh (New York), November 2020. https://www.cityofplattsburgh-ny.gov/department/community-development/downtown-revitalization-initiative/durkee-street-site-development.
Dvorak, Petula. "Protests in the Rural U.S. Do Small Towns Justice." *Washington Post*, July 13, 2020. https://www.washingtonpost.com/local/yes-even-in-small-single-stoplight-towns-theyre-saying-his-name/2020/07/13/1abae5a6-c4a2-11ea-b037-f9711f89ee46_story.html.
Edelman, Marc. "Hollowed Out Heartland, USA: How Capital Sacrificed Communities and Paved the Way for Authoritarian Populism." *Journal of Rural Studies* 82 (2021): 505–517. https://doi.org/10.1016/j.jrurstud.2019.10.045.
Edelman, Marc. "How Capitalism Underdeveloped Rural America." *Jacobin*, January 2020. https://jacobin.com/2020/01/capitalism-underdeveloped-rural-america-trump-white-working-class.
Egan, Timothy. "Vanishing Point" (series). *New York Times*. December 1–3, 2003.
"Ellensburg Comprehensive Plan Update." City of Ellensburg (Washington), 2006.
Falconer Al-Hindi, Karen, and Caedmon Staddon. "The Hidden Histories and Geographies of Neotraditional Town Planning: The Case of Seaside, Florida." *Environment and Planning D: Society and Space* 15, no. 3 (1997): 349–372. https://doi.org/10.1068/d150349.
Ferrier, Pat. "Fort Collins Home Prices Continue to Soar in First Two Months of 2022." *The Coloradoan*, March 10, 2022. https://www.coloradoan.com/story/news/2022/03/10/fort-collins-single-family-home-price-hits-record-highs-2022/9437909002.
"First & Main." Fairmount Properties. Accessed July 27, 2022. https://fairmountproperties.com/hudson.
Fisher, Ann. "Horror and Small Towns." All Sides with Ann Fisher (audio). WOSU, July 25, 2019. https://news.wosu.org/show/all-sides-with-ann-fisher/2019-07-25/horror-and-small-towns.
Fishman, Robert. "New Urbanism." In *Planning Ideas That Matter: Livability, Territoriality, Governance, and Reflective Practice*, edited by Bishwapriya Sanyal, Christina D. Rosan, and Lawrence J. Vale, 65–90. MIT Press, 2012.
FitzPatrick, Terry. "Toxic Fertilizer." *Living on Earth*, December 25, 1998. https://www.loe.org/shows/segments.html?programID=98-P13-00052&segmentID=4.
Florida, Richard. *Cities and the Creative Class*. Routledge, 2005.
Florida, Richard, and Joel Kotkin. "America's Post-Pandemic Geography." *City Journal*, Spring 2021. https://www.city-journal.org/americas-post-pandemic-geography.
Florida, Richard, Marie Patino, and Rachael Dottle. "How Suburbs Swung the 2020 Election." Bloomberg News, November 17, 2020. https://www.bloomberg.com/graphics/2020-suburban-density-election.
Fluck, Timothy Alan. "*Euclid v. Ambler*: A Retrospective," *Journal of the American Planning Association* 52, no. 3 (1986): 326–337. https://doi.org/10.1080/01944368608976439.
Flusty, Steven. *De-Coca-Colonization: Making the Globe from the Inside Out*. Routledge, 2004.
Foote, Nathan S. "Beyond Studentification in United States College Towns: Neighborhood Change in the Knowledge Nodes, 1980–2010." *Environment and Planning A* 49, no. 6 (2017): 1341–1360.
"For Nearly Half of America, Grass Is Greener Somewhere Else." Pew Research Center, January 29, 2009. https://www.pewresearch.org/social-trends/2009/01/29/for-nearly-half-of-america-grass-is-greener-somewhere-else-denver-tops-list-of-favorite-cities/.
Ford, Scott, Stacey Kramer, and Jennifer Mapes. "Community Indicators." Yampa Valley Partners, 2009.

Francaviglia, Richard. *Main Street Revisited: Time, Space, and Image Building in Small Town America*. University of Iowa Press, 1996.
Franklin, Nancy. 2003. "Western Exposure." *New Yorker*, January 20, 2003.
Franz, Scott. "Life after Coal: How a NW Colorado Town Is Bracing for a Future without a Power Plant." KUNC, January 14, 2020. https://www.kunc.org/politics/2020-01-14/life-after-coal-how-a-nw-colorado-town-is-bracing-for-a-future-without-a-power-plant.
Fraser, Emma. "How 2018's TV Shows Explored the Horror of Misplaced Nostalgia." *Collider*, December 13, 2018. https://collider.com/2018-tv-shows-horror-nostalgia.
Frazier, Ian. "Rural America Could Stand Remembering." *New York Reviews*, November 19, 2020. https://www.nybooks.com/articles/2020/11/19/election-rural-america-could-stand-remembering.
Frey, William. "New Census Data Shows a Huge Spike in Movement out of Big Metro Areas during the Pandemic." Brookings Institute, April 14, 2022. https://www.brookings.edu/blog/the-avenue/2022/04/14/new-census-data-shows-a-huge-spike-in-movement-out-of-big-metro-areas-during-the-pandemic.
Fries, Laura. "'Ed' Rolls a Strike." *Variety*, October 2008.
Frosch, Dan, Kris Maher, and Zusha Elinson. "Murder Rates Soar in Rural America." *Wall Street Journal,* June 19, 2022. https://www.wsj.com/story/murder-rates-soar-in-rural-america-bb431022.
Fuguitt, Glenn, David Brown, and Calvin Beale. *Rural and Small-Town America: The Population of the United States in the 1980s*. Russell Sage Foundation, 1989.
Fulton, William. "The New Urbanism: Hope or Hype for American Communities?" Lincoln Land Institute, 1996. https://www.lincolninst.edu/sites/default/files/pubfiles/the-new-urbanism-full.pdf.
Gao, Jie, Yan Song, Jiang Zhou, and Dingxin Wu. "Locating New Urbanism Developments in the U.S.: Which Cities Have New Urbanism and Why?" *Land* 11, no. 1 (2021): 44. https://doi.org/10.3390/land11010044.
Garcia, Adrian. "Wellington's First Brewery Opening Valentine's Day." *The Coloradoan*, February 11, 2016. https://www.coloradoan.com/story/money/2016/02/11/old-colorado-brewing-company-wellington/80194300.
Garron, Barry. "Everwood." *Hollywood Reporter*, September 16, 2002: 10–11.
Gee, Brandon. "City Sees Future West of Town: Trip to Denver Gives Eye-Opening Look at Urbanist Design." *Steamboat Pilot and Today*, June 1, 2008. https://www.steamboatpilot.com/news/city-sees-future-west-of-town.
Georges, Salwan, Julie Vitkovskaya, and Joshua Partlow. "Yellowstone Is This Town's Golden Ticket. Climate Change Risks That." *Washington Post*, July 25, 2022. https://www.washingtonpost.com/climate-environment/interactive/2022/climate-change-national-parks-yelllowstone.
"Gerald 'Jerry' Hansen." Obituary. Longfellow Finnegan Riddle Funeral Home, December 12, 2014. https://www.longfellowfinneganriddle.com/obituaries/Gerald-Hansen.
Ghose, Rina. "Big Sky or Big Sprawl? Rural Gentrification and the Changing Cultural Landscape of Missoula, Montana." *Urban Geography* 25, no. 6 (2004): 528–549.
"Global Human Settlement Layers." Joint Research Centre, European Commission. Accessed January 5, 2023. https://ghsl.jrc.ec.europa.eu.
Goodnough, Abby. "Vermont Towns Have an Image, and They Say Dollar Stores Aren't Part of It." *New York Times*, May 14, 2012. https://www.nytimes.com/2012/05/14/us/dollar-store-plans-divide-vermont-residents.html.
Gosnell, Hannah, and Jesse Abrams. "Amenity Migration: Diverse Conceptualizations of Drivers, Socioeconomic Dimensions, and Emerging Challenges." *GeoJournal* 76 (2011): 303–322. https://doi.org/10.1007/s10708-009-9295-4.

Gottsacker, Erin. "The Ramifications of Exploding Interests in Small Town Living during the Pandemic." NPR, January 21, 2022. https://www.npr.org/2022/01/21/1074664401/the-ramifications-of-exploding-interests-in-small-town-living-during-the-pandemi.
Gould, Peter, and Rodney White. *Mental Maps*. Penguin, 1974.
Grabar, Henry. "The Real Story of the Affordable Housing Development That Dave Chappelle Helped Kill." *Slate*, February 5, 2022. https://slate.com/business/2022/02/dave-chappelle-affordable-housing-ohio-yellow-springs.html.
"Growth Policy Statement of Vision." Anaconda-Deer Lodge County Department of Planning. 2005.
Grudowski, Mike. "Outside's Best Towns 2004: 100-Proof Americana." *Outside*, 2004. https://www.outsideonline.com/adventure-travel/destinations/100-proof-americana/.
Gumprecht, Blake. "The American College Town." *Geographical Review* 93, no. 1 (2004): 51–80.
Gumprecht, Blake. *The American College Town*. University of Massachusetts Press, 2008.
Gumprecht, Blake. "College Towns in the United States: Table 1." *The American College Town*, 2008. https://scholarworks.umass.edu/umpress_act/1.
Gura, David. "Guns and God: A Bitter Brew." NPR, April 14, 2008. https://www.npr.org/sections/talk/2008/04/guns_and_god_a_bitter_brew.html.
Haffey, Vera. "Contractor Sues Developers for Non-Payment of Failed Hotel Project." *Montana Standard*, May 21, 2006. https://mtstandard.com/news/local/contractor-sues-developers-anaconda-for-non-payment-of-failed-hotel-project.
Hajela, Ashad. 2019. "Film Studio, Tech Park, Yoga Retreat: Some Shuttered New York Prisons See New Life While Others Await Development." *Gotham Gazette*, April 24, 2019. https://www.gothamgazette.com/state/8466-some-shuttered-new-york-prisons-see-new-life-while-others-await-development-cuomo.
Halbwachs, Maurice. *On Collective Memory*. Trans. by Lewis Coser. The Heritage of Sociology. University of Chicago Press, 1992.
Hancock, Lynnell. "The Anonymous Town That Was the Model of Desegregation in the Civil Rights Era." Hechinger Report, October 3, 2016. https://hechingerreport.org/anonymous-town-model-desegregation-civil-rights-era.
Hardy, Kevin. "Rural America Yearns to Get Glory Days Back." *USA Today*, October 4, 2016. 1A.
Hart, John Fraser. "Small Towns and Manufacturing." *Geographical Review* (1988): 272–287.
Harvey, David. "From Managerialism to Entrepreneurialism: The Transformation of Urban Politics in Late Capitalism." *Geografiska Annaler B* 71 (1989): 3–17.
Hathorn, Taylor McKay. "'My Hometown Too': Laurel's Downtown Blossoms Despite City's Complicated History." *Mississippi Free Press*, December 13, 2021. https://www.mississippifreepress.org/18922/my-hometown-too-laurels-downtown-blossoms-despite-citys-complicated-history.
Haupt, Wolfgang, Peter Eckersley, and Kristine Kern. "How Can 'Ordinary' Cities Become Climate Pioneers?" In *Addressing the Climate Crisis*, edited by C. Howarth et al. Palgrave Macmillan, 2022. https://doi.org/10.1007/978-3-030-79739-3_8.
Heinrich, Martin. "Town of Silver City." Solar Toolkit. https://www.heinrich.senate.gov/solar-toolkit/success-stories/town-of-silver-city.
Herndon, Astead, and Shane Goldmacher. "In Rural Areas, Prospects Sink for Democrats." *New York Times*, November 7, 2021. https://www.nytimes.com/2021/11/06/us/rural-vote-democrats-virginia.html.
Herron, Ima. *The Small Town in American Literature*. Pageant Books, 1939.
Hesse, Tom. "Steamboat Voters Reject Plan to Annex Land for Affordable Housing." Colorado Public Radio, March 27, 2024. https://www.cpr.org/2024/03/27/steamboat-voters-reject-plan-to-annex-land-for-brown-ranch-affordable-housing.

Hilfer, Anthony. *The Revolt from the Village, 1915–1930*. University of North Carolina Press, 1969.
Hines, J. Dwight. "In Pursuit of Experience: The Postindustrial Gentrification of the Rural American West." *Ethnography* 11, no. 2 (2010): 285–308.
Hines, Sandra. "Trouble in Timber Town." *Columns* (University of Washington), 1990. https://www.washington.edu/alumni/columns/top10/timber_town.html.
Hirsch, Zach. 2016. "Plattsburgh Mayoral Candidates Battle over $10 Million Grant." North Country Public Radio, August 5, 2016. https://www.northcountrypublicradio.org/news/story/32339/20160805/plattsburgh-mayoral-candidates-battle-over-10-million-grant.
Holbling, Walter. "From Main Street to Lake Wobegon and Half-Way Back: The Mid-West Small Town as a Literary Place in 20th Century U.S. Literature." In *The Small Town in America: A Multidisciplinary Revisit*, edited by Hans Bertens, Theo d' Haen, and Hans Bak, 97–108. European Contributions to American Studies 32. VU University Press Amsterdam, 1995.
"Housing with Dignity: 75 Years with the Akron Metropolitan Housing Authority." Akron Metropolitan Housing Authority, 2013. https://www.akronhousing.org/files/12648/file_upload/seventy-five-years-with-the-akron-metropolitan-housing-authority.pdf.
Hubbard, Phil. "Space/Place," in *Cultural Geography: A Critical Dictionary of Key Concepts*, edited by David Atkinson, Peter Jackson, David Sibley, and Neil Washbourne. I. B. Tauris, 2005. Pp. 41–48.
"HUD Hope IV." Congress for the New Urbanism. Accessed August 15, 2022. https://www.cnu.org/our-projects/hud-hope-vi.
Hummon, David. *Commonplaces: Community Ideology and Identity in American Culture*. SUNY Series in the Sociology of Culture. State University of New York Press, 1990.
Ibbitson, Ross. "Rural America Is Now Experiencing 'Disaster Gentrification.'" *Daily Mail*, April 2, 2020. https://www.dailymail.co.uk/news/article-8180805/Rural-america-experiencing-disaster-gentrification-wealthy-Covid-19-evacuees-flee.html.
"Ideal Community Type" (Table 3.2). In "2014 Political Polarization Survey." Pew Research Center, June 12, 2014. https://www.pewresearch.org/politics/2014/06/12/ideal-community-type.
Ingram, Christopher. "I Called This Place 'America's Worst Place to Live.' Then I Went There." *Washington Post*, September 3, 2015. https://www.washingtonpost.com/news/wonk/wp/2015/09/03/i-called-this-place-americas-worst-place-to-live-then-i-went-there.
Jakle, John. *The American Small Town: Twentieth-Century Place Images*. Archon Books, 1982.
Jakle, John. "America's Small Town/Big City Dialectic." *Journal of Cultural Geography*, 18, 1999.
Jakle, John, and David Wilson. *Derelict Landscapes: The Wasting of America's Built Environment*. Geographical Perspectives on the Human Past. Rowman and Littlefield, 1992.
Jayne, Mark, Chris Gibson, Gordon Waitt, and David Bell. "The Cultural Economy of Small Cities." *Geography Compass* 4, no. 9 (2010): 1408–1417.
"John Mellencamp: My Life in 15 Songs." *Rolling Stone*, December 23, 2013. https://www.rollingstone.com/music/music-lists/john-mellencamp-my-life-in-15-songs-11308/i-need-a-lover-208807.
Johnson, Kenneth M. "Demographic Trends in Rural and Small Town America." Carsey School of Public Policy, University of New Hampshire, March 15, 2006. https://scholars.unh.edu/cgi/viewcontent.cgi?article=1004&context=carsey.
Johnson, Steven Ross. "States with the Most Rural Hospital Closures." *US News and World Report*, June 22, 2023. https://www.usnews.com/news/healthiest-communities/slideshows/states-with-the-most-rural-hospital-closures.
Judis, John B., and Ruy Teixeira. *The Emerging Democratic Majority*. Scribner, 2002.
Juran, Robert. *Find Your Small-Town Paradise: The 450 Best Small Towns in America*. Paradise Press, 2005.

Kaján, Eva, and Jarkko Saarinen. "Tourism, Climate Change, and Adaptation: A Review." *Current Issues in Tourism* 16, no. 2 (2013): 167–195.
Katz, Peter. *The New Urbanism. Toward an Architecture of Community*. McGraw Hill, 1994.
Keck, Nina. "Rutland Honors Two Men Who Died in Tropical Storm Irene." Vermont Public Radio, September 8, 2011. https://archive.vpr.org/vpr-news/rutland-honors-two-men-who-died-in-tropical-storm-irene.
Key, David Stanton. "Laurel, Mississippi: A Historical Perspective." Unpublished dissertation. East Tennessee State University, 2001. https://dc.etsu.edu/etd/121.
Kleiner, Sarah. "Race Relations in Yazoo City, Mississippi: A Brief History." Center for Public Integrity, October 19, 2018. https://theworld.org/stories/2018-10-19/race-relations-yazoo-city-mississippi-brief-history.
Knox, Paul, and Heike Mayer. *Small Town Sustainability: Economic, Social, and Environmental Innovation*. Birkhäuser Verlag, 2013.
Krieger, Alex. *City on a Hill: Urban Idealism in America from the Puritans to the Present*. Harvard University Press, 2019.
Kunstler, James Howard. *The Geography of Nowhere: The Rise and Decline of America's Man-Made Landscape*. Simon and Schuster, 1993.
Kunstler, James Howard. "Schuylerville Stands Still." *New York Times Magazine*, March 25, 1990. https://www.nytimes.com/1990/03/25/magazine/schuylerville-stands-still.html.
Kunstler, James Howard. *World Made by Hand*. Grove Press, 2009.
Lane, Charles. "What Will It Take for Democrats to Woo the White Working Class?" *Washington Post*, November 23, 2016. https://www.washingtonpost.com/opinions/what-will-it-take-for-democrats-to-woo-the-white-working-class/2016/11/23/42d90508-b1a6-11e6-8616-52b15787add0_story.html.
"Laurel High School." *US News and World Report*. Accessed January 5, 2023. https://www.usnews.com/education/best-high-schools/mississippi/districts/laurel-school-district/laurel-high-school-11326.
Lee, Barrett A., and Gregory Sharp. "Ethnoracial Diversity across the Rural-Urban Continuum." *The Annals of the American Academy of Political and Social Science* 672, no. 1 (2017): 26–45. https://doi.org/10.1177/0002716217708560.
Lee, Michelle Ye Hee. "Donald Trump's False Comments Connecting Mexican Immigrants and Crime." *Washington Post,* July 8, 2015. https://www.washingtonpost.com/news/fact-checker/wp/2015/07/08/donald-trumps-false-comments-connecting-mexican-immigrants-and-crime.
Lefebvre, Henri. *The Production of Space*. Translated by D. Nicholson-Smith. Blackwell, 1991.
Leland, John. "Off to Resorts, and Carrying Their Careers." *New York Times*, August 13, 2007. https://www.nytimes.com/2007/08/13/us/13steamboat.html.
Lenker, Maureen Lee. "Romance Author Robyn Carr on Bringing Her Virgin River Series to Life with Netflix." *Entertainment Weekly*, October 3, 2018. https://ew.com/books/2018/10/03/robyn-carr-virgin-river-netflix-interview.
Levy, Emanuel. *Small-Town America in Film: The Decline and Fall of Community*. Continuum, 1991.
Lew, Alan. "Authenticity and Sense of Place in the Tourism Development Experience of Older Retail Districts." *Journal of Travel Research* 27, no. 4 (1989): 15–22.
Lewis, Peirce. "Small Town in Pennsylvania." *Annals of the Association of American Geographers* 62, no. 2 (1972): 323–351.
Lewis, Sinclair. *Main Street*. Harcourt, Brace and Howe, 1920.
Liberatore, Wendy. "Residents Sue over Saratoga Excelsior Park." *Times Union*, September 13, 2022. https://www.timesunion.com/news/article/Residents-sue-Spa-Planning-Board-over-Excelsior-17438454.php.
Lichter, Daniel. "Immigration and the New Racial Diversity in Rural America." *Rural Sociology* 77, no. 1 (2012): 3–35.

Lichter, Daniel, Domenico Parisi, Steven Michael Grice, and Michael Taquino. "Municipal Underbounding: Annexation and Racial Exclusion in Small Southern Towns." *Rural Sociology* 72 (2009): 47–68.

Lingeman, Richard. *Small Town America: A Narrative History, 1620–the Present*. Putnam, 1980.

Llera, Elliott. "The Need for Big Box Retailers in Ellensburg." *Central Washington University Observer*, December 6, 2015. https://cwuobserver.com/6661/news/the-need-for-big-box-retailers-in-ellensburg.

Loewen, James. *Sundown Towns: A Hidden Dimension of American Racism*. The New Press, 2005.

Logan, John, ed. *Diversity and Disparities: America Enters a New Century*. Russell Sage Foundation, 2014.

Lorentzen, Anne, and Bas van Heur, eds. *Cultural Political Economy of Small Cities*. Routledge, 2012.

LoTemplio, Joe. "Napoli: Plattsburgh 'Looking Real Good.'" *Press Republican*, May 18, 2022. https://www.pressrepublican.com/news/dinapoli-plattsburgh-looking-real-good/article_34b9e4e8-d6bb-11ec-9e18-075323fc93cb.html.

Love, Hanna, and Tracy Hadden Loh. "The 'Rural-Urban Divide' Furthers Myths about Race and Poverty—Concealing Effective Policy Solutions." Brookings Institute, 2020. https://www.brookings.edu/blog/the-avenue/2020/12/08/the-rural-urban-divide-furthers-myths-about-race-and-poverty-concealing-effective-policy-solutions.

Lowenthall, David. "Past Time, Present Place: Landscape and Memory." *Geographical Review* 65, no. 1 (1975): 1–36.

Lu, Ruoxi, and Rebekkah Dudensing. "What Do We Mean by Value-Added Agriculture?" *Choices: The Magazine of Food, Farm, and Resource Issues* 30, no. 4 (2015): 1–8.

Lucey, Catherine. "JD Vance Accepts GOP Nomination for Vice President." *Wall Street Journal*, July 18, 2024. https://www.wsj.com/livecoverage/trump-biden-rnc-election-2024/card/vance-argues-democrats-have-abandoned-small-town-america-wgw60ZwyZwuIG3x9DPJe.

Lutz, Andrew. "Up and Down Main Street: An Examination of Character, Place, Myth, Community, and Culture through Contemporary Small Town American Fiction." Unpublished doctoral dissertation. State University of New York at Stony Brook, 1998.

Lynch, Kevin. *Image of the City*. MIT Press, 1960.

MacKenzie, Steven. "What Home Means to David Lynch." *Street Roots*, July 26, 2019. https://www.streetroots.org/news/2019/07/26/what-home-means-david-lynch.

Macy, Beth. *Dopesick: Dealers, Doctors, and the Company That Addicted America*. Little, Brown and Company, 2019.

Mann, Bryan, and Annah Rogers. "Segregation Now, Segregation Tomorrow, Segregation Forever? Racial and Economic Isolation and Dissimilarity in Rural Black Belt Schools in Alabama." *Rural Sociology* 86 (2021): 523–558.

Mapes, Jennifer. "Developing Excelsior Park." *The Saratogian*, December 9, 2001. https://www.saratogian.com/2001/12/09/developing-excelsior-park.

Mapes, Jennifer. "Landscapes of Nostalgia: Place Marketing and the Cultural Economy in the American Small Town." In *Cultural Political Economy of Small Cities*, edited by Anne Lorentzen and Bas van Heur. Routledge, 2012.

Mapes, Jennifer. "Urban Revolution: Rethinking the American Small Town." Unpublished dissertation. University of Southern California, 2009.

Mapes, Jennifer. "Using Big Data to Study Small Places: Small-Town Voting Patterns in the 2020 U.S. Presidential Election." *Growth and Change* 55, no. 3 (2024).

Marsh, Ben. "Continuity and Decline in the Anthracite Towns of Pennsylvania." *Annals of the Association of American Geographers* 77, no. 3 (1987): 337–352.

Martínez, Amanda Marie. "Jason Aldean's 'Small Town' Is Part of a Long Legacy with a Very Dark Side." NPR, July 22, 2023. https://www.npr.org/2023/07/22/1188908968/jason-aldean-small-town-vs-city.
Massey, Doreen. "A Global Sense of Place." In *The Cultural Geography Reader*, edited by Timothy Oakes and Patricia Price, 257–263. Taylor and Francis, 2008.
Massey, Doreen. *Space, Place, and Gender*. University of Minnesota Press, 1994.
Mattson, Kevin. "President Trump's 'American Carnage' Speech Fit into a Long American Tradition." *Vox*, January 26, 2017. https://www.vox.com/the-big-idea/2017/1/26/14393288/trump-inaugural-american-carnage-speech.
Mayer, Heike, and Paul L. Knox. "Slow Cities: Sustainable Places in a Fast World." *Journal of Urban Affairs* 28, no. 4 (2006): 321–334.
McGranahan, David, and Timothy Parker. "The Opioid Epidemic: A Geography in Two Phases." Economic Research Report 287. USDA, April 2021. https://www.ers.usda.gov/webdocs/publications/100833/err-287.pdf.
"Meet the ICLEI USA Network." International Council for Local Environmental Initiatives. https://icleiusa.org/network.
Meinig, Donald. "Symbolic Landscapes: Models of American Community." In *The Interpretation of Ordinary Landscapes*, edited by Donald Meinig, 164–194. Oxford University Press, 1979.
Mitchell, Clare J. A. "Making Sense of Counterurbanization." *Journal of Rural Studies* 20, no. 1 (2004): 15–34.
Molotch, Harvey. "The City as a Growth Machine: Toward a Political Economy of Place." *American Journal of Sociology* 82, no. 2 (1976): 309–332.
Montanaro, Domenico. "Trump Escalates Racist Rhetoric and Plays on White Grievance at Recent Rallies." NPR, February 1, 2022. https://www.npr.org/2022/02/01/1077166847/trump-escalates-racist-rhetoric-plays-on-white-grievance-at-recent-rallies.
Montlake, Simon. "Politics of Pessimism: Why Neither Party Is Selling the American Dream." *Christian Science Monitor*, March 1, 2022. https://www.csmonitor.com/USA/Politics/2022/0301/Politics-of-pessimism-Why-neither-party-is-selling-the-American-dream.
Moore, Noreen, and Scott Ford. "Location-Neutral Businesses." Survey results. Routt County Economic Development Cooperative, 2006.
Moore, Susan, and Dan Trudeau. "New Urbanism: From Exception to Norm—The Evolution of a Global Movement." *Urban Planning* 5, no. 4 (2020): 384–387.
"Morenci Copper Mine, Arizona, USA." *Mining Technology*, September 1, 2022. https://www.mining-technology.com/projects/morenci.
Morrill, Richard, John Cromartie, and Gary Hart. 1999. "Metropolitan, Urban, and Rural Commuting Areas: Toward a Better Depiction of the United States Settlement System." *Urban Geography* 20, no. 8 (1999): 727–748. https://doi.org/10.2747/0272-3638.20.8.727.
Motamayor, Rafael. "Twin Peaks Inspired a Lasting Legacy of Smalltown Weirdness in Television." SyFy Wire, April 20, 2020. https://www.syfy.com/syfy-wire/twin-peaks-inspired-legacy-smalltown-weirdness-riverdale-westworld.
Munsell, Kenneth. "Small Town." In *Rodeo Town: Stories of the Kittitas Valley*, edited by John Bennet. Vagabond Press. 1997.
Murray, Sara. "Election 2012: Economy in South to Test Campaigns." *Wall Street Journal*, January 11, 2012. A5.
Nelson, Garrett Dash. "'The Town Was Us.'" *Places Journal*, July 2018. https://doi.org/10.22269/180731.
Nelson, Lise, and Nancy Hiemstra. "Latino Immigrants and the Renegotiation of Place and Belonging in Small Town America." *Social and Cultural Geography* 9, no. 3 (2008): 319–342.

Nelson, Peter B. "Geographic Perspective on Amenity Migration across the USA: National, Regional, and Local Scale Analysis." In *The Amenity Migrants: Seeking and Sustaining Mountains and their Cultures*, edited by Laurence A. G. Moss, 55–72. CAB International, 2006.

Nelson, Robert, and Edward L. Ayers, eds. "Renewing Inequaltity: Urban Renewal, Family Displacements, and Race, 1950–1966." *American Panorama*. Digital Scholarship Lab, University of Richmond. Accessed August 20, 2022. https://dsl.richmond.edu/panorama/renewal/#view=0/0/1&viz=cartogram.

Neuhaus, Jessamyn, and John Neuhaus. "'Sometimes It Feels More Like a Commune Than a Town': Envisioning Utopian Possibilities in Robyn Carr's Virgin River Romance Novels." *Studies in Popular Culture* 37, no. 2 (2015): 25–42. http://www.jstor.org/stable/43940356.

Newport, Frank. "Americans Big on Idea of Living in the Country." Gallup, December 7, 2019. https://news.gallup.com/poll/245249/americans-big-idea-living-country.aspx.

Norton, Joni, Glen Howze, and Laura Robinson. "Regional Comparisons of Timber Dependency: The Northwest and the Southeast." *Journal of Rural Social Sciences* 19, no. 22 (2003): 40–59.

Odell, Jonathan. "Returning to Laurel." *Progressive Magazine*, June 23, 2023. https://progressive.org/magazine/returning-to-laurel-odell.

Oehler, Kay, Stephen Sheppard, and Blair Benjamin. "Mill Town, Factory Town, Cultural Economic Engine: North Adams in Context." C^3D, Williams College, 2006. https://web.williams.edu/Economics/ArtsEcon/library/pdfs/NA%20History%20and%20Ethnography%202006.pdf.

Oldenburg, Ramon, and Dennis Brissett. "The Third Place." *Qualitative Sociology* 5, no. 4 (1982): 265–284.

Olson, Richard, and Thomas. Lyson, eds. *Under the Blade: The Conversion of Agricultural Landscapes*. Westview Press, 1999.

Palmer, Doug. "Trade 'Disaster' Worsens under Trump." *Politico*, July 18, 2018. https://www.politico.com/story/2018/02/06/trump-trade-disaster-325749.

Paradis, Thomas. "The Transformation of Place: Historic Theme Development in Small Town Commercial Districts." Unpublished doctoral dissertation. University of Illinois at Urbana-Champaign, 1997.

Park, Alice, Charlie Smart, Rumsey Taylor, and Miles Watkins. "An Extremely Detailed Map of the 2020 Election." *New York Times*, 2021. https://www.nytimes.com/interactive/2021/upshot/2020-election-map.html.

Parker, Kim, Rich Morin, and Juliana Horowitz. "Looking to the Future, Public Sees an America in Decline on Many Fronts." Pew Research, March 21, 2019. https://www.pewresearch.org/social-trends/2019/03/21/public-sees-an-america-in-decline-on-many-fronts/.

Perry, Kati, Tim Meko, and Kevin Uhrmacher. "Small Towns Don't Vote Like Other Rural Areas." *Washington Post*, August 9, 2023. https://www.washingtonpost.com/politics/2023/08/09/small-town-voting-trump.

Pesaresi, Martino, Daniele Ehrlich, Stefano Ferri, Aneta Florczyk, Sergio Freire, Matina Halkia, Andreea Julea, Thomas Kemper, Pierre Soille, and Vasileios Syrris. "Operating Procedure for the Production of the Global Human Settlement Layer from Landsat Data of the Epochs 1975, 1990, 2000, and 2014." JRC Technical Reports, European Commission, 2016. https://doi.org/10.2788/253582.

Pilkington, Ed. "'American Carnage': Donald Trump's Vision Casts Shadow over Day of Pageantry." *The Guardian*, January 21, 2017. https://www.theguardian.com/world/2017/jan/20/donald-trump-transition-of-power-president-first-speech.

Pipa, Anthony, and Natalie Geismar. "The New 'Rural'? The Implications of OMB's Proposal to Redefine Non-Metro America." Brookings Institute, 2021. https://www.brookings

.edu/research/the-new-rural-the-implications-of-ombs-proposal-to-redefine-nonmetro-america.

"The Plan of Chicago: A Regional Legacy." Chicago Metropolis 2020, 2008. https://burnhamplan100.lib.uchicago.edu/files/content/documents/Plan_of_Chicago_booklet.pdf.

"Presidential Precinct Data for the 2020 General Election." The Upshot. *New York Times*, 2022. https://github.com/TheUpshot/presidential-precinct-map-2020.

"Proposed Urban Area Criteria for the 2010 Census." *Federal Register*, August 24, 2010. https://www.federalregister.gov/documents/2010/08/24/2010-20808/proposed-urban-area-criteria-for-the-2010-census.

Quammen, David. "A Drink of Death." *New York Times*, November 12, 2006. https://www.nytimes.com/2006/11/12/books/review/Quammen.t.html.

Quinones, Sam. *Dreamland: The Story of America's New Opiate Epidemic*. Bloomsbury Press, 2014.

Ratcliffe, Michael. "A Century of Delineating a Changing Landscape: The Census Bureau's Urban and Rural Classification, 1910 to 2010." Paper presented at the Annual Meeting of the Social Science History Association, 2015. https://www2.census.gov/geo/pdfs/reference/ua/Century_of_Defining_Urban.pdf.

Rau, Nate. "After Sellout, Bonnaroo Navigates Tenuous Relationship with Coffee County." *The Tennessean*, June 17, 2019. https://www.tennessean.com/storya/entertainment/music/bonnaroo/2019/06/17/bonnaroo-future-in-manchester-coffee-county-tenn/1419129001.

Redmon, Kevin Charles. "The Man Who Reinvented the City." *The Atlantic*, May 18, 2010. https://www.theatlantic.com/personal/archive/2010/05/the-man-who-reinvented-the-city/56853.

Reeves, Jay. "Alabama Cotton Gin Factory's Transformation Haunted by Slavery's Ghost." Associated Press, November 22, 2022. https://apnews.com/article/business-alabama-race-and-ethnicity-slavery-433dc0c956607a400b6b8b00c5c366fc.

Relph, Edward. *Place and Placelessness*. Pion, 1976.

Reynnells, Mary Louise. "Rural Resources and Funding." USDA webinar, December 10, 2014. https://www.webjunction.org/events/webjunction/rural-resources-funding-RIC.html.

Roberts, Bill. "New Urbanism Is Just Growth by Another Name." *High Country News*, April 7, 2003. https://www.hcn.org/wotr/13898.

Robertson, Campbell. "Protests against Racism Reveal Hidden Diversity in Small Towns." *New York Times*, July 15, 2020. https://www.nytimes.com/2020/07/15/us/black-lives-matter-protests-small-towns.html.

Robinson, Eugene. "What Happens When President Trump Has to Face Reality?" *Washington Post*, November 9, 2016. https://www.washingtonpost.com/opinions/what-happens-when-president-trump-has-to-face-reality/2016/11/09/e138dec0-a6b2-11e6-ba59-a7d93165c6d4_story.html.

Robinson, Jennifer. *Ordinary Cities: Between Modernity and Development*. Routledge, 2006.

Rodden, Jonathan. "'Red' America Is an Illusion. Postindustrial Towns Go for Democrats." *Washington Post*, February 14, 2017. https://www.washingtonpost.com/news/monkey-cage/wp/2017/02/14/red-america-is-an-illusion-postindustrial-towns-go-for-democrats-heres-the-data.

Rodden, Jonathan. *Why Cities Lose: The Deep Roots of the Urban-Rural Political Divide*. Basic Books, 2019.

Romano, Aja. "Gilmore Girls' Final Words Change Everything We Believe about Rory and Stars Hollow." *Vox*, November 28, 2016. https://www.vox.com/culture/2016/11/28/13760018/gilmore-girls-final-four-words-review-bad.

Roney, Marty. "Crowd Gets Sneak Peek at Prattville's $37 Million 'Gin Shop' Project." *Montgomery Advertiser*, November 24, 2022. https://www.montgomeryadvertiser

.com/story/news/crime/progress/2022/11/25/prattville-alabama-the-mill-real-estate-downtown-apartments-housing/69631229007.

Rothman, Hal. *Devil's Bargains: Tourism in the Twentieth-Century American West.* University Press of Kansas, 1998.

Rudolf, John Collins. "Copper's Every Dip is Felt in Arizona." *New York Times,* November 27, 2008.

Russo, David J. *American Towns: An Interpretive History.* Ivan R. Dee, 2001.

"Rutland, Vermont: Time to Shine." *Business View Magazine,* February 4, 2021. https://businessviewmagazine.com/rutland-vermont-time-shine.

Saad, Lydia. "Country Living Enjoys Renewed Appeal in U.S." Gallup, January 5, 2021. https://news.gallup.com/poll/328268/country-living-enjoys-renewed-appeal.aspx.

Sablik, Tim. "Growing Rural America through Startups." Econ Focus. Federal Reserve Bank of Richmond, 2022. https://www.richmondfed.info/-/media/RichmondFedOrg/publications/research/econ_focus/2022/q1/feature2.pdf.

"Safford Downtown Vision Plan." City of Safford (Arizona), 2006.

Said, Edward. "Invention, Memory, and Place." *Critical Inquiry* 26, no. 2 (2000): 175.

St. James, Emily. "Gilmore Girls: A Year in the Life Takes Place in a Beautiful, Perfect Bubble. Let It Never Burst." *Vox,* November 23, 2016. https://www.vox.com/culture/2016/11/23/13720452/gilmore-girls-review-netflix-a-year-in-the-life.

Sanders, Jaquin. "Norman Rockwell: A Serious Artist at Last." *Tampa Bay Times,* September, 30, 2005. https://www.tampabay.com/archive/1999/11/23/norman-rockwell-a-serious-artist-at-last.

Sassen, Saskia. "A New Geography of Centers and Margins: Summary and Implications. In *The City Reader,* edited by Richard LeGates and Frederic Stout, 69–74. Routledge, 1996.

Schultz, Jack. *Boom Town USA: The 7½ Keys to Big Success in Small Towns.* National Association of Industrial and Office Properties, 2006.

Semuels, Alana. "America Needs to End Its Love Affair with Single-Family Homes. One Town Is Discovering It's a Tough Sell." *Time,* June 2, 2022. https://time.com/6183044/affordable-housing-single-family-homes-steamboat-springs.

Semuels, Alana. "'They're Trying to Wipe Us Off the Map.' Small American Farmers Are Nearing Extinction." *Time,* November 27, 2019. https://time.com/5736789/small-american-farmers-debt-crisis-extinction.

Sen, Conor. "Booming 'Zoom Towns' Should Ease City Housing Costs." Bloomberg, August 5, 2020. https://www.bloomberg.com/opinion/articles/2020-08-05/remote-work-from-resort-towns-eases-housing-costs-in-big-cities.

Sisson, Patrick. "Craft Beer's Big Impact on Small Towns and Forgotten Neighborhoods." *Curbed,* June 13, 2017. https://archive.curbed.com/2017/6/13/15788960/brewing-economic-development-craft-beer.

Slack, Tim, and Leif Jensen. "The Changing Demography of Rural and Small-Town America." *Population Research and Policy Review* 39 (2020): 775–783.

Sodja, Elizabeth. "Boom Town: Amenity Migration in the Rural West and the Rise of the 'Zoom Town.'" Gateway and National Amenity Region Initiative, Utah State University, 2021. https://digitalcommons.usu.edu/cgi/viewcontent.cgi?article=3181&context=extension_curall.

Sorenson, Matthew. "Location Analysis of Lifestyle Centers: Uncovering Patterns and Potential Driving Factors behind Site Selection." Unpublished MS thesis. University of North Texas, 2019. http://www.murrayrice.com/uploads/1/2/9/6/12967989/sorenson-thesis-2019.pdf.

Speier, Michael. "Everwood." *Variety,* September 16–22, 2002. 45.

Stephenson, Bruce. "The Roots of the New Urbanism: John Nolen's Garden City Ethic." *Journal of Planning History* 1, no. 2 (2002): 99–123. https://doi.org/10.1177/153132001002001.

Stevens, Hampton. "'Parks and Recreation': Finally, a Sitcom That Loves Middle America." *The Atlantic*, November 17, 2011. https://www.theatlantic.com/entertainment/archive/2011/11/parks-and-recreation-finally-a-sitcom-that-loves-middle-america/248645.
Stoker, Phillip, Danya Rumore, Lindsay Romaniello, and Zacharia Levine. "Planning and Development Challenges in Western Gateway Communities." *Journal of the American Planning Association* 87, no. 1 (2021): 21–33.
Swanson, Bert, Richard Cohen, and Edith Swanson. *Small Towns and Small Towners: A Framework for Survival and Growth*. Sage Library of Social Research 79. Sage Publications, 1979.
Tan, Tiffany. "A Record 2010 Vermonters Died of an Opioid Overdose Last Year." *VTDigger*, April 5, 2022. https://vtdigger.org/2022/04/05/210-vermonters-died-of-an-opioid-overdose-last-year-first-time-death-toll-topped-200.
Taylor, Laura. "No Boundaries: Exurbia and the Study of Contemporary Urban Dispersion." *GeoJournal* 76, no. 4 (2011): 323–339.
Teixeira, Ruy. "Demography Is Not Destiny." *Persuasion*, July 16, 2020. https://www.persuasion.community/p/demography-is-not-destiny.
Thill, Mary. "Shorter Winters Chip Away at New York State Logging Town's Future." *Scientific American*, March 28, 2013. https://www.scientificamerican.com/article/shorter-winters-chips-away-at-new-york-logging-towns-future.
Thomas, G. Scott. "Study: Small Cities in the West Tops for Best Quality Of Life." *Albuquerque Business First*, August 17, 2006. https://www.bizjournals.com/albuquerque/stories/2006/08/21/story10.html.
Thompson, Jonathan. "Reluctant Boomtown." *High Country News*, February 18, 2008. https://www.hcn.org/issues/issue-364.
Thurston, Steve. 2022. "Planning Ready on Excelsior Park, Residents File Suit." *Foothills Business Daily*, October 3, 2022. https://foothillsbusinessdaily.com/springs-planning-ready-on-excelsior-park-residents-bring-sui.
"Top 20 Urban Planning Books (of All Time)." *Planetizen*. Accessed July 15, 2022. https://www.planetizen.com/books/20.
Tournier, Robert. "Small Towns at the Crossroads: Outcome Scenarios in Non-Metropolitan Change." In *Change and Tradition in the American Small Town*, edited by Robert Craycroft and Michael Fazio, 31–48. Small Towns series. University Press of Mississippi, 1983.
Towler, Sureva. "Obituary of the Old Town." *Denver Post*, October 6, 2002. A9.
"Town of Silver City Sustainability Plan 2030." Office of Sustainability, Silver City (New Mexico), 2013. https://www.townofsilvercity.org/DocumentCenter/View/200/Silver-City-Sustainability-Plan-2030-PDF.
"Town of Wellington Comprehensive Plan." Town of Wellington, Colorado, 2008.
"Town of Wellington Comprehensive Plan." Town of Wellington, Colorado, 2012.
Trudeau, Dan. "A Typology of New Urbanism Neighborhoods." *Journal of Urbanism: International Research on Placemaking and Urban Sustainability* 6, no. (2013): 113–138.
Tuan, Yi-Fu. *Topophilia: A Study of Environmental Perception, Attitudes, and Values*. Columbia University Press, 1974.
Tucker, Ken. "Widower's Peak." *Entertainment Weekly*, September 20, 2002.
Tuff, Sarah, and Greg Melville. "50 Best Places to Live: The Next Great Adventure Towns." *National Geographic Adventure*, September 2008.
Turner, V. Kelly. "Green New Urbanism." In *A Research Agenda for New Urbanism*, 63–80. Edward Elgar Publishing, 2019.
Uhlenbrock, Kristan. "You Knew." *Coal at Sunset* (podcast). Institute for Science and Policy, November 15, 2021. https://coalatsunset.org/episodes/episode-3-you-knew.
"Urban Area Criteria for the 2020 Census—Final Criteria." *Federal Register*, March 24, 2022.
Urbanska, Wanda, and Frank Levering. *Moving to a Small Tow: A Guidebook for Moving from Urban to Rural America*. Simon and Schuster, 1996.

Van Allen, E. "Carmel Grows Up: The History and Vision of an Edge City." Carmel Clay Historical Society, 2017. https://carmelclayhistory.org/wp-content/uploads/2023/06/Carmel-history-FINAL-2.pdf.

Van Doren, Carl. *Contemporary American Novelists, 1900–1920*. Macmillan, 1931.

Van Green, Ted. "Majority of Americans Prefer a Community with Big Houses Even If Local Amenities Are Farther Away." Pew Research, August 2, 2023. https://www.pewresearch.org/short-reads/2023/08/02/majority-of-americans-prefer-a-community-with-big-houses-even-if-local-amenities-are-farther-away.

Verlaan, Tim, and Cody Hochstenbach. "Gentrification through the Ages: A Long-Term Perspective on Urban Displacement, Social Transformation, and Resistance," *City* 26, no. 2–3 (2022): 439–449. https://doi.org/10.1080/13604813.2022.2058820.

Villani, John. *The 100 Best Art Towns in America: A Guide to Galleries, Museums, Festivals, Lodging, and Dining*. Countryman Press, 2005.

Viser, Matt. "Officially in, Romney All about the Economy." *Boston Globe*, June 3, 2011. A1.

"Vision 2030: Heart and Soul of Our Community." Final Report. Steamboat Springs, Colorado, 2009.

Weber, Bruce. "Richard Russo, Happily at Home in Winesburg East." *New York Times*, July 2, 2004. https://www.nytimes.com/2004/07/02/books/richard-russo-happily-at-home-in-winesburg-east.html.

"What Carmel, Indiana, Can Teach America about Urbanism." *The Economist*, September 29, 2022. https://www.economist.com/united-states/2022/09/29/what-carmel-indiana-can-teach-america-about-urbanism.

Willer, Christopher. "Towards a 'National' Main Street: Networks, Place Marketing, and Placemaking in U.S. Small Towns." Unpublished dissertation. Kent State University, 2022.

Williams, Kevin. "Reaction Goes beyond Major Cities." *Washington Post*, June 5, 2020. https://www.washingtonpost.com/national/ohio-small-towns-see-something-missing-for-decades-protests/2020/06/05/34e174ea-a756-11ea-bb20-ebf0921f3bbd_story.html.

Williamson, Kevin. "The Father-Führer." *National Review*, March 28, 2016. https://www.nationalreview.com/magazine/2016/03/28/father-f-hrer.

Wilson, Duff. *Fateful Harvest: The True Story of a Small Town, a Global Industry, and a Toxic Secret*. HarperCollins, 2001.

Woods, Lynn. "Lost Newburgh: The Tragedy of Urban Renewal." Lynn Woods (blog), January 17–19, 2018. http://www.lynndwoods.com/lost-newburgh-the-tragedy-of-urban-renewal.

Woods, Michael. *Rural*. Routledge, 2011.

Wuthnow, Robert. *The Left Behind: Decline and Rage in Small-Town America*. Princeton University Press, 2019.

Wyly, Elvin K., and Daniel J. Hammel. "Gentrification, Segregation, and Discrimination in the American Urban System." *Environment and Planning A* 36, no. 7 (2004): 1215–1241.

Yagley, James, Lance George, Cequyna Moore, and Jennifer Pinder. "They Paved Paradise . . . Gentrification in Rural Communities." Housing Assistance Council, 2005. https://ruralhome.org/wp-content/uploads/storage/documents/gentrification.pdf.

"Yazoo City Comprehensive Plan 2019." Yazoo City, Mississippi, 2019. http://www.cityofyazoocity.org/images/Yazoo-City-Comp-Plan-2020.pdf.

Yuko, Elizabeth. "The Three Subversive Messages of 'Schitt's Creek.'" CNN, January 7, 2020. https://www.cnn.com/2020/01/07/opinions/schitts-creek-final-season-utopia-yuko/index.html.

Zak, Dan. "Rep. Matt Gaetz Wants You to Know Who He Is, and His Plan Is Working." *Washington Post*, February 20, 2018. https://www.washingtonpost.com/lifestyle/style

/rep-matt-gaetz-wants-you-to-know-who-he-is-and-his-plan-is-working/2018/02/20/2dfce71e-126a-11e8-8ea1-c1d91fcec3fe_story.html.

Zimmerman, Jeffrey. "From Brew Town to Cool Town: Neoliberalism and the Creative City Development Strategy in Milwaukee." *Cities* 25, no. 4 (2008): 230–242.

Zipp, Samuel. "The Roots and Routes of Urban Renewal." *Journal of Urban History* 39, no. 3 (2013): 366–391.

Zitner, Aaron, and Paul Overberg. "Rural Vote Fuels Trump." *Wall Street Journal*, November 9, 2016.

Zito, Salena. "How Trump Made Small-Town America Matter Again." *New York Post*, January 22, 2017. https://nypost.com/2017/01/22/how-trump-made-small-town-america-matter-again.

Zukin, Sharon. *The Cultures of Cities*. Blackwell, 1995.

INDEX

Agenda 21, 123
agricultural towns. *See* farm towns
Akron (OH), 10, 14–15, 20, 54, 59
Aldean, Jason, 78
Alliance (OH), 14–15, 17
amenities in small towns, 29, 81, 88, 89–91
    cultural, 30, 93–96
    natural, 89, 122
amenity migration, 88–92, 94–95, 98, 120–21, 123
American Community Survey, 11, 22
American small towns:
    adapting to change, 108, 110, 123–26
    critiques of, 33, 38–40
    as escape for urbanites, 33, 41, 43, 91
    future of, 96, 107–10, 122–23, 130
    history of, 35–38
    idealized, 3, 8, 35, 38–44, 48–50, 107
    as role model for planning, 49–50
    and sense of place, 6, 33, 38, 41, 96
    See also perceptions of small towns
Anaconda (MT), 7, 31–32, 119, 121
    copper mining in, 71–72, 110–12
    Main Street restoration in, 57–58
anti-urban sentiment, 3, 89
Appalachian small towns. *See* coal towns
Ashville (NC), 54
Asian residents in small towns, 23, 26, 30, 82
Aspen (CO), 89
Athens (OH) 84
Aubrey (TX), 30
automobile dependence, 5, 37, 55

basic services, 19, 36–37, 109, 125
    loss of, 75–76
Beckley (WV), 94
Bellefonte (PA), 21
Bend (OR), 92
Bennington and Brattleboro (VT), 29
Biden, Joseph, 70, 72, 82, 83
Black residents in small towns, 5, 23–24, 26, 28–31, 60, 80–82
Bonnaroo Music Festival, 24
Bowling Green (OH), 84
breweries, 64, 95, 115, 117–18

Bristol (CT), 54
Brown Ranch (Steamboat Springs CO), 99–100
brownfields, 61, 117, 130

Carmel (IN), 63–64
Cascade Agenda, 129
census blocks, 12–13
census-designated place (CDP), 10, 16, 21, 22
central place functions, 19, 35–37, 125
Chappelle, Dave, 29
Chardon (OH), 15, 17
Chicago (IL), 53–54, 129
City Beautiful movement, 54, 59
Clayton, John, 42
Cleveland (OH), 14, 15, 20
climate change, impact on small towns 122, 127
cluster analysis, 23–24, 26–27
cluster types, 24, *25*, 26–32
coal and mining towns, 36, 73–75, 84, 90, 118, 125–26
    environmental impacts of, 109–12
Cody (WY), 29
college towns, 4, 14, 25, 29–30, 36, 83–84, 93–94
community:
    building, 45, 57, 131–33
    sense of, 4, 8, 38–39, 49–52, 68, 87, 101, 104, 108, 120, 126
    See also place, sense of
Community Development Block Grant, 9
community master plans, 2, 52–53, 93
commuting, 11, 23, 96, 128–29
    See also rural-urban commuting area codes
company towns, 36, 118
Congress for the New Urbanism (CNU), 1, 51, 59
counterurbanization, 89, 94–95
county-based urban identification, 10–11
COVID-19 pandemic, 48, 68, 80–81, 88, 91, 94–95, 130
Craig (CO), 111
Crampton, Norman, 42
Crocker Park (Westlake, OH), 61–63

Delaney, Patrick and Tammie, 98, 131–33
Democratic voters in small towns, 82–85
demographic diversity, 4, 23, 39, 92
  See also race and ethnicity
density. *See* population density
Detroit (MI), 55, 75, 125
Duany, Andrés, 2, 51, 52, 59

economic development, 2, 56–57, 87–93, 103, 106, 117
economies of small towns, 26, 37, 57, 71, 108, 118–22
  cultural, 89, 117
  diversity of, 5, 93
  See also coal and mining towns; college towns; factory towns; farm towns; timber towns; tourist towns
education level in small towns, 24, 27, 30
Ellensburg (WA), 7, 30–32, 94, 102–3, 118, 121–22, 127–30
  downtown redevelopment in, 58
  rodeo, 104, 115
employment in small towns, 7, 19, 26–28, 37, 49, 89, 109–10, 128
environmental health, 2, 38, 50, 59–60, 106–7
environmental impacts on small towns, 74–75, 110, 112, 122–24
Euclid (OH), 55
Everwood, 43–44
exurbs, 5, 25, 30, 38, 84, 91–93, 105

factory towns, 24–28, 36, 74–75, 113
  reviving, 116–18
farm towns, 5, 27, 28, 37, 112–15
Florence (SC), 94
Florida, Richard, 88, 93
Forks (WA), 74
Fort Collins (CO), 30, 92–93, 109, 114

gentrification, 68, 87, 95, 101, 121
Geography of Nowhere, The (Kunstler), 1
Gilmore Girls, 43, 47–48
global human settlement layer (GHSL), 11–13, 15, 17, 22
global economy, 7, 74, 94, 111, 125, 133
globalization, 3, 74–76, 127–28
greenfields, 52, 60–61, 130
Greenwich (NY), 18
guidebooks on small towns, 42–43, 48

hamlets, 5, 9, 10, 17–19
Hayden (CO), 7, 98, 131–33
Hazelton (PA), 105
Hillbilly Elegy (Vance), 80, 86
Hispanic residents in small towns, 5, 23–24, 26, 28–31, 80–82, 105
historic preservation, 56–57, 103–4, 121
home values, 23, 27, 29, 92–93, 110

Hope IV program, 59
housing developments, 9, 19, 32, 67–68, 88, 92, 100
Hudson (OH), 64–65

International Council for Local Environmental Initiatives, 123–24
internet access, 23, 31, 89–90, 108

Jackson (WY), 89, 121

Kent (OH), 4, 14, 17, 20, 64–66, 116–17
Kent State University, 4, 14, 66, 116
King, Stephen, 46
Kingsport (TN), 54
knowledge economy, 94, 129
Kunstler, James Howard, 1, 3, 108

Lake Tahoe (CA), 121
large cities, characteristics of, 22–23, 37, 39, 82–83, 87
Laurel (MS), 28–29
Leadville (CO), 29
Lewis, Peirce, 37–38, 49
Lewis, Sinclair, 39–40
lifestyle center, 61–63
location neutral businesses, 90, 91, 121–22
Los Angeles, 8–9, 61, 120
Lovecraft Country, 46–47
Lynch, David, 40–41, 48
Lyon Mountain (NY), 72–73

Madras (OR), 92
"Main Street," as American ideal, 37, 38, 56, 59
Main Street America program, 56, 58, 88
majority-minority town, 28, 80, 82, 124
"Make America Great Again" slogan, 3, 69, 79
Manchester (TN), 24
manufacturing towns. *See* factory towns
master plans. *See* community master plans
McCain, John, 77
media coverage of small towns, 6, 50, 69–71, 75–76, 80–82, 85–88
median income in small towns, 23–24, 27, 30–31, 85
mental maps, 34
metropolitan and micropolitan areas, 10–11, 15
Midwestern towns, 36, 74, 81–82, 129
mining towns. *See* coal and mining towns
Missoula (MT), 40
mixed-use development, 1, 19, 50, 51, 67, 128
Moab (UT), 89, 91
Monessen (PA), 80
Montauk (NY), 29
Morehead (KY), 30
municipal boundaries, 8–12, 16, 19, 22, 96

Munsell, Ken, 33, 42
mythologizing small towns. *See* perceptions of small towns

national retail chains, 108–10
natural environment, protecting, 122–24
Nature's Metropolis (Cronon), 112, 129
New Deal, 55
New England towns, 36, 38
New Urbanism, 1–3, 5, 50–53, 67–68, 130
   history of, 59–61
   ideal characteristics of, 1–2, 51, 67–68
   impact on city planning, 2, 50
New Urbanist development, 2, 19, 51–52, 59–61, 64–66, 128
   infill development, 52, 60, 61
   retail projects, 61–64
   See also Seaside (FL)
North Adams (MA), 116–17
nostalgia for small towns, 7, 33–35, 103, 112, 114, 125

Oberlin (OH), 30, 84
Ohio Village (OH), 39
Ohio voting patterns, 83
Old Sturbridge Village (MA), 39
Old Town (ME), 117
"Old West" image, 103–4, 120
open space, preserving, 2, 99, 103, 123, 129–30
opioid crisis, 28, 75
Oxford (OH), 84

Palin, Sarah, 77, 82
Paradise (CA), 122
Parks and Recreation, 45
perceptions of small towns, 3–7, 33–34, 68
   as declining, 1, 41, 70–71, 79–80
   as homogeneous, 4
   as isolated, 33, 38–39, 45, 49, 95, 107–9
   in literature, tv, and film, 33–35, 38–41, 43–47, 69
   as Republican-leaning, 3, 70, 72, 82
   as safer than cities, 1, 33, 39, 42, 44, 49, 54, 80–81
   as sustainable alternative to suburbs, 49–50
   as white, 3, 23, 49, 80–81
   See also media coverage of small towns
Pew Research Center surveys, 48, 49, 80
Pittsburgh (PA), 52
place, sense of, 6, 33–34, 59, 96, 103, 107, 119, 122
   See also community
planned towns, 50
plant closings, 3, 74, 111
Plater-Zyberk, Elizabeth, 2, 51, 52
Plattsburgh (NY), 30. 66–67
political diversity of small towns, 84–86
population decline in small towns, 13, 25–28, 37, 71, 74–76, 87, 106

population density, 2, 9–12, 16–18, 23, 88, 125, 129–30
population growth in small towns, 22, 87–88, 92, 96, 106
   problems resulting from, 97–106
Portsmouth (OH), 117
postindustrial cities, 84, 125
Prairie Crossing (Grayslake, IL), 52, 53
Prattville (AL), 118
presidential elections, voting patterns in, 7, 69–70, 76–79, 82–85
Prineville (OR), 92
prisons, 13, 16–17, 73

quality of life in small towns, 33, 42, 75, 91, 108, 122
Quincy (WA), 31–32, 81–82, 99–103, 124
   agricultural heritage of, 104–5
   Hispanic population in, 31, 81, 105

race and ethnicity in small towns, 4–5, 23–24, 26, 48–49, 80–82, 105
railroad towns, 36–37, 75, 90
Redmond (OR), 92
remote work, 89–90, 94–96
resort towns, 37, 59, 90–91, 95, 101, 118, 120
resource extraction, 70–76, 109–12
   See also coal and mining towns; timber towns
retirees in small towns, 25, 29, 57, 109, 119, 121
Rise of the Creative Class, The (Florida), 93–94
risk assessment, 123
Rockwell, Norman, 39
Rocky Mount (NC), 117
Romney, Mitt, 76, 78
rural areas:
   defining, 5–6, 12–13, 17–18, 76, 92, 129–30
   as distinct from small towns, 4, 9, 23, 69
rural-urban commuting area (RUCA) codes, 11, 14–15, 22, 80
Russo, Richard, 41
Rust Belt, 4, 74–75, 80, 82, 106, 129
Rutland (VT), 28

Safford (AZ), 31–32, 111–12, 119–20, 122
   Main Street redevelopment in, 58, 111
Sanders, Bernie, 78–79
Santorum, Rick, 78
Saratoga Springs (NY), 67–68, 95–97
Sauk Centre (MN), 39
Schenectady (NY), 54
Schitt's Creek, 45
Schuylerville (NY), 1–2, 18, 82, 108, 113–14
Seaside (FL), 52, 59, 60
Sebastopol and Sonoma (CA), 106
segregation, 5, 29, 48, 54–55, 68, 80, 82
shopping malls, 3, 16, 55, 61, 96

Silver City (NM), 31–32, 109, 118–121, 123
    downtown revitalization of, 56–57, 122
Slow City movement, 106
small town character, 90, 97
    loss of, 101–7
small town characteristics, 1–2, 10, 22–32, 126
small town replication. *See* New Urbanist development
small towns:
    as distinct from suburbs, 9–10, 12–13, 52
    federal definitions of, 10–14, 16–18
    identifying, 5–6, 8–22
    national and global impacts on, 6–7, 74, 107–9, 113, 128
    See also urban clusters
Snoqualmie (WA), 30, 32
social equity, 2, 106, 107, 130
socioeconomic characteristics of small towns, 23–24, 109
Southern towns, 36
space vs. place, 34
sprawl, 2, 13, 59–60, 68, 87, 99
    commercial, 102–3
    suburban and exurban, 53, 60, 63, 92, 112, 128
St. James (PA), 105
State College (PA), 21
Steamboat Springs (CO), 7, 29, 31–32, 64, 101–4, 109
    agricultural heritage of, 103–4
    housing problems in, 98–99
    as tourist town, 89–91, 118, 120–21
    Vision 2030 project, 98–99, 101, 108, 122
stereotypes about small towns. *See* perceptions of small towns
Stow (OH), 20, 64
Stranger Things, 46
suburbs, 3, 5, 7, 55, 64, 83, 128
    dependence on cities, 9–10, 19–20, 52
sundown towns, 47, 82
SUNY Plattsburgh, 72
Superior (AZ), 125–26
sustainable urbanism, 2, 7, 49, 88, 106–7, 123–24, 128–30
    "three E's" of, 106, 107

telecommuting. *See* remote work
timber towns, 73–74
tourism, environmental threats to, 122–24
tourist towns, 118–22
    See also resort towns
townscape mall. *See* lifestyle center
Trump, Donald, 3, 69–70, 76, 78–81, 84–85, 123
Tuskegee (AL), 30

urban, definition of, 9, 12, 16
urban clusters, 12–15, 16–21, 22–27
    See also cluster analysis
urban growth boundaries, 90, 92
urban problems and responses, 53–56
urban renewal, 55–56, 96, 116–17
urban-to-rural migration. *See* counterurbanization
U.S. Census data, 6, 9–11, 13, 22, 30
U.S. Department of Agriculture (USDA), 9, 11

Vail (CO), 91, 121
Vance, J. D., 80
Virgin River, 45

walkable communities, 2, 18, 23, 48–49, 64, 87, 130
    as goal of New Urbanism, 51, 67–68, 128
Walmart, 102–3, 108
Wellington (CO), 30–32, 76–77, 92–93, 114–15, 121
Western Reserve Land Conservancy (WRLC), 129
white flight, 55, 89
Windber (PA), 74
work from home. *See* remote work
world cities, 3

Yazoo City (MS), 118
Yellow Springs (OH), 29
Youngstown (OH), 14–15

zoning restrictions, 2, 52–55, 58–59, 92, 102

www.ingramcontent.com/pod-product-compliance
Lightning Source LLC
Chambersburg PA
CBHW040253170426
43191CB00019B/2394